THE RHIZOME OF BLACKNESS

Rochelle Brock and Richard Greggory Johnson III
Executive Editors

Vol. 68

The Black Studies and Critical Thinking series
is part of the Peter Lang Education list.
Every volume is peer reviewed and meets
the highest quality standards for content and production.

PETER LANG
New York • Washington, D.C./Baltimore • Bern
Frankfurt • Berlin • Brussels • Vienna • Oxford

AWAD IBRAHIM

THE RHIZOME OF BLACKNESS

A Critical Ethnography of
Hip-Hop Culture, Language, Identity,
and the Politics of Becoming

PETER LANG
New York • Washington, D.C./Baltimore • Bern
Frankfurt • Berlin • Brussels • Vienna • Oxford

Library of Congress Cataloging-in-Publication Data

Ibrahim, Awad.
The rhizome of Blackness: a critical ethnography of Hip-Hop culture,
language, identity and the politics of becoming / Awad Ibrahim.
pages cm. — (Black studies and critical thinking; volume 68)
Includes bibliographical references and index.
1. African Americans—Race identity. 2. African Americans—Social conditions—1975–
3. African Americans—Languages. 4. African Americans—Education (Higher)
5. Hip-hop—United States. 6. African diaspora. 7. Identity politics—United States.
8. Ethnology—United States. 9. United States—Race relations.
10. Racism—United States. I. Title.
E185.625.I27   305.896'073—dc23   2014000349
ISBN 978-1-4331-2603-1 (hardcover)
ISBN 978-1-4331-2602-4 (paperback)
ISBN 978-1-4539-1276-8 (e-book)
ISSN 1947-5985

Bibliographic information published by **Die Deutsche Nationalbibliothek**.
Die Deutsche Nationalbibliothek lists this publication in the "Deutsche
Nationalbibliografie"; detailed bibliographic data is available
on the Internet at http://dnb.d-nb.de/.

© 2014 Peter Lang Publishing, Inc., New York
29 Broadway, 18th floor, New York, NY 10006
www.peterlang.com

All rights reserved.
Reprint or reproduction, even partially, in all forms such as microfilm,
xerography, microfiche, microcard, and offset strictly prohibited.

*Of course, to you and your beautiful memory:
my mother, Fatima Salih Mohamed*

CONTENTS

Acknowledgments ix

Introduction: **Black Don't Crack**
   Marking the Unmarked: A Critical Ethnography of Becoming 1

Chapter One: **We Got a Situation Herre**
   Race, Culture, Language, and Identity: Theorizing the Rhizomatic Third Space . 31

Chapter Two: *"Wallahi, ils sont tous des racistes!"*
   Striated Racialization and the Rhizomatic Process of Becoming Black 59

Chapter Three: *"Si tu allais faire un sondage, ça vient souvent de l'orientation ou des personnels"*
   Teachers, Curriculum, and Pedagogy 98

Interlude: *Homeless Urban Dreams* by Reenah L. Golden 124

Chapter Four: **"Oh, I Got It, It Gives Me Great Pleasure!"**
   Hip-Hop Culture and Language, Post/Coloniality, and the Imaginary 125

Chapter Five: **"Peace and One Love!"**
   A Rhizomatic Third Space:
   Race, Language, Culture, and the Politics of Identity 154

Conclusion: **What's the Dillio?**
   Towards a New "Ticklish Subject":
   Pedagogy of the Imaginary as Integrative Antiracism 192

Appendix I: Notes on Transcription of Interviews 215

Appendix II: Profiles of Students Interviewed for This Book 217

References 221

Index 235

ACKNOWLEDGMENTS

My thanks and gratitude go to a friend whose refusal to be a "big name" made him an awesome human being: George Dei. Thanks to my friends: Nicholas, Rebecca, Handel, Boulou, Emmanuel T., Tamari, Tim, Joel, Marie-Josée, Francis, Meredith, Carole, Emmanuel D., Douglas, and Giuliano. Thanks to my friends in Ottawa: Galal, Hamid, Fadil, Abugargas, Sayed, Osama, Hatim, M. Khalifa, Nashwa and the kids, T. Khazin, Hassan and Hiba, Hana and Haneen, Mohamed and Mojtaba, Samah, M. Bashir, and all our kids in Ottawa. My mother-in-law, big up! Hafiz, Elmala and Rayed, thanks for the many conversations we had on this book. Kelsey, Annette, Shenin, graduate students, keep the hope! Back home in Sudan, thanks family: my sisters Osailat and Aziza, my brother Hassan, and my nieces (Swsan, Ishraga, Najat, Selma, Oula, Roa, Alaa, Bona, Malaz) and nephews (Hatim, Mohaied, Hisham, Mohamed M., Ahmed, Mohamed A., Mohamed H., Musa, Mazin). Ihab, Yasir, Zeinab and Zeinat and the kids—much love. My family in Sennar and Halaween, love you. Finally, I would like to acknowledge the schools where I conducted my research. Without their permission and generous hospitality, this research would not have been possible. My friends, Shirley, Rochelle, Reenha, Hodari, Tricia, Pierre, and of the Freire Institute—thank you. You keep me smiling, and for this I am utterly grateful. Thank you Alim and Alastair very much indeed. I want to thank a mentor whom I met only once: the late Stuart Hall. His work has been inspiring, and it came into my life at the right time. Paulo Freire and Joe Kincheloe, you will never die. Thank you Phyllis Korper, Sophie Appel and the incredible anonymous editor at Peter Lang. Finally, my partner, Hala, suffered quite a bit while I finished this book, so I am more than grateful for her patience and love. For the young women and men who lovingly welcomed me in their lives, keep the hope. Ya makin it BIG. I got lotsalove for y'all.

Black popular culture does not determine the formation of social and cultural identities in any mechanistic way, but it supplies a variety of symbolic, linguistic, textual, gestural, and, above all, musical resources that are used by people to shape their identities, truths, and models of community. That culture has struggled over a long period of time with its transmutation into the closed form of commodity. It is used in dynamic ways that liberate it from the logic of commodification and supplement the original creative input of its producers with further contributions.

—Gilroy, *The Black Atlantic* (1995)

"*Je suis une combinaison de plusieurs choses*" [I am a collage of things] (Hassan, 17-year-old boy of Somali descent). Yet, "I am an invisible man. No, I am not a spook like those who haunted Edgar Allan Poe; nor am I one of your Hollywood-movie extoplasms. I am a man of substance, of flesh and bone, fiber and liquids — and I might even be said to possess a mind. I am invisible, understand, simply because people refuse to see me. Like the bodiless heads you see sometimes in circus sideshows, it is as though I have been surrounded by mirrors of hard, distorting glass. When they approach me they see only my surroundings, themselves, or figments of their imagination—indeed, everything and anything except me."

—Ralph Ellison, *Invisible Man* (1952)

Let me begin with a caveat to any and all who find these pages. Do not trust large bodies of water, and do not cross them. If you, dear reader, have an African hue and find yourself led toward water with vanishing shores, seize your freedom by any means necessary. And cultivate distrust of the color pink. Pink is taken as the colour of innocence, the colour of childhood, but as it spills across the water in the light of the dying sun, do not fall into its pretty path. There, right underneath, lies a bottomless graveyard of children, mothers and men.

—Aminata Diallo in *The Book of Negroes*, Lawrence Hill (2007)

INTRODUCTION

Black Don't Crack[1]

Marking the Unmarked:
A Critical Ethnography of Becoming

In speaking, the act that the body is performing is never fully understood; the body is the blindspot of speech...[Therefore] there is what is said, and then there is a kind of saying that the bodily "instrument" of the utterance performs. (Butler, 1997, p. 11)

They are seen as *black*, therefore they *are* black; they are seen as *women*, therefore, they *are* women. But before being seen that way, they first had to be *made* that way. (Wittig, 2003, p. 159)

When Blackness encounters the syntactic structure of identity, it seems that a new becoming spills over, a rhizome[2] is given birth to. This book is about the rhizomatic structure of identity when it encounters Blackness. It is about the unspoken, that which is speaking so loudly: the Black body. Specifically, it is about more than "saying ego"[3]—the capacity to posit oneself as a subject; it is about the grammar of *how* displaced and migrant subjects posit, "speak" their subjectivity. Fittingly, this book is about the following exchange. In a cold February afternoon—typically Canadian—Aziza[4] and I have set up an interview at the school, one of the three sites for my research, which I will call Marie-Victorin (hereafter cited as MV). Aziza, one of the research participants, is an 18-year-old female of Somali origin, and we were discussing which language to use in conducting the interview:

Awad: You have the time? I have all the time in the world. *Ahm tu veux le faire en français ou en anglais*? [Ahm, would you like the interview to be in English or in French?]

Aziza: Oh, in French.

Awad: In French.

Aziza: But I don't know, I might also talk in English, I don't know.

Awad: Ah that's exactly what I want, choose the language you like; it doesn't matter to me.

Aziza: So, like, both?

Awad: You can; oh yah, switch in and out, yah if you want to.

Aziza: O.K. I do it in both, because I know 'm gonna slip in French and in English; 'm gonna talk in both. (individual interview, English, 1996)

This exchange is not simply about deciding on a language to use; more significantly, for me, it is about how we decide to *speak our identities*, how we come to terms with them. "Slipping in" or "slipping out" of English or French, for example, is not a simple linguistic act. It is a "performative act" of culture and identity (Butler, 2004, 2011), an act through which we "tell" others where we are located—or where we want them to locate us—socially, culturally, linguistically, and in terms of sex, nationality, gender, and/or race. English and French are not, and never were, exterior entities and simple instruments or mediums of communication, as linguists would have us believe (Bourdieu, 1991). These languages, I will argue, are expressing the complexity and the inseparability of Aziza's identity or, better yet, identities. They *are* performed identities and, hence, to paraphrase Jacques Derrida (1996), *une langue est une identité* (language is identity). On the one hand, language is where power is instituted, formed, and performed, and on the other, it is that "thing" that "is so organized that it permits each speaker to *appropriate to himself* an entire [apparatus] by designating himself as *I*" (Beneviste, 2000, p. 42; original emphasis). Language is where Aziza is enabled to "say ego," where she becomes a subject-in-language and a subject-of-language (Heller, 2011; Hewson, 2009; du Gay et al., 2000).

"Slipping," here, is code-switching, and code-switching is about living in-between languages, cultures, and social cartographies *and* the temporality and the plurality of the *I*, the subject. Using each language as *an* identity *within* the speaking subject, this book is about translating, translated, and translatable identities; how the symbolic is appropriated, cited, posited, mimed, transposed, and per/formed on and through the (Black) body; how the global is negotiated locally; and how this translation and negotiation takes place through race, language, culture, and the politics of identity. In short, the book is about the processes—the politics—of becoming Black.

These processes, I intend to show, are "rhizomatic." In Deleuze and Guattari's *A Thousand Plateaus* (1987), the rhizome is a crabgrass-like figuration that Deleuze and Guattari contrast to a tree-and-root system of power distribution as it functions on individuals and society at large. A rhizome, for them, is a weblike fabric that "must be produced, constructed, a map that is always detachable, connectable, reversible, modifiable, and has multiple entryways and exits and its own lines of flight" (p. 21). Working against facile notions of "roots" and "origins," a rhizome is always in "a middle (*milieu*) from which it grows and which it overspills" (p. 21). As such, the rhizome resists verticality and chronological "lines of flight," where its growth is contained and conceived in a linear, arborescent and systematic line. Line of flight means a path, a line of possibilities. Both in the plural and the singular forms, in the end, line of flight is about pursuing and following paths where the end result is either unknown (rhizome) or assumed to be known, binary, and totalizing (arborescent). As such, Deleuze and Guattari (1987) argue, the rhizome is altogether different than the arborescent. It is more complex, complicated, fluid, multiple, and multiplying, and forever becoming. The rhizome is a constant flow or movement of deterritorialization. It is not a point we reach, and finally say, We are finally there! Rather, it is a way of becoming that we are forever struggling to attain. Being open to the unkown, the rhizome is an uncontainable dimension "or rather directions in motion" (p. 21) that are forever in "between things, interbeing, intermezzo" (p. 7). This is how I am approaching the process of becoming Black and the general politics of identity in this book. There is no simple reading and definitely no simple identity into which we slot ourselves; we are forever becoming. If we reach anything, as we shall see in the next chapters, we reach what I am calling *rhizomatic identity*: a rhizomatic "assemblage" that is welcoming sociality, with everything that it brings (the good and the ugly), but with no guarantees as to what it might finally look like or what maze it has to go through to get there. It is a tree that is welcoming the sun, the rain, the snow, and so on, whose branches and leaves are growing horizontally. There are no certainties about what shape or form they will take, or how green they will turn out to be. This rhizomatic assemblage thus finds itself in a constant state of flow, deterritorialization, and multiplicity.

> Every rhizome contains lines of segmentarity according to which it is stratified, territorialized, organized, signified, attributed, etc., as well as lines of deterritorialization, down which it constantly flees.... These lines always tie back to one another. That is why one can never posit a dualism or a dichotomy, even in the rudimentary form of the good and the bad. (p. 9)

Based on a series of "critical ethnographic research projects" (1996, 2007, 2011), which I shall outline later, this book will trace this rhizomatic identity: immigrant and refugee groups of French- and English-speaking continental African youths[5] living in southwestern and northeastern Ontario, Canada, who were in the process of becoming Black. On one hand, this process was marked by an *identification* with and a *desire* for North American Blackness; on the other, it was as much about gender and race as it was about language, displacement, identity, and cultural performance. I shall delineate these youths' desire for and identification with Blackness through language. They were learning Black English as a Second Language (BESL), as we shall see, which they accessed in and through Black popular culture, namely Hip-Hop cultural identity, language practices, and ways of "being." The rhizomatic assemblage of their identity, to paraphrase Deleuze and Guattari (1987), demonstrates KRS-One's well-known contention: Rap is something we do, Hip-Hop is who we are!

These youths are part of the population of political refugee and economic immigrant continental Africans who, especially since the 1990s, have been crossing the Atlantic Ocean to North America in considerable numbers (Ibrahim, 2008; Statistics Canada, 2014; for the United States, see Fisher & Model, 2012; Harushimana & Awokoya, 2011). Once in North America, they join the African diaspora by becoming part of it. In a sense, one might argue that when continental Africans "join" diasporic Africans (in North America or Europe), and when the latter group "go back" to Africa (mostly, interestingly, for tourism, or sometimes in search of their "roots"), both are performing a symbolic act of defiance that they rub into the face of historical colonialism, imperialism, and the Middle Passage. But before joining diasporic Africans, continental Africans have to confront this history—the history of the present (Foucault, 1980)—where their bodies are *already assembled,* in an *assemblage* that is set and in turn sets itself against a "striated" (Deleuze & Guattari, 1987, p. 474)[6] and "hegemonic" (Gramsci, 1971) gaze that functions as a technology of semiotic control (Foucault, 1980). This striated gaze, I intend to show, turns their bodies into "Black" bodies, thus making them Black. As they *become Black*, however, they have to translate, negotiate, and answer two questions. First, what does "being Black" really mean in North America; that is, when Blackness is spoken, either through the body or otherwise, what kind of history and social order does it invoke? And second, if one is "becoming Black," what does this call for, entail, and hence produce? These are two of the questions I shall answer in this book.

Although the autobiographical is neither central to nor the center of this research, it is a *ma'ja playa* (Alim & Smitherman, 2012). After all, it is worth remembering that all discourses are placed, and the heart has its reasons and desires: I am a continental African living in what is for me, to paraphrase Stuart Hall (2006), the New Diaspora of North America. I am motivated on the one hand by Frantz Fanon's idea of "passionate research"; a research "directed by the secret hope of discovering beyond the misery of today, beyond self-contempt, resignation and abjuration, some very beautiful and splendid era whose existence rehabilitates us both in regard to ourselves and in regard to others" (1963, p. 170). On the other hand, I am inspired by Pierre Bourdieu's assumption "that the autobiographical narrative is always at least partially motivated by a concern to give meaning, to rationalize, to show the inherent logic, both for the past and for the future" (2000, p. 298). Furthermore, if discourses are placed, then the *experiential narrative*—the intense stories we tell from that location—is epistemology. After all, "experience can be a way to know and can inform how we know what we know," bell hooks (1994) argues, and "personal testimony...is such fertile ground for the production of liberatory [praxis] because it usually forms the base of our [knowledge and] theory making" (p. 168). And so, I hope, modestly, is the narrative in this book.

Here, I shall narrate a significant incident in my own journey of becoming Black. I find myself thus smuggled, as it were, into the research, through the backdoor. Assembling my research participants' and my own experiential narratives, I want to further complicate the following ontological questions. As a continental African living in North America, am I a Black man? Conjugating the verb *to be* in the present tense is central, and I am using Blackness as "imagined in North America" (see especially Baker, 1993; Henry, 2012; Jackson & Moody-Freeman, 2011; Kennedy, 2002; West, 2001). If the answer is no, what does it mean "not to be" a Black man while materially possessing the socially defined Black male body? That is, at the essence of identity formation, how is one translating and negotiating one's own sense of self vis-à-vis the already pronounced, assembled social order? Or, if the answer is yes, I am a Black man, when did I become one?

I shall use the autobiographical, but concentrate primarily—if not exclusively—on the biographical, the empirical, and the ethnographic. I argue that my research participants and I were not "Black" before emigrating to North America, but we became Black after emigration; indeed, we became one. On this point, South Africa stands outside this postulation. In South Africa, Blacks did in fact become Black in their own homeland. But outside the legacy of apartheid in South Africa, there is hardly any overt African context in which one's skin color has ever been such a social concern as it is in North America. Otherwise conceived, an African does not become Black in an African country where there is no history of racial discrimination (H. Wright, 2004).

In sum, this book is a significant exploration of these rhizomatic processes of becoming Black: the cultural, linguistic, and sociopsychic implications of what it means to possess the Black body in North America (and the Western world in general). These processes and the narratives they engender, I will argue, are applicable not only to continental Africans (including myself), but also to most if not all émigrés and displaced subjects who move to North America and who are "visibly" black. This is what I want to call the "politics of ineffable visibility": an ultravisibility whose reading is so historically ingrained that it becomes a fait accompli, already signified, named, and normalized. It is when the unmarked—our Blackness in Africa—is marked and made visible (see Hall, 1997, for the idea of "marking"). This marking takes place in and through language and is felt on the surface of our "Black" bodies.

To explain further, if the "norm"—Whiteness in North America, for example—is made obscure and invisible through processes of normalization and naturalization (Abdi, 2008; Chan & Mirchandani, 2002; Fine et al., 2004; Frankenberg, 1993; Essed & Goldberg, 2002; Ibrahim, 2011), and if these processes are embedded in language and work by "hailing" and pointing towards the Other and away from the self (Althusser, 1971; Woodward, 1997), and furthermore, if the hailer or the speaker possesses the authorized language and the authorized power to speak and to be listened to (Bourdieu, 1991), then the *hailed Other*—Blackness in this study—can only be made excessively visible, a visibility that is ineffable because it just *is*. Here, the singular "I" stands for the plural "they," expressing what Laclau and Mouffe (1986) call an "axis of equivalence." One hailed Other would fetishistically stand for, and in place of, all Others. This, I contend, is implicated directly in how African youths enter this specter of ultra-, not to say ulterior, visibility, and in how people relate to their bodies, and in whom they then identify with, and why and how. In order to explore this ineffability, I shall begin with the autobiographical and then discuss the biographical.

Falling Under the Eyes of Power: Being or Becoming?

In his preface to Althea Prince's (2000) *Being Black*, Clifton Joseph, a West Indian, talks about the axis of equivalence, the *présence africaine* in West Indianness, or what it means to become Black in Canada. He writes:

> We were a politicized grouping of student/activists, athletes, those looking for a place to hang/out, street-wise players & partiers, and people who were just dissatisfied with not seeing enough blackness in school and in the society, generally. We *weren't* [italics added] "Black" where we came from in the west indies, but in toronto we had to confront the fact that we were seen as "Black," and had to check/out for ourselves what this blackness was. (pp. 16–17)

Succinctly, Joseph is describing the tug of war, the first encounter between the Black body and the syntactic structure of identity, the central focus of this book. Coming face to face with hailed Otherness, the West Indian experience, then, is no different from the continental African experience. Joseph has also encapsulated what can be termed the *politics of becoming Black*: "… we had to check/out for ourselves what this blackness was." And the negation and the past tense in his notion "We weren't 'Black' where we came from in the west indies" assume that we have "become" and hence we "are" now. It is a notion that requires a distinction between *being* and *becoming,* and since the rest of book depends on it, a definition is in order.

Hamlet famously observed, "To be or not to be—that is the question." Or is it? At a philosophical and phenomenological level, it has been argued, *being* can never be (in full and in complete), since it is always-already a *sujet-en-procès*, a work-in-progress, a continuous act of becoming (Butler, 2011; Hall, 2006; Ibrahim, 1999, 2011; Kristeva, 1974; Sartre, 1980; Woodward, 1997). Being as a continuous act of becoming deploys not a fixed entity but a production, a signifier that is already open for signification, a performative category that is never saturated (Deleuze & Guattari, 1987). Borrowed from Judith Butler (1999, 2009), performativity is a central concept of/for my research, and one that I shall explore further in chapter 1. It is a concept that does not assume *idées fixes*; quite the opposite, it requires repetitive, parodic, and continual acts of becoming. For Butler, there is nothing fixed about, for example, gender or the category "woman"—and I would add race (see also Minh-ha, 2011). Gender (or race) therefore for Butler is the repeated stylization of the body, a set of recurrent acts, words, and gestures, or what Roland Barthes (1983) calls *complex semiological languages*. These are signs that are open for signification and different readings because they cannot produce verbal utterances yet are ready to speak. According to Butler (2009), we produce and perform these complex languages on the surface of our bodies: in and through our modes of dress, walk, and talk; in our hair, *maquillage*, lip gloss; and in architecture, photographs, and so on. We perform, I contend accordingly, who we are, our identities, desires, and investments, at least in part, in and through these complex semiological languages: our modes of dress, walk, and talk. Following Simone de Beauvoir, Monique Wittig (2003) thus concludes that there is nothing inherent or guaranteed about being a woman. Indeed, one is not born a woman at all, one becomes one. If this is so, then *one is not born Black* either, *one becomes one*, where Blackness is a set of norms, narratives, and everyday performative roles and acts (Jackson & Moody-Freeman, 2011; Ibrahim, 2004; Kennedy, 2002; M. Wright, 2004).

Using the analogy of language learning, *being* can be equated to a mother tongue while *becoming* to a second language. Although no one can fully and completely master one's mother tongue, one is comfortable enough within it to know its nuances and even to know that which is beyond language, the excess (Klein, 2000; Rose, 2000). With a second language, by contrast, one enters—so to speak—that language as an outsider, in the hope that that which is outside will eventually belong to the self, that a second language will become a first. In short, *being* is an accumulative memory, an understanding, a conception, and an experience with which individuals interact with the world around them, whereas *becoming* is the process of building this memory—experience. As a continental African, for example, I was not (considered) Black in Africa; other terms served to patch together my identity, such as *tall, Sudanese, academic, basketball player,* and so on.

In other words, as I already indicated, race is not *the* defining social identity in Africa. However, in direct response to the historical representation of Blackness and the social processes of racialization where my "Black" body was (and still is) assembled and mapped in relation to and against the hegemonic White state of mind ("Oh, they all look like Blacks to me!"), the above antecedent signifiers, adjectives, became secondary to my Blackness, and I retranslated my being: I became Black. My main contention, then, is that in North America, my Black body speaks a language of its own, it cheats me, it ritualizes me, where I become a condensed moment of historicity, an inscribed repetition of convention, a passerby who turns to the policeman to acquire an identity, "one purchased, as it were, with the price of guilt" (Butler, 1997, p. 25). Here, Butler continues, the act of being recognized becomes an act of identity formation: The address animates me into an existence, constituting me within the possible circuit of recognition. Thus, to be recognized is to be interpellated, hailed within the terms of language, and it is only there that my social existence becomes possible (Althusser, 1971; Austin, 1962; Butler, 2009). My Blackness, put otherwise, was not marked in Africa. It was taken for granted; it was at the shadow, the blind spot, the outside of the speech act of the dominant North American other, refusing the latter's regulation, interpellation, subjection, normative gaze and even recognition. Simply, it was—a radical autonomy. However, as a refugee in North America, falling within the address of the other, I was given a new spelling of my name: I was rendered and addressed as Black. Clearly, the negativity around which Blackness is assembled in the West does not coincide with my contention here; far from it. I am interested, indeed, first, in the everyday, how people negotiate their identities and psychic, linguistic, cultural and social practices; second, in the pain and the triumph allied with these practices; and, finally, in the outcome of these practices and in detailing how they might look ethnographically and how we end up performing them, on our bodies or otherwise.

It is from this perspective that I tell the following story. It is meant to testify, and in moments like these, as Jacques Derrida (1996) has argued, "one can testify only to the unbelievable. To what can, at any rate, only be believed; to what appeals only to belief and hence to the given word...[here] when we ask others to take our word for it, we are already in the order of what is merely believable" (p. 20). An apogean experience, the story is an intense moment of becoming, a semantic moment that helped me solidify my understanding of what it means *to be* (a) Black (man) in North America, especially in Canada. It was the day I was hailed (as Black?) by an authorized speaker who possessed an authorized language. Published elsewhere (2003), it is an extract from my diary, where I titled it "Being Under Surveillance: Who Controls My 'Black' Body?" It is cited here for several reasons: first, to demonstrate how my body is hailed, constituted, and ritualized; second, to show the speech act my body produces in others, or what it makes them "say"; third, to delineate how much this writer is implicated in the research; and, finally, to explore the social context—of everyday racism (Essed & Goldberg, 2002)—where my research participants form, perform, and circulate their identities. For Dan McAdams (1993), it is only through personal narrative—what he calls "personal myth"—that we make meaning of our surroundings, ourselves, and of life itself. In order for others to know us, to know our desires, and in order for us to know ourselves, we need to tell our stories (see also Ladson-Billings, 2009). One may argue, in the end, that in this research there is quite a fine line between the biographical (my research participants' experiential narratives) and the autobiographical (how much this research is speaking about my own body). My story follows.

May 16, 1999: The Story of the "Dark Man"

Today was the last day of my trip to Toronto after a five-month absence in Ottawa. I had, to say the least, a wo(a)nderful time during my sojourn in Toronto: visited friends, had flavorful meals, and yes saw *The Mummy*, too. It was 1:10 p.m. on a sunny and an unexpectedly hot Sunday. I was more in the mood for poetry than for prose, and bicycling on St. George Street had never been so light. However, it is frightening how lightness can so easily whirl into an unbearable heaviness, and how heaviness can cause so much pain. It all began when I had just crossed the yellow light of Bloor Street West. I saw a white car curving into the bicycle lane and afterwards I heard a siren coming from it. Since I was bicycling, I was able to fully verify neither the car nor

> If you want to know me, then you must know my story, for my story defines who I am. And if *I* want to know myself, to gain insight into the meaning of my own life, then I, too, must come to know my own story....It is a story I continue to revise, and tell to myself (and sometimes to others) as I go on living (McAdams, 1993, p. 11, original emphasis).

who was driving it nor why it was requesting that I stop. However, when it was fully halted before my bicycle, I realized it was a police car. From it came veering a rangy White man in full gear and a pair of sunglasses, with a clean and handsome gun. My immediate thought was that it must be about the bicycle helmet, since I was not wearing one; and seeing that there is always a first time for our social experiences, I whispered to myself, "Oh my God, this is the first ticket of my life." I was deadly mistaken.

He approached my bicycle and said, "Have you ever been in trouble with the law before?" Shocked beyond any imaginable belief, I said, "No." "Can I know why am I asked the question?" I added. "You fit the description of a man we are looking for, who just snatched a bag from Yorkville; and I just saw you around the Yorkville area," he said. Could I have avoided Yorkville, since to buy a muffler or a bandana in Yorkville one needs at least a few hundred, and I had only $42 in my pocket? Coincidences have their own logic, which is beyond my humble understanding. At this point, he began a walkie-talkie conversation with a dispatcher, and I realized when he said, "I am talking to him right now" that it was a continuation of a previous dialogue. I was already under surveillance; I was already "talked" about; I had become intensely visible. Looking sternly into his eyes, I repeated one more time, "Can I know why I was stopped?" In a panoptic regime, I now understand, the redundancy of the question may mean one is thrown into a "White hole." His face turned red and he loudly regurgitated, "I TOLD you Sir that you fit the description of a man we are looking for."

Calmly, I wondered, "And what is that description?" "We are looking for a dark man with a dark bag," he said. First, I was curious about the "we." Who are "we"? I can hazard guesses, but my complex knowledge of this category makes the answer difficult. Second, I looked at my backpack, which I was carrying because I would be leaving Toronto at 3:00 p.m., and it occurred to me that my bag was light blue, with one very small black (or, as he said, "dark") stripe at the edge. More with my eyes than with my voice, I repeated after him, "A DARK man?" Self-consciously, but annoyingly, he exclaimed "A Black man with a dark bag!" He insisted that my bag was "dark"; now I was significantly metamorphosed from "dark" into "black." Not that it matters either way, I reflected after, but it seems that some people either cannot see or have a "color problem." "Do you live around here, Sir?" he asked. "I don't," I responded. Until now, I had no idea why his eyes stared out and his face changed when I said I did not live in Toronto. "Where do you live, Sir?" "Ottawa," I said. "What are you doing in Toronto?" What, indeed, are you doing in Toronto? I repeated to myself. Some questions, I guess, are meant to be repeated for their banality, if not stupefaction. I told him none of this; "I am visiting friends," I said. Looking unconvinced, he murmured "Ohha!"

During this conversation, I saw another police car stopping behind the first, and from it came another White policeman. I was then asked for a piece of identification. I gave the first policeman my citizenship card. Before I did so, he asked me to lay down my (dark?) bag, which I did. On his order, I widely opened my bag for all on the street to see. Since it was a tourist area, near the well attended Bata Shoe Museum, everyone was looking into my bag. Some, I observed, sympathized with my plight, and one White woman was smiling. I was upset not only by my situation, which was abstrusely absurd, but also that Toni Morrison's *Paradise*, Margaret Atwood's *Alias Grace,* and Julia Kristeva's *Reader* had to endure the same humiliation. These books were on top of my clothes. Not that these books mattered in and of themselves, because they didn't; disrespect of the authors was what bothered me. Anyway, it was getting closer to 2 p.m., and my ride to Ottawa was to leave at 3 p.m. At this point, I decided to use my University of Ottawa professor identification. I am still debating whether it was a good or bad decision not to use it from the beginning. After writing down my name and date of birth, the policeman announced to the dispatcher, "All is OK now." With no apologies, I was ordered to collect my affairs and my bag, and he uttered, "You are free to go now."

To be assembled under the eyes of power is to become an "abstract machine," a "Body without Organ,"[7] a signifier whose signification is determined not by the speaker but squarely by those who are authorized to speak. Nonetheless, I am still wondering if the reasons for which I was stopped would be enough to stop a White man. Who among White men would be stopped? Probably an unsmartly dressed man, with long hair in a ponytail. Moreover, I am wondering, what if I could not look the policeman in the eye and ask why I was stopped in a calm manner (which was not an evoked personae but my natural character)? What if I was a shy man who is genuinely frightened by the police? As well, one might ask, did my Hip-Hop dress, my emerging dreadlocks, and my youthfulness (at the time of the arrest) form part of the reasons why I was stopped? Given my panic, terror, and fright, what would have happened if I had run? Given the antagonistic relationship between the Black body and the police in Canada and North American in general, the wrath I saw in that man's eyes was not reassuring.

Again, to fall under the eyes of power—the gaze—is to find oneself within *discourses of closure* where the Black body is already authored, read, and constantly stabilized across time, language, culture, and space. Here, "I" becomes fixed, known, and already spoken and talked about; an open book, a canvas to be drawn on. This book will try to map out, both theoretically and ethnographically, these moments of being under the eyes of power, and I shall offer a theoretical proposition that links my vignette with the research upon which this book is based. It is a framework connected to the *gaze*: How am I perceived or imagined, and what impacts does this imaginary have on how I am gazed upon, consumed, and related to? Even if, as Rousseau would have argued, we "live very much in the public gaze" (Taylor, 1994, p. 86), what is the nature of this public gaze, and how much impact does it have on our identities, identification, investments, and desires? In what follows, I shall discuss the research's main questions and contentions, its methodology, and the progression of the chapters.

The Problem of the Twenty-First Century: Research Questions

W. E. B. Du Bois forecasted in 1903 that "the problem of the twentieth century is the problem of color-line" (p. 13). As far as the "imaginary of Blackness" is concerned (Jackson & Moody-Freeman, 2011), has anything changed since then? Should we and/or could we enunciate a similar prophecy for the twenty-first century? Though without the definite article *the* (in Du Bois's sentence above), and despite Obama's presidency (Giroux, 2012), the answer in the present book tilts more toward the affirmative. If this is so, what are the implications of Du Bois's prophetic statement for the process of identity formation in general, and the process of learning in particular, especially learning a second language? That is, how do displaced subjects form their identities, and what is the role of popular culture representation in this formation? What happens to Old Identities *in* the New geocultural, linguistic, and social space?[8] And how and in what way do our differently raced, gendered, sexed, abled, and classed social identities enter the process of learning? Under what social conditions do students learn what they learn? Put differently, at the dawn of the twenty-first century, known as late modernity, postmodernism, and/or after postmodernism (Faye, 2012; Jameson, 1991; Lyotard, 1984; Trifonas, 2004), when identity formation is increasingly mediated by technological media, who learns what, and how is it learned? How are these mediated identities formed and performed?

In her discussion of the network of relationships between perception and reality, the mental and the physical, matter and language, and especially gender and race, Monique Wittig (2003) raises epistemological and ontological questions that are very significant for my research. The central problem with race and sex for Wittig is that they are taken as immediate and sensible givens, physical features belonging to a natural order. Yet, as she puts it, "what we believe to be a physical and direct perception is only a sophisticated and mythical construction, an 'imaginary formation'" (p. 159). In the epigraph that opens this chapter, she writes, "They are seen as *black*, therefore they *are* black; they are seen as *women*, therefore, they *are* women" (p. 159). They are seen by whom, I want to ask, and what is the translatability or conversion of being seen into "is"—that is, the psychic relation between visuality and reality? "But before being seen that way," she continues, "they first had to be *made* that way" (p. 159). How does one make a woman, *woman*, or a Black person, *Black*? More importantly, what is the psychic and consequently ethnographic result of being made a woman or being made Black?

That is, in the case of African youths, how is becoming Black implicated in who they identify with, and how and why? What is the role of race and racism in their identification and social identity formation in general? At a time when North American Blackness is governed by how it is negatively located in a race-conscious society, what does it mean for an English as a Second Language (ESL) learner to acquire Black English as a Second Language (BESL)? In other words, what symbolic, cultural, pedagogical, and identity investments would learners have in locating themselves politically and racially at the margin of representation? Given their "Blackness," how are continental African youths assembled, positioned, imagined, and constructed inside and outside the school? What are the implications of this construction in students' social identity formation, identification, and processes of learning? Finally, in a postcolonial era when postcolonial subjects are constituting part of the metropolitan centers, what critical pedagogy is required in order not to repeat the colonial history embedded in the classroom relationship between White teachers and students of color? This research is guided by and simultaneously a response to these questions, where each question will be discussed in detail.

Being Made: Research Contentions

The central working contention of the research is that once in North America, continental African youths enter, so to speak, or will be subject to a *social imaginary*: an assemblage of ideas, a discursive or symbolic space in which they are already constructed, imagined, assembled, and positioned, and thus treated by the hegemonic discourses and dominant groups, respectively, as Blacks. Here, I address the arborified and dominant White everyday communicative state of mind: "Oh, they all look like Blacks to me!" This state of mind, one must note, should not be seen as racist, though it always-already has the potential of becoming so. Per contra, it is a racial discursive framework that invokes, works within, and makes use of racial history; a history that is deeply marked by modernity[9] and racial stratification (cf. Stanley, 2011). This social imaginary is best described as *racialization* (Chan & Mirchandani, 2002; Essed & Goldberg, 2002; Minh-ha, 2011; Winant, 2004). Offered to continental African youths through netlike praxis in exceedingly complex and mostly subconscious ways, this discursive framework is a racial positionality that does not and is unwilling to acknowledge the differences in the students' ethnicities, languages, nationalities, and cultural identities and backgrounds. Fanon (1967, p. 116) sums up this striated, arborified and netlike praxis brilliantly in writing about himself as a Black *Antillais* coming to the metropolis of Paris:

> I am given no chance, I am overdetermined from without. I am the slave not of the "idea" that others have of me but of my own appearance....I *progress* [italics added] by crawling. And *already* [italics added] I am being dissected under white eyes, the only real eyes. I am *fixed*. Having adjusted their microtomes, they objectively cut away slices of my reality. I am laid bare....When people like me, they tell me it is in spite of my color. When they dislike me, they point out that it is not because of my color. Either way, I am locked into the infernal circle.

Obviously, one's imagined community (Anderson, 1983) is someone else's racial nightmare. As such, one is turned into what Trinh Minh-ha (2011) calls the "new color of fear." Henceforth, continental African youths find themselves in a racially conscious society that, wittingly or unwittingly, and through fused yet rigid, striated, circumscribed, normalized, and arborified social mechanisms such as racisms and racial representations, *asks* them to racially fit somewhere. To fit somewhere signifies choosing or becoming aware of one's own being, which is partially reflected in one's language practice. Choosing, I will argue, is a question of agency, which itself is governed and disciplined—in the Foucauldian (1979) sense—by social conditions. For example, to be Black in a racially conscious society such as the Euro-Canadian and U.S. societies means that one is expected to be Black and act Black, and thus be the marginalized Other (Chideya, 2000; Dei, 2010; Hill, 2008; Nelson, 2010). As will become clear, under such disciplinary social conditions, continental African youths express their *moments of identification*—where they see themselves mirrored—in relation to African American cultures and languages, thus becoming Black. Alternatively, since these moments of identification are contextually Canadian, the impact of African Canadians can also be ethnographically traced.

Interestingly, considering that continental African youths do not have many African American friends, nor do they have everyday contact with them, channels of Black popular culture—namely, Hip-Hop and Rap, and Black magazines, newspaper, television, and cinema—emerge as crucial sites to access these mediated cultural identities and language practice. One may dispute the uniqueness of this phenomenon, since the global impact of African American culture and music, especially contemporary Hip-Hop, is well documented (see especially Alim, Ibrahim, & Pennycook, 2009; Terkourafi, 2010). What renders it unique, for me, surprisingly, are the Elvis Presleys, Eric Claptons, and Eminems of the White world. That is to say, when a White person takes up Black culture and music, it becomes a cause célèbre, and a whole industry is created around them. In contrast, when K'naan (Somali Canadian), Emmanuel Jal (Sudanese Canadian), or Akon (Senegalese American) take up Hip-Hop, it is almost expected. The aim of this book is to complicate this reasoning and look at its cultural, linguistic, and psychic implications. That is, I want to ask, why does this reasoning exist in the first place, and what does it mean for African youths?

It is significant to note that, as far as African youth identity formation is concerned, Black popular culture is identified with, related to, assembled, and read within a framework of *translation* and *negotiation*. In other words, while African youths were translating, paraphrasing, and mapping the meaning of the new North American culture and language, a peculiar supplementarity and resignification was happening to the cultures, languages, histories, and memories they brought with them from their homelands. The "Old" is being translated simultaneously as the "New." As I discuss in the next chapter, the end result is a "bricolage" (Kress, 2011), a "rhizomatic assemblage" (Deleuze & Guattari, 1987), a "new flâneurie" (Ibrahim, 2008), a hybrid "third space" (Bhabha, 1994), which results from a subconscious negotiation between the two. Here, the African will be founded side by side with the North American: in the same sentence, in the same garment, at the same time.

Obviously, the unsatisfactory integration of African youths into the New Canadian dominant groups, the public spaces they occupy, and their arborified symbolic cultural and linguistic capital has influenced their moments of identification. That they take up, identify with, and cite Rap and Hip-Hop and acquire BESL is by no means a coincidence. On the contrary, these actions are semiotic articulations of the youths' desire to belong to a location, a politics, a memory, a history, and hence a representation. It is their way of saying, "We too are Black!" and "We too desire Blackness!"

Hanging Out Methodology: A Critical Ethnographic Research Project

Following Sandra Harding (2009), I make a distinction between method and methodology (see also Denzin & Giardina, 2010). Classically, Harding (1987) defines methodology as "a theory and analysis of how research does or should proceed; it includes accounts of how the general structure of theory finds its application in particular scientific disciplines" (p. 3). Method, on the other hand, "is a technique for (or way of proceeding in) gathering evidence" (p. 2). Bonny Norton (2000) refers to this distinction as "the theory of the methodology" and "the methodology of the theory." In another context, she argues that "[t]heory (implicit or explicit) informs the questions researchers ask, the assumptions they make, and the procedures, methods, and approaches they use to carry out projects. *How* data is collected," she continues, "will inevitably influence what kind of data is created, and in turn, what conclusions are drawn on the basis of data analysis" (Norton, 1993, p. 22; original emphasis). But how data is collected and what conclusions are drawn, I would submit, are contiguously and discursively (co)authored by the researcher's subject location. Indeed, they are a direct expression of that location. I want to refer to this as the *politics of embodiment*: Who the researcher is and what her or his racial, gender, sexual, and social class embodiments are will necessarily influence, if not govern, the research questions and findings. It is a politics that calls for a subjective notion of research where "the class, race, culture, and gender assumptions, beliefs, and behaviors of the researcher her/himself must be placed within the frame of the picture that she/he attempts to paint" (Harding, 1987, p. 8; see also Denzin, Lincoln, & Smith, 2008).

Methodologically, the present research project is located within what Monica Heller (2011) defines as *critical ethnography*, which Simon and Dippo (1986) prototypically call a *critical ethnographic research project*. For both Heller and Simon and Dippo, a critical ethnographic research project is a set of activities situated within a political and pedagogical *project* that seeks and works its way towards social transformation. It has "an underlying set of assumptions, a structure of relevance, and a form of rationality," and it is "determined both by real and present conditions, *and* certain conditions still to come which it is trying to bring into being" (Simon & Dippo, 1986, pp. 195–196; original emphasis). The assumption underpinning my project is that Canadian (and U.S.) society is "inequitably structured and dominated by a hegemonic culture that suppresses a consideration and understanding of why things are the way they are and what must be done for things to be otherwise" (Simon & Dippo, 1986, p. 196). My "critical ethnographic research project" therefore, at least in part, is a deconstruction of these hegemonic institutional and cultural practices and norms.

The critical ethnographic research project upon which this book is based is a complicated one. In fact, it is not one study in one place. It is a series of research projects that I carried out in the mid-1990s, in 2007, and in 2011.

These projects took me from a relatively small French-language intermediate and high school in southwestern Ontario to two large urban English-language high schools in northeastern Ontario. The determining factor in choosing these sites was their populations: They all had sizeable continental African student populations. In the French-language intermediate and high school, for example, they constituted more than one-third of the student population. I was, and still am, interested in how this population experiences what I will call the *rhizomatic process of becoming Black* across language and geography. In this sense, then, my research is demonstrably "archaeological" (Foucault, 1972).

Apparently, Foucault tells us, at any given period in a given domain, we are surrounded and engulfed by discourses; discourses that are restraining and constraining what we do, what we think, and how we think the "unthinkable." These discourses are a set of *énoncés*, an ensemble of announcements, statements, concepts, and ideologies that govern and act as technologies of control that materially restrict the range of thought. The role of "archaeological analysis," then, is to uncover these implicit rules: that which is symbolically intangible yet materially felt on our bodies. Once we uncover these seemingly arbitrary constraints, along with their rules and expectations, Foucault contends, we will be able to see that they are neither arbitrary nor nonsensical. Indeed, they make total sense in the framework defined by these rules. Here, the idea is not simply to analyze the individual act but to archaeologically dig deep into the underlying structures that form the context where that act is possible. The dilemma for Foucault is that our primary access to these *deep* structures is the *énoncé*, the linguistic event, the specific *surface* use of language.

In themselves, these *énoncés* are significant, but they are more illuminating collectively. Together, they act like "monuments" (Foucault, 1972, p. 7), where the emphasis, according to archaeological methodology, is not (on) what X says but what X + the people around him or her, of the same time and place, say. Their *énoncés* are then taken, collectively, as clues to the general deep structure of the system in which they live, think, learn, and circulate their desires and identities. This system, significantly, is not linear, but heterogeneous and multiple; it is not simplistically organizational, but complexly "rhizomatic" (Deleuze & Guattari, 1987). As such, it resists chronology and organization in favor of a "nomadic" system of "interbeing," where we are forever in the middle in terms of subjectivity and identity, as we shall see in the next chapter. Archaeologically, I will use significant *énoncés* (interview transcripts), incidents, and moments to "think through" (Derrida, 2000) the notion and the process of becoming Black as a story, a narrative, and a plot. This narrative exposes what Trinh Minh-ha (2011) calls "the (ugly) nature of the system" (p. 42). Here, Blackness becomes a perfect illustration of how what Deleuze and Guattari (1987) call "arborescent model" works. By "arborescent," Deleuze and Guattari are referring to a vertical and linear way of becoming. In contrast to the rhizomatic model, where things are fluid, complex, always multiple, and in constant motion, the arborescent model is a rigid and a determined cartography, whose "line of flight" or possibilities are limited and limiting. Simply put, similar to Timothy Stanley (2011), I intend to argue that Whiteness has become an arborescent category: a rigid map and a clearly demarcated cartography against which Blackness is mapped, categorized, and signified.

I first started my systematic—ethnographic—inquiry into these cartographies, their norms, rituals, and subsequent speech and bodily performance from January to June 1996 at Marie-Victorin, a small French-language high school in a large metropolis in southwestern Ontario, Canada. This was followed by a second study from May to June 2007 in a large English-language urban high school in a large city in northeastern Ontario. This study was used as an archaeological moment to dig deeper and better understand the process of becoming Black. In 2011 I conducted a third study in the same large city at a different large English-language urban high school. I will give a relatively short description of each of these schools below, but for now it is worth noting that all through these studies, I was not (and still am not) interested in comparing schools, linguistic experiences, or cultural geographies. I am interested in how young people experience, work their way into, make use of, impact, and are impacted by the process of becoming Black across time, geographies, and linguistic cartographies. Moreover, I am interested in how people experience this process from the bottom up. That is, my investigation does not center on structural and grand analysis; instead, I am focusing on what the everyday say about grand narrative and structure. Put otherwise, I am investigating how people take up, translate, make sense of, and perform the so-called structure and, in turn, what their everyday practices and performances say about the structure. Reciprocally understood, my access to the grand narrative and structure is through the everyday *énoncés* and doings.

To access these *énoncés*, I am introducing a framework that accounts for both archaeology and ethnography: *hanging out methodology*. In a true anthropological spirit and tradition of ethnography, one "hangs out" in a place to get the "full" picture, if ever that is possible, of the place, the people, the culture, and the sense of being and becoming in it. This is especially true with young people. Whether one is studying the "lad" in England (Willis,

1977), Shaker High in the U.S. Midwest (Ogbu, 2003), "Hiphopography" in Oakland, California (Alim, 2006), Hip-Hoppers in Hong Kong (Lin, 2009), or the African youths of this study, the aim has been to investigate what young people *actually* do, say, and perform on their bodies and, in turn, what their doings "say" about who they are, and their identities, desires, and futures. According to Willis (1977), this should give us a complex picture of the space in which these identities circulate. In this sense, *hanging out* is neither aimless nor rigid nor without a theoretical grounding. It attempts to understand the complex through the banal, the structural through the everyday, the infinite possibilities of identities through daily utterances, performances, and "doings" (Foucault, 1972). As a methodology, it sees the classic research notions of reliability and validity as useful, but from an archaeological point of view, as Ladson-Billings (1998) argues, all stories, especially the "minoritarian" (Deleuze & Guattari, 1987), deserve special attention. The reliability and validity of minoritarian stories stem from their juxtaposition, triangulation, and the metanarrative they attempt to tell collectively (Duncan-Andrade & Morrell, 2008). Yet, the individual story is as significant as the collective. In the critical pedagogy tradition (Kincheloe, 2008), all stories and research are situational, contextual, and tied to space and time. Hence, not only are all stories contingent and contextual, but the very definition of reliability and validty is also contextual and contingent. There is no universally valid definition in all time and in all places. Therefore, as it seeks meaning in the everyday, the hanging out methodology is mindful of this contingency of the everyday, and as such, it has to do the difficult balancing act of paying homage to individual stories as it attempts to tell a collective story. It asks not only, Is this story true? but also, and more significantly, What does the story mean? "What new thoughts does it make possible to think? What new emotions does it make possible to feel? What new sensations and perceptions does it open in the body?" (Massumi, 1992, p. 8).

For hanging out methodology, the everyday is a feast, a theater of the marvelous, where one should always be open to the pleasant surprises of daily life. Yet, as this book shows, life is not always pleasant and marvelous; indeed, for the minoritarian, it is puzzlingly absurd, affectively painful, and psychically haunting. The hanging out methodology is proposed here specifically in order to live this tension between the marvelous and the absurd, where there are no simple readings and thus no simple solutions. In the words of van Manen (1997), hanging out is a "poetic activity," and "as in poetry it is inappropriate to ask for [simple] conclusion" (p. 13). This is why I am addressing becoming Black as a rhizomatic process and not a conclusion.

To be sure, hanging out methodology requires the researcher to hang out, to stay in/within a space for an extended period of time to *truly* familiarize herself or himself with the place, its people, and their ways of being in that space. In my case, these sites were sometimes formal (classrooms) but mostly informal areas within schools, such as hallways, the schoolyards, the school steps, the cafeteria, the gymnasium, and especially the basketball court, where students were comfortable enough to speak their minds. Because I hung out in these schools for so long, in one school I became the assistant to the school basketball coach; in another school, I became a tutor and academic help; and in the third, I became an advocate for the students before the school administration. In traditional ethnography, I am considered a "participant-observer," whose role is to become part of the research scene and then report my findings (Carspecken & Walford, 2001; Denzin & Giardina, 2010). Given the "participatory" and "advocacy" nature (Kress, 2011) of this research, however, where the line between the so-called researcher and research participants is fine, the very definition of research is reconceptualized. In hanging out methodology, research "becomes an act of love" (Ibrahim, 2014); findings are turned into a series of advocacy *énoncés* for social change and social justice; and all participants, including the person institutionally defined as researcher, become co-constructors and co-researchers. As an act of love, we research the communities we research because we have an expressed love for them and we want the best for them. This is not the colonial desire, or "going native," or simply collecting data for our research. Here we become advocates *with* the people with whom we are co-researching. They let us into their classrooms, into their homes, and into their hearts, so hanging out as a methodological event becomes a reciprocal act of love.

> [B]ecause it [rhizoanalysis] has given up on intentions, it cannot see very far down the road. It stalls, gets stuck, thumbs its nose at order, goes someplace the [researcher] did not know existed ahead of time, stumbles over its sense, spins around its middle foregoing ends, wraps idea around idea in some overloaded imbrication that flies out of control into a place of no return…. Writing, then, is an exquisitely brazen, ethically astute rhizome that deterritorializes subjects and method. Rhizomatic, nomadic writing, in fact, writes its authors. (St. Pierre, 1997, p. 414)

In terms of method, that is, the actual techniques for data collection, hanging out requires extensive, thick, lengthy, extended periods of hanging out. It requires diligence and thorough notes (be it ethnographic observations or interviews or document analysis). For example, for the present study, in 1996 I spent the entire day in the school two or three times a week, on average, for six months. Intensively, I attended classes and observed curricular and extracurricular activities. Prior to conducting this research, significantly, I was involved in another research project in the same school for almost two years; so, in actuality, the findings reported from the 1996 study are an extended product of two and a half years of research. This explains, in part, why most of what is reported in this book is based on that study. Although I conducted the research from January to June 1996, like archaeological and rhizoanalysis (Foucault, 1972; Johnson, 2004; Alverman, 2000), the research did not have a beginning, a middle, and an end. Hanging out methodology is always working in the middle: that productive space where linkages are possible and ruptures and discontinuities proliferate to open up new "tracings, possibilities of analysis and 'lines of flight'" (Johnson, 2004; St. Pierre, 1997). Therefore, constantly I needed to make connections and linkages, to be open to the surprises and the delays in the road ahead, and to be on the lookout for the "exquisitely brazen" (Johnson, 2004) and its infinite rhizomatic deterritorializations.

With the permission of the students as well as their parents and the school administration, I started to hang out in Marie-Victorin in January 1996. To this day, I remain grateful for the students and their parents who signed individual permissions and participation consents to 'hang out' and interview them. I spent countless hours in the school. I took extensive field notes, which I wrote immediately after each visit. I video- and/or audiotaped classes, sports activities, picnics, ceremonies, graduations and festivals, and free interactions during lunchtimes; on two occasions, I gave a tape recorder to students to capture their "natural" interactions among themselves, without me present (O'Toole & Were, 2008; Rampton, 1995). My interest was in part in their linguistic code-switching, and subsequently I interviewed them in French or English and transcribed these interviews thoroughly, using margin spaces for theme grouping. I used what Neuman and Robson (2012) and De-Poy and Gitlin (2011) call an *emergent coding system.* Following this system, after transcribing all the interviews and observation notes, I read through them three times to find the big commonalities across people and contexts, and then categorized these commonalities into themes with related subthemes. In the third reading I identified quotes and important passages that followed the themes. In the 1996 study, all interviews were conducted on the school grounds except for one group interview with the boys, which was conducted in the home of one of the students. They were either individual or group interviews, and I translated the French-language interviews into English. I also consulted official school documents. Composed of open-ended questions, the interviews became both moments of verifying my conclusions and/or initiating new ideas or lines of flight.

In 2007 I hung out in a large English-language urban high school for eight weeks from May to June and "soak[ed] up every detail in case it might be of some particular significance in later analysis" (Troman, Jeffry & Walford, 2004, p. 538). I will call this school Sunnyside (see next section). I went to school every day during those eight weeks; I attended classes, and hung around the cafeteria, library, gym, parking lot, bus stop (where a large number of students hung out as they waited for the school bus or public transport), and so on. All interviews were conducted in English at the school, and the procedure I used for data analysis was similar to that of the 1996 study.

In 2011, I conducted a study similar to the 1996 and 2007 studies. For this one, however, I was invited by the school to conduct an in-depth ethnographic study of the school from February to June. With their permission, in this book I use some of the ethnographic notes I took during the study. I will refer to this school as Maxwell High (see next section). As in the 1996 and 2007 studies, I used hanging out methodology and found myself in classrooms, the cafeteria, hallways, on city buses, and at a local shopping plaza. Although there is a multilayered level of data, for the sake of clarity I will focus primarily on the 1996 study and use data from 2007 and 2011 as supplementary data. In my discussion of my research findings, the year of data collection is implicit in the name of the school under study: Marie-Victorin (data collected in 1996), Sunnyside (2007), or Maxwell High (2011).

In all three sites, I used what I call *ethnography of performance*. A central tenet of the hanging out methodology, ethnography of performance contends that the ethnographer's best access to the research participant's rhizomatic identity and subjectivity is the participant's verbal and nonverbal performance. That is, what people actually and materially perform on and through their bodies and what they say and the meaning they put onto those performances combine to give the ethnographer a more complete—or the least distorted—picture of the research participant's identity. Put otherwise, I did a thorough interpretive analysis of these triangulated data from all three studies: my reflective journal entries, interview conversations, video-/audiotape analysis, and school official documents. I was able to see students over an extended period of time, in different places, doing multiple activities, which allowed me access to the rhizomatic process of becoming Black and a better understanding of its epiphenomenon: learning Black English as a Second Language (BESL). Since my interest was in the students' everyday lives, a shortcoming of this research was that I was not able to interview parents or

White persons, and only one teacher, one counselor, and two multicultural workers across all three studies.

Unité dans la diversité: Research Sites

1996: The first site of the research was a small French-language intermediate and high school (grades 7–13) in the affluent north side of a large urban metropolitan city in southwestern Ontario, Canada: Marie-Victorin (MV). MV had a population of approximately 400 students from various ethnic, racial, cultural, religious, and linguistic backgrounds. Although it is a French-language school, the language predominantly spoken by students in the school corridors and hallways was English; Arabic, Somali, and Farsi were also spoken sometimes. The school had 27 teachers (19 for the high school—*l'école secondaire*—and 8 for the intermediate school—*intermédiaire*), all of whom were White, except for one counselor and one teacher of colour; and the school archives showed that up until the 1990s, almost all students were White, too, except for a few students of African (read Black, mainly Haitians) and Middle Eastern descent.

Opened in the late 1960s, MV is the first French-language public high school in this metropolitan area. It is a two-story building with a gymnasium and three playgrounds, and it has seven academic departments and two academic streams: *niveau général* (general level) and *niveau avancé* (advanced level).[10] The mission of the school is clearly stated in a posting at its entrance:

La mission de l'école Marie-Victorin consiste à offrir aux jeunes francophones de la région Métropolitaine une programmation de base, solide et unique, dans une atmosphère de respect mutuel entre tous, et toutes, grace à un cadre éducatif efficace et propice à la réussite.

[The mission of the school Marie-Victorin consists of offering to young francophones of the metropolitan region a basic program, strong and unique, in an atmosphere of mutual respect between everyone, thanks to an effective and success-oriented educational framework].

Significantly, at the time of this research, students who were born outside Canada or were children of parents born outside Canada made up 70% of the student population at MV. Continental Africans constituted the majority of that 70% and, indeed, MV's population in general, though their numbers fluctuated slightly from year to year. For its part, the school emphasized the theme of unity in this multicultural and multiethnoracial population, with the slogan *unité dans la diversité* (unity in diversity). This discourse of unity, as we shall see, remained at the level of rhetoric, and had little material bearing on the students' lives. The absence of people of color in the school personnel was a case in point. Indeed, it was the Frenchness of the school that seemed to be the capital of its promotion. That is, the French language, especially in Canada, represents a form of extremely important *symbolic capital* which, according to Bourdieu (1991), can be the key for accessing *material capitals*—jobs, business, and so on. Given their postcolonial educational history, most African youths in fact come to Franco-Ontarian schools already possessing a highly valued symbolic capital: *le français parisien* (Parisian French).

2007: The second site of the research is a large urban high school with close to 900 students: Sunnyside. The school is located in a metropolitan city in northeastern Ontario in an extremely ethnically diverse neighborhood. Sunnyside was established in the late 1950s as one of the schools built to accomodate children of the baby boom and to increase school attendance. Sunnyside offers many programs including English as a Second Language (ESL), French immersion, mechanics, woodworking, both general and university-bound academics, Everyday Community Living (a program for special needs students), and international languages (e.g., Spanish, Somali, and Arabic). Sunnyside is well known in the city for its ethnic diversity. In 2007 there were more than forty-five languages spoken at the school, and each was represented with a flag in the school cafeteria. Hence, it was the norm to hear languages other than English in the school. Interestingly enough, one can already observe what Ben Rampton (1995) calls "crossing." In this context, this occurs when unilingual English speakers are so immersed in a particular clique in the school that speaks a language other than English (Somali or Arabic, for example) that they start code-switching, using certain words and terms from that language. It is their way of "signaling" their desire to belong, or in some cases, following Rampton, they are "just kidding around" (as one student told me). Three or four times, I witnessed English-language teachers slipping in Somali and Arabic words, for example, to get students' attention in class. This proved to be extremely effective pedagogically, because it gets the students' full attention.

2011: The third and last site of research is another urban high school of close to 700 students: Maxwell High. Opened at the same time as Sunnyside, Maxwell High is located in the east end of a large city in northeastern Ontario. Historically, the east end tended to be working-class and occupied by French-language speakers. Since late 1990s it was radically transformed into an exceptionally ethnically diverse neighborhood, yet it kept its "working-class vibe" (as the school vice principal calls it). Almost all the students at the school come from this immediate neighborhood. The school was designed to house more than 1,200 students, but in 2011 it had about 700 students. The physical environment of the school is welcoming, with a big display case in the foyer of the school containing more than forty flags from a variety of nations, representing the national origins of the student population. Maxwell High is equipped with a multicultural, multifaith prayer room that was designed and built by a team of students and one teacher. There is a mixed stream offering academic (advanced), applied (general), and essential-level courses. The school also has a significant ESL program, with about 15% of the student population enrolled. Its specialization in ESL programs makes it one of the most ethnically diverse schools in the city. Maxwell High also has programs for special needs students and strong technological programs. It is not surprising to see adult ESL learners in the hallways or teenage mothers bringing their kids to the daycare housed in the school. This sense of structure yet openness is what makes the school a "community hub," as the principal calls it. Student-generated art lines the walls in the hallways all through the school; a huge display case at the front of the school is large enough to house the flags representing the home nations of all the students.

All three schools have between 15 and 25 clubs, from sports to academic to social clubs. They each have a substantial population of continental African students, my co-researchers. But this population is represented in neither the teaching staff nor the school personnel. MV had one teacher and one counselor of color (out of 27 teachers); Sunnyside had three teachers of color and one multicultural worker who liaises between the school, parents, and the community, providing translation and academic help (out of 65 teachers); and Maxwell High had a vice principal of color, one teacher of color, one multicultural worker and three First Nation teachers (out of 52 teachers).

From Ethiopia to Sénégal: Research Participants

My research participants in all three sites encompass groups of youths who are part of a growing continental francophone, anglophone, and allophone African population in French-language and English-language schools. Francophone here refers to youths who come from postcolonial countries where French is designated by the state as the national or official language of the state and/or as the language of instruction and education (e.g., Côte d'Ivoire, Sénégal, or Togo). Similarly, anglophone refers to youths from states where English is the national or official language (e.g., Kenya, Nigeria, or Zimbabwe); whereas allophone refers to youths whose countries and frames of reference are neither English nor French (e.g., Sudan).

The numbers of continental Africans have grown exponentially since the beginning of the 1990s all across Canada, but particularly in Ontario (Statistics Canada, 2011). The research participants varied in several ways, the first of which was the length of their residence in Canada: in 1996 it ranged from one to six years, but in 2007 and 2011 almost 90% were Canadian born. Yet, 100% of the parents had been born outside Canada, in all three studies. Second, they varied in legal status (some were immigrants but the majority were refugees in 1996, and 100% were Canadian citizens in 2007 and 2011) and, third, in their sexes, classes, ages, languages, and national backgrounds. They came from diverse places including Democratic Republic of Congo (formerly Zaïre), Djibouti, Gabon, Ghana, Senegal, Somalia, South Africa, Sudan, South Sudan, Sierra Leone, and Togo. With no exceptions, all of the African students in all three schools were at least bilingual, and in MV, they were trilingual, speaking English, French, and a mother tongue or first language,[11] with various (postcolonial) histories of language learning and degrees of fluency in each language.

Marie-Victorin: After three weeks of extensive 'hanging out' at the school in January 1996, I made a purposeful sampling (Troman et al., 2004): I chose 10 boys and 6 girls for extensive ethnographic observation inside and outside the classroom—especially language arts and ESL classes—and inside and outside the school, and I interviewed all 16. Although I shall closely interpret the stories and narrative of these 16, their narrative, it should be noted, is horizontally applicable, holds sway, and is ethnographically verifiable and emotionally felt in all three studies. Of the 10 boys, 6 were Somali speakers (from Somalia and Djibouti), 1 was Ethiopian, 2 were Senegalese, and 1 was from Togo. A considerable number of them bore witness to traumas of war and violent displacement; some came to Canada, underage, by themselves, while others came with their parents. Their ages ranged from sixteen to twenty. The 6 girls were all Somali speakers (also from Somalia and Djibouti), aged fourteen to eighteen. As already mentioned, the students chose the language in which the interviews were conducted (either English or French). The only Black counselor and a former Black teacher were also interviewed; given the highly sensitive issues addressed in this study, and the teacher-student relationships at the school, I chose not to interview White teachers.

Sunnyside and Maxwell High: In contrast to MV, at Sunnyside and Maxwell High I chose to simply hang out with African students without a tight following of a particular group of students. So, my interviews were conducted whenever and wherever the occasions arose, and usually took the format of informal conversations. They were conducted at the schools, in English, and they mostly lasted 45 minutes to 1 hour. I conducted 10 interviews, involving 8 students (4 boys and 4 girls), one vice principal (an African Canadian), one teacher assistant (an African Canadian), and a multicultural liaison (Canadian of Somali origin). I transcribed these interviews and used emergent coding system.

Progression of Chapters

Chapter 1 theorizes and investigates the interrelation between race, identity, and culture, with specific attention to youth popular culture. It brings together Stuart Hall's (2006) "new ethnicity" and "articulation," Homi Bhabha's (1990) "hybridity," Pierre Bourdieu's (1977, 1991) "market" and "capitals," and Deleuze and Guattari's (1987) "rhizome" to build a new landscape that Homi Bhabha calls the *third space,* and I call *rhizomatic identity* and *rhizomatic third space.* In the process, I discuss Kristeva's (1974) "transposition" and Bakhtin's (2000) "heteroglossia," "dialogue," and "translation." Ultimately, the goal in this chapter is to experiment theoretically with the *rhizomatic process of becoming Black.*

Chapter 2 is where I set the stage through a discussion of the racial climate of/in the schools. Here, I discuss what is happening on stage—read, to students—and what is happening behind the scene—read, to Black teachers and staff. Focusing on MV, I will recount a particular, significant incident that happened to a Black teacher, who experienced one of the most violent symbolic utterances and anger. These experiences, in the cases of the students, were crucial moments in the odyssey of becoming Black and BESL learning.

Chapter 3 addresses questions of pedagogy, the lack of Black teachers, and the absence of Black people from history books. Building on their experiences of schooling in their homelands, African youths show a clear understanding of the Eurocentric nature of textbooks, pedagogy, and school personnel. There is nothing but agony and rules and regulations that are imposed solely on a group of students that constitutes one third to one half of the school population (in the case of MV); a group whose sizeable representation is only in the lower academic level. Either the youths themselves or their parents have experience of success in their homelands, and they know they *are* capable of it in Canadian schools, too.

Chapter 4 is divided into two sections. The first section focuses on language: the historical memories of language learning, students' relation to and emotional investment in language, and the diverse sites of language learning. The site of their BESL learning was Black popular culture: Hip-Hop and Rap. The second section introduces culture as found in the students' narratives. This encompasses *cultural representation* and *separatist culture.* The former speaks to the *présence africaine* in the imaginary of the nation: that is, how Africans and Africa are imagined in popular representation and the impact of this imaginary on students' articulatory sense of belonging. Explored briefly in Solomon and Sekayi (2007; see also Solomon, 1992), "separatist culture" explores how cultural zones are demarcated through cultural practices, language, and religion.

Using my ethnographic gaze, in Chapter 5 I demonstrate the visuality of the rhizomatic third space: its shape and form. In this space, racial, gender and sexual identities are manifested through linguistic and cultural performances. Finally, I offer a conclusion about the need to rethink the intersection of displacement, culture, language, identity, and Blackness. I introduce the "pedagogy of the imaginary" to address the multidimensional nature of Blackness: an already-always multicultural, multinational, multilingual, and multiethnic category. The pedagogy of the imaginary questions the unidimensional, colonized imaginary of Blackness in late modernity and seeks pedagogical ways to decolonize, imagine, or mark it differently.

Notes

1 I am indebted to Phong Kuoch (2013) for reminding me of certain Hip-Hop expressions. Explaining what "Black don't crack" means, Kuoch put it thus: "On one level the expression 'black don't crack' refers to the versatility of black skin in disguising the aging process in black people's physique. 'Black don't crack' is also 'cracking' a joke at its white counterpart, whose 'pale' skin tends to highlight rather than cover up signs of aging, such as wrinkles. In this rare case, blackness is actually seen as desirable, which is often the other ways around when traditionally contrasted with whiteness. On another level, 'crack' is urban vernacular for cocaine, which, used in this context, is actually addressing the stereotype that all black people either use or sell drugs—'black DON'T crack' is refuting this stereotype. Most importantly, 'black don't crack' speaks to the resilience of black people who although they have faced and continue to face atrocities, oppressions and injustices, refuse to 'crack' under the constant pressures put on them and their identities" (p. 46).

2 Inspired by Deleuze and Guattari (1987), this is a notion I will explore and explain later in the Introduction and Chapter 1.

3 For Émile Beneviste (2000), "'Ego' is he who says 'ego.'" That is, the foundation of subjectivity is ritualized and given a name at the moment of utterance; henceforth, Beneviste argues, "there is no objective testimony to the identity of the subject except that which he himself thus gives about himself" (p. 40). Subjectivity, as we shall see all through this book, is a narrative, a story that is producing our identities, our sense of self, and simultaneously is produced in and through language, that is to say, at the moment of utterance.

4 Except for the author's name, all names in this book are pseudonyms. Each excerpt indicates the participant's school, gender, age, and country of origin; the interview type (individual versus group); and the language in which the interview was conducted.

5 Given the arbitrary nature of the social construction, I use the term *youths* interchangeably with *students*, *boys*, and *girls*. By *continental African*, I mean Africans from the continent of Africa, as opposed to *diasporic African* (e.g., African Canadians or African Americans).

6 For Deleuze and Guattari (1987), *striated* is used to refer to the power that controls, sedates, imposes, and limits. The opposite of striated is *smooth*, where people are free to become themselves and to assemble themselves, and with others, as they desire. Within the smooth, they contend, we become "nomads," and their notion of "assemblage" comes into play. Deleuze and Guattari do not use the term *identity*. They prefer *assemblage* as a metaphor that captures the duality of identity; that is, we assemble ourselves, but since we do not do it in total freedom from the striated, we are also assembled. When taken together, one ends up with a complex, "rhizomatic," and forever deterritorialized sense of self and subjectivity. Thinking about this contention in simultaneity and nonoppositional terms of space, Deleuze and Guattari (1987) write, "Smooth space and striated space—nomad space and sedentary space—the space in which the war machine develops and the space instituted by the State apparatus—are not of the same nature. No sooner do we note a simple opposition between the two kinds of space than we must indicate a much more complex difference by virtue of which the successive terms of the oppositions fail to coincide entirely. And no sooner have we done that than we must remind ourselves that the two spaces in fact exist only in mixture: smooth space is constantly being translated, transversed into striated space; striated space is constantly being reversed, returned to a smooth space. In the first case, one organizes even the desert; in the second, the desert gains and grows; and the two can happen simultaneously" (pp. 474–475). I will return to this notion in Chapter 1.

7 For Deleuze and Guattari (1987), with an "abstract machine" one can imagine oneself as one likes, but one is also imagined based on social normal and historical patterns. Here, Blackness becomes an abstract machine, a Body without Organs (BwO). For the purpose of my research, BwO is an assemblage, a collection, an empty signifier that is signified as the reader likes. My Blackness for the policeman was a BwO; that is to say, he decided to lock and imprison its meaning to signify certain things.

8 See Stuart Hall (2006) for the idea of the Old and New identity, which I will revisit in chapter 1.

9 Modernity is understood here as an integral part of the "Enlightenment Project," where human classification and stratification was one of the main objectives of the so-called "science" (Goldberg, 1994).

10 *Niveau avancé* prepares students for university studies, whereas *niveau général*, by and large, prepares them for community and technical colleges.

11 For linguistic purposes, I distinguish between "mother tongue" and "first language." The former is the language first heard, understood, and spoken with the parents, especially the mother, whereas the latter is the language one masters the best. One's mother tongue might be one's first language, but not necessarily; this is the case in some postcolonial contexts. In my case, for instance, my mother tongue is Nubian but my schooling was in Arabic, the language that ended up replacing my mother tongue, hence, becoming my first.

CHAPTER ONE

We Got A Situation Herre[1]

Race, Culture, Language, and Identity: Theorizing the Rhizomatic Third Space

> Race works like a language, and signifiers…gain their meaning not because of what they contain in their essence, but in the shifting relations of difference which they establish with other concepts and ideas in a signifying field. Their meaning, because it is relational and not essential, can never be finally or transhistorically fixed.… That is, there is…always something about race left unsaid. (Hall, 2002, n.p.)

The Signifying Economy of Race[2]

In the Saussurean linguistic tradition, to argue that "race works like a language" is to presuppose that race has a syntactic structure, grammar, morphology, phonology, message, speaker, and receiver (Kristeva, 1989). And although Stuart Hall in the epigraph above is interested in the excess of race—that which cannot be neatly formulated in language, the left over, the unsaid—I on the other hand am interested in *race as language*, specifically in the phonology of race: how we speak it, what we "say" through our bodies, and what our bodies "say" to others. In the latter case of what our bodies "say," clearly we do not have control over that language; our bodies are open for different readings, translations, and interpretations. As such, we speak race as much as it speaks us. Race, moreover, is not a possession or ontological being that persons *have*. It is relational; indeed, it is a set of relations and not an individual attribute. It is a *symbolic capital* in a *signifying economy of exchange* whose signification and value are marked differently. Thus Whiteness is an unmarked, transcendent, and universal signifier and Blackness is a subaltern and stable category that is already-always "one": "Fixed in a dimension where it has only itself as term," as Levinas (1998, p. 60) put it in a different context. That is, it becomes a unidimensional category. For Jean-Paul Sartre (1980), Whiteness becomes the "signifying-subject" while Blackness becomes the "signified-Other."

Race, I am contending, is a discursive category, a social script and an unofficial but firmly expected role we play, a plot, a representational language that is beyond our individual control, and because, as Wittig (2003, p. 159) has argued, "there is no nature in society," it is a historical, political, and social product (Back & Solomos, 2000; Baker, 1991; Hassaskhah, 2011; Johnson, 2006; Yon, 2000). Defined within an economy of exchange, race then is relational, transactional, and both symbolic and material. Being relational means that it becomes meaningful only in relation to—and in fact its meaning depends on—other categories such as gender, class, sexuality, and ability. In contrast, being symbolic, Lacan (1977) explains, requires, first, a distinction between "having" and "being" and, second, a temporal structure that transcends the individual. Whiteness is not a possession like a pair of sunglasses or a category one neatly occupies or slots oneself into. It is a conceptual map, an imaginary, a signifying economy, and in North America, it is a set of privileges that one draws from—whether the individual actor likes it or not (McIntosh, 1998).[3] As a temporal structure that transcends the individual, race is a set of norms that one enters, as it were, at birth, and through repetition, (re)citation, identification, marking, and everyday compulsory and normative acts, one eventually becomes. For Lacan (1977), "I have Blackness" is a statement that lacks meaning because of the nonpossessive nature of Blackness, whereas "to be Black" is meaningful only because it builds on two axes: first, because it centralizes the body, the performed, the ethnographically observable, and second, because it invokes identity. To be Black, I have already argued, is a coming into being, a continuous act of becoming, a production that is never complete. One becomes Black, I want to emphasize, in the univocal and hegemonic signifying economy of power, that is, of Whiteness. The incident with the police that I described in the introduction is a case in point, where I became Black in the eyes of power (cf. Henry, 2012; Wilson, Gutierrez, & Chao, 2013).

Within this economy of power, Frantz Fanon (1967) argues, three epiphenomena appear on the scene as far as Blackness is concerned. First, Blackness finds itself sealed into objecthood, where its meaning is closed,[4] and its multiethnic, multinational, multicultural, and multilingual nature is repudiated. It is no longer a free-floating signifier, or a multiple and contested site of meaning. It becomes, instead, a "phantasmatic one" (Rose, 2000), whose meaning *is* and is already known. Again, my incident with the police is a case in point. The "real" (the-thing-in-itself) and the "imaginary" (the-thing-for-me) are not only colliding and consolidating, but they become—that self-naturalizing—reality itself (Pascale, 2012). Second, Blackness is defined and hence treated as a lack, a negative capital, an Other: that which is not White (the transcendent) (Gaarder, 1996). This, for Fanon (1967), is not an imposed act, in the face of which I am paralyzed or possess no agency of resistance, but schema that create "a third-person consciousness" (p. 110). That is to say, my body is displaced by an atmosphere of certain uncertainty, it becomes hyperconscious of itself. Thus, third and finally, this body no longer represents only itself, but becomes responsible for a whole race and ancestors.

Based on the above, in sum, the Black body is a closed canvas, already signified, and thus is turned into an objectified Other. This signifying economy creates a context where those who possess the Black body become hyperconscious of it, and subsequently feel the burden of representing not only themselves but every Black person. At this point, the metaphors of *economy* and *capital* are in need of further explanation. According to Pierre Bourdieu (1991), they suggest the need for a *market*: a social context where transactions are possible. In this market, Bourdieu argues, not all capitals are treated equally, and not everyone has access to the authorized and legitimized capital. As a capital and a currency in an economy of exchange, race gains its meaning through transactions between and through bodies. In the case of the Black body, for example, given its long and troubled career in the West, it invokes the *présence africaine*, the semiotic third name of a presence both perceived and treated by hegemonic discourses and groups, respectively, as an undesired phenomenon from its inception, as a negative and liable currency, one which is said to be restituted by one's proving oneself capable of performing intellectual tasks (cf. Back & Solomos, 2000; Essed & Goldberg, 2002; Hardt & Negri, 2000; Henry, 2012).[5]

To be sure, *race as language* also needs further explanation. I will start with the very category of language. Approached in a broad semiotic sense, Roland Barthes (1983) explains, language is more than what people say. In fact, he contends, most of what we communicate is nonverbal: through our bodies, clothes, hair, makeup, etc. He calls these "signifiers," which in turn constitute "texts" that are open for different interpretations depending on the context, the message, the sender, and the receiver. In a semiotic sense, language does not work in mimesis; that is to say, like a mirror, where the faithful correspondence is one-to-one between language and the so-called real world (Minh-ha, 2010; Rose, 2000; Woodward, 1997). Here, language does not work by simply reflecting or imitating the truth that is already out there and fixed in the real world. This is because meaning does not lie in the object, person, or event. "Things don't *mean*," Stuart Hall (1997) argues, "we *construct* meaning, using representational systems" (p. 25, original emphasis). If this is so, where then does meaning lie? I contend that meaning is produced at the borderline between two interdependent yet dialectic entities: language system (or any other representational system) and social actors (those who create, use, and make meaning of that system) (see also Beneviste, 2000). On the one hand, when it comes to raciology (Gilroy, 2000) and especially the racialization of Blackness in North America, White social actors govern (Foucault, 1980) and in so many ways completely close its meaning. When it comes to subject formation, on the other hand, language always has the fantastic dual task of *constructing* and *representing*. Language allows us to re/present ourselves, and while doing so, we come to form ourselves. Put otherwise, our subjectivities are constructed and formed in and through language, and it is only in language that we are able to talk about and/or "speak" them.

But if meaning does not lie in the object, race/Blackness then is an empty signifier, unless it is perceived, acknowledged, and situated within a historical, social, political, symbolic, and signifying system. This system is performed in the grammar of the everyday, and its meaning is both unconsciously internalized and fixed through an exercise of power. Outside this grammar, race/Blackness is stripped of any market value. This is precisely the reason why my emphasis is not on race per se, but on racialization—the processes of becoming Black—and on racism.[6] In fact, according to my research, it is only within this signifying economy that race/Blackness can gain any value; and given its performative nature, this value is ever changing. In sum, read as language, race then is a complex syntactic, morphological, phonological, and semantic system that is forever dual: conscious and unconscious, forming and performing, constructing and representing.

In addition to race being a symbolic capital and language, the metaphor of transaction presupposes *race as a performative category*. For Butler (1999), there is a tension, if not contradiction, in race being a performative category that researchers need to be mindful of. Butler first introduced the notion of performativity precisely to haul down categorization and to raise different questions: For example, how is race/Blackness performed, and how are other social categories—gender, class, ability, and sexuality—articulated among and within Blackness? The significance of these questions, for Butler, stems from the idea that categories such as race have a form of staticism attached to them (Laclau & Mouffe, 1985), whereas performativity has a constantly changing context: a moment, a situation, an interaction, a transaction. Ethnographically, this moment is observable and context is describable. So, for my research, instead of looking at Blackness as a category, I will look at the moments and the different ways in which Blackness is performed by continental Africans. This is significant in that it helps me locate and ethnographically observe the intersection of race, gender, sexuality, and class.

Positing it as a nonstatic category, Butler (1999) argues that gender "is always a doing" (p. 33).[7] If this is so, then race is also always a doing. Moreover, as Simone de Beauvoir aptly argued, if "one is not born a woman, but, rather, becomes one" (cited in Butler, 1999, p. 12), then one is not born

Black either, but rather becomes so. This is because Blackness, like gender, is "a process, a becoming, a constructing that cannot rightfully be said to originate or to end" (Butler, 1999, p. 43). It is a discursive category I perform, do, and speak in the semiological language of the everyday, that is, in the dress, in the walk and in the talk. Similar to Stuart Hall, Butler then argues,

> As an ongoing discursive practice, it [Butler is referring to gender and I am referring to Blackness] is open to intervention and resignification...[and it is] sustained and regulated by various social means....[It] is the repeated stylization of the body, a set of repeated acts within a highly rigid regulatory frame that congeal over time to produce the appearance of substance, of a natural sort of being. (1999, pp. 43–44)

Central to this repeated stylization of the body is the process of racialization, a product of what Lopez and Espiritu (1990) call "racial lumping," which, in turn, produces a "panethnic" formula. For Omi and Winant (1994, p. 64), racialization is an ideological concept that is used to "signify the extension of racial meaning to a previously racially unclassified relationship, social practice or group." This is what I called "marking the unmarked" in the Introduction. Robert Miles (2003) refers to it as "racial categorization," which he defines as "a process of delineation of group boundaries and of allocation of persons within those boundaries by primary reference to (supposedly) inherent and/or biological (usually phenotypical) characteristics" (p. 157). After the Middle Passage, Omi and Winant (1994) explain, Africans whose specific identity was Ibo, Yoruba, or Fulani before the arrival of the Europeans in Africa were rendered "Black" once in North America, based on the racial logic of "the establishment and maintenance of a 'color line'" (p. 64).

For Fisher and Model (2012), this color line is framed within a panethnic formula where race and ethnicity (where "ethnicity" is defined in terms of language, culture, national origin, and religion) are conjugated and fused together, and the internal difference among and within the so-called racial groups is erased because, from the outsider's point of view, "They all look alike!" According to the panethnic formula, continental and diasporic Africans are assumed to be one, a unidimensional category (hooks, 1992).[8] The "groups that...are most racially homogeneous," Lopez and Espiritu (1990, pp. 219–220) concluded, "are also the groups with the greatest panethnic development." Within the context of the present research, then, it is important to ask: What happens *within* the subgroups; that is, what is the outcome when continental Africans are lumped with diasporic Africans? This is a central question in my research and one to which I shall respond throughout this book. Lopez and Espiritu (1990) remind us in their conclusion that panethnic formation is not merely an "alliance of convenience"—where continental Africans in this study find it convenient to identify themselves with diasporic Africans—but a necessary means of everyday survival, accessing resources, and even individual and group identity formation.

Culture: Popular/Youth Culture and the Black Diaspora

In his seminal work *There Ain't No Black in the Union Jack*, Paul Gilroy (1991) argues that "The [Black] cultural forms...cannot be contained neatly within the structures of the nation-state....Analysis of black politics must therefore...move beyond the field of inquiry designated by concepts which deny the possibility of common themes, motives and practices within diaspora history" (p. 154). Following a similar line of arguments, Hebdige (1997) contends that the politics of Black culture in general and Black youth culture in particular "is a politics of gesture, symbol, and metaphor, that it deals in the currency of signs and that the subcultural response is, thus, always essentially ambiguous" (p. 403). As such, he adds, it "translates the fact of being under scrutiny into the pleasure of being watched, and the elaboration of surfaces which takes place within it reveals a darker will towards opacity, a drive against classification and control, a desire to exceed" (p. 403). Being so, however, does not come without danger or a price to be paid, because probably not for the very first time in its long history in North American (see my discussion of Elvis Presley in the Introduction) Black popular culture, Black popular music, especially, is "in danger of being completely absorbed by the mainstream it had previously defied" (Williams, 1992, p. 164).

Before reporting on this "dangerous" context, I want to conceptualize what Raymond Williams (1988) considers one of the two or three most complex words in the English language: *culture.* When dealing with culture, de Certeau (1997, p. 102) warns us, we are dealing with "a field of strategic possibilities" that "moves on a ground of unstable words." This is because the meaning of these strategic possibilities is tied to functions in disparate ideologies, systems, languages, geographies, nations, narrations, histories, races, genders, classes, sexualities, ethnicities, and so on. Much like race, culture is constructed in *and* through language. That is, if race is not a category independent from gender, class, sexuality, and ability, then it is a socialized category that is performed in and through *culture*, language, garments, and other "complex semiological signs" (Barthes, 1983).

By complex semiological signs, Roland Barthes (1983) is referring not only to linguistic signs, as I already argued, but also to anything that cannot produce verbal utterance yet is ready to speak: the body, modes of dress, hair, architecture, photography, and so on. These signs, according to Barthes (1983), constitute "if not *languages*, at least systems of signification" (p. 9, original emphasis). These systems of signification, Barthes adds, then patch together to create and produce "maps of meaning" or "*régimes du savoir*" (Hall, 1997, and Foucault, 1979, respectively). And the sharing of these "maps of meaning" is our only guarantee for interpersonal communication. Put otherwise, no two individuals—or cultures—are able to communicate without shared maps of meaning. Culture, therefore, is "a field of strategic possibility" that is ever-changing, dynamic, interdependent, and complex.

For Raymond Williams (1988), the complexity of culture stems both from the different historical passages that the concept has encountered, hence transforming its meaning, and from the different utilizations of the term in several distinct intellectual disciplines. Middleton (2002) relates this complexity more to the ineffable connection between culture and the everyday, from sports to shopping, food, Hollywood, language, religion, music, literature, and so on. Here, the relation is dialectic; the everyday is where culture is expressed and, simultaneously, where it is produced. It becomes both a formative and a performative site. According to Jenks (1993), there are four discursive or hermeneutic approaches to culture. The first celebrates culture as a cerebral or *cognitive category*, as a state of mind, something we vividly carry in our heads. The second sees culture as an embodied and *collective category*. Culture here encompasses a Darwinist notion of evolution, out of which came some pioneering anthropological research, and it is also linked to nineteenth-century imperialism: the "imagined community" (Anderson, 1983) of the "civilized" versus the "uncivilized/primitive/savage." This approach also accentuates culture as belonging to the sphere of the collective rather than the individual consciousness.

The third discursive approach addresses culture as a descriptive and *concrete category*, where culture represents the collective body of arts and intellectual work within any given society. It is the "authorized/legitimized" language where the particular, exclusive, elitist, and specialized knowledge of any one society are incorporated—creating a "high" culture.[9] The fourth and final approach is where culture is reconfigured as a *social category*. This is Raymond Williams's (1988) "whole way of life": the pluralist and potentially democratic concept that became the focus of anthropology, sociology, and, more recently, cultural studies (Atlas, 2014; During, 2005; Grossberg, 2014; Grossberg et al., 1992; Hall, 1997; Wilson et al., 2013).

My approach to culture is better conceived within cultural studies. For me, culture is a set of sociohistorical patterns of life whose meaning depend on groups, nations, generations, and power relations within which the individual self is formed and performed. These patterns are dynamic, dialectic, and socially performed. Culture, therefore, is not a "thing" we carry in our heads, but a set of practices. It is that whole way of life that acquires its meaning only at the "dirty crossroads" (Hall, 1989; Pascale, 2012) where the mass and the popular intersects with "high" art: "That place where power cuts across knowledge, or where cultural processes anticipate social change" (Hall, 1989, p. 1). It is that map of meaning that makes things intelligible and identity formation possible. Identity becomes possible, I argue, only within and in relation to it.

Culture, in sum, is complex codes, maps, or networks of meaning through which people can and do communicate, and can and do make sense of the social environment that surrounds them. Enabling us to encode and decode, these networks of meaning eventually become "capitals," "régimes" and "mythologies" (Bourdieu, 1977; Foucault, 1979; Barthes, 1983, respectively). These mythologies govern our possibilities in life and the markets we access. These networks are dynamic, changing, dialectic, fluid, and ever-hybrid (Bhabha, 1994). The dynamic and fluid nature of culture is a product of the ongoing *wars* (Gramsci, 1971) at the "dirty" intersection between "the popular" and "high arts." In conclusion, no culture exists in and for itself, and no high culture, despite its powerful networks of meaning, is not influenced by popular or mass culture, or vice versa (Ryan & Musiol, 2008; Wilson et al., 2013).

But what is *popular culture,* and how does it relate to the theater of the everyday? Up until the 1980s, Tony Benett (1986) explains, popular culture was approached either from a structuralist or culturalist perspective (see also Eagleton, 2000; Gelder & Thornton, 1997). For the structuralist, popular culture is an ideological machine that, in complex ways, dictates people's thoughts. This was the dominant theoretical approach when it came to the study of cinema, television, and popular writing. For the culturalist, popular culture—say, sports or youth subcultures—is the "authentic interests and values" of subordinate social groups and classes. Unsatisfied with this distinction, Tony Benett (1986) suggested a third way, a "turn to Gramsci."

Gramsci (1971) mounted a principled critique against the classic Marxist ideology of class struggle because, for him, it reified the techniques and physics of power as an unresistable, unintersticed, and top-down regime. For Gramsci, power is neither universal nor given. Rather, it is organic and works through "hegemony."[10] Hegemony "refers to the processes through which the ruling class seeks to negotiate opposing class cultures into a cultural and ideological terrain which wins for it a position of leadership" (Benett, 1986, p. xv). In capitalist societies, Gramsci (1971) explains, cultural and ideological relations between ruling and subordinate classes consist less in the *domination* of the latter by the former than in the struggle for *hegemony*, seeking and negotiating consent. Popular culture in the Gramscian sense, then, "is viewed neither as the site of the people's cultural deformation nor as that of their cultural self-affirmation or...of their self-making; rather, it is viewed as a force field of relations shaped, precisely, by these contradictory pressures and tendencies" (Benett, 1986, p. xiii). No power, dominance, culture or ideology is absolute, or without resistance, opposition, and contradiction (Pascale, 2012).

Thus, for me, popular culture is a dialectic production that is dynamic, shifting, relational, plural, historical, and temporal. It "always has its base in the experiences, the pleasures, the memories and the traditions of the people," and "has connections with local hopes, local aspirations, local tragedies, local scenarios that are the everyday practices and the everyday experiences of ordinary folks" (Hall, 1992, p. 25). It is connected to the Bakhtinian (2000) notion of "the vulgar": the popular, the informal, the underside, the grotesque. It is the contradictory site where today's radical symbol is tomorrow's fashion and next year's nostalgia. It is where the populace's desires are *expressed* and *shaped*. It is the theater of popular fantasies and desires, "where we discover and play with the identifications of ourselves, where we are imagined, where we are represented, not only to the audience out there who do not get the message, but to ourselves for the first time" (Hall, 1992, p. 32).

When the above definitions of culture and popular culture are applied to the social category of youth, they give birth to what some have called "youth culture," "youth subculture," or simply "subcultures" (Center for Contemporary Cultural Studies, 1982; Dimitriadis, 2001; Gelder, 2007; Hebdige, 1979/2003; Sagert, 2010; Weaver et al., 2001). Critiquing the Birmingham School and its classic studies of youth culture as a ferocious always-already resisting subculture, Amit-Talai and Wulff (1995) delineated the need to see youth culture not as a subculture, but as a culture "in its own right" (p. 3; see also McRobbie, 2009). And in any society, Amit-Talai (1995) contended, "to operate effectively, people have to be multicultural" (p. 227). In the case of youth culture, it is multicultural in light of the fact that it occurs "at home, at schools, at work, at play, on the street, with friends, teachers, parents, siblings and bosses," and "draws elements from homegrown as well as transnational influences, and intertwines with class, gender, ethnicity and locality with all the cultural diversity that such a multiplicity of circumstances compels" (Amit-Talai, 1995, p. 231).

Whether it is "youth subculture" or "youth culture" (Weaver et al., 2001), or whether it is teenagehood or adolescence (Danesi, 2009),[11] there is common agreement that youth perform a *sui cultura,* a unique and often temporal cultural production. From style to image to demeanor to argot, youth cultural production has its own mannerisms, attitude, particularity, and historicity (Ryan & Musiol, 2008). For me, then, youth culture is a culture in its own right, but it draws its language, authority, and identity from a parental culture, so, after all, it is a subculture. My position therefore tends to oscillate between *youth subculture* (Gelder, 2007) and *youth culture* (Amit-Talai & Wulff, 1995; Brake, 2003; Savage, 2007). I shall thus use both interchangeably.

In everyday language, youth and youthfulness is linked to sexuality, and is sexually active or even promiscuous when it comes to the female body (Danesi, 2009; Wulff, 1995). This is more so when it comes to the Black (female) body (hooks, 2005; Jackson & Moody-Freeman, 2011). Besides sexuality and erotica, youth is also demarcated by age, spontaneity, energy, exploration, risk-taking, vivaciousness, and playfulness (Savage, 2007). When it comes to age, youth is typically between thirteen and twenty-four years old. However, there are certain professions in which "looking young" is prolonged, such as acting, singing, or sports. The blurred boundaries between childhood and youth, on the one hand, and youth and adulthood, on the other, should therefore shed light on the *constructed* nature of these categories. For precisely this reason, following Wulff (1995), I equate youth with young people. In the final analysis, youth and their culture are products of a social context where peers, neighborhood, schools, the immediate circle of kin, community, and locality act as decisive players in constructing, deconstructing, and interpreting symbols and signs around youths' lives. These include language, (popular) media, religion, gender, race, class, consumption, narration, garments, books, and music. In interpreting the world around them, however, and as they attempt to "resolve collectively experienced structural problems," youths "experience a gap between what is happening and what they have been led to believe should happen" (Brake, 2003, p. 27). This is especially true with Black (popular) culture.

Diaspora Project and Black Cultural Expression

In his comparative study of youth cultures in Britain, the United States, and Canada, Brake (2003, pp. 116–142) found it necessary to devote an entire lengthy chapter to Black youth cultural expression. For Gilroy (1991), this is unsurprising given the fact that Black "cultural forms…cannot be contained neatly within the structures of the nation-state" (p. 154). They need a "framework of a diaspora" (Gilroy, 1991, p. 155), "a project of hybridization" (Mercer, 1994, p. 26). In short, they need alternative frameworks to the varieties of absolutism that confine culture in racial, ethnic, or national essence. The currency of Black culture is multi- and transnational—it can be understood only within Black Atlantic history (Gilroy, 1993)—and youth are its insignia: performing, producing, and inventing and reinventing its cultural forms (Huq, 2001; Ibrahim, 2005; Jackson & Moody-Freeman, 2011; Lemelle, 1995; Walcott, 2000). Indeed, I am contending, youth constitute the border post and the front line in the continuation of the specificity of the diasporic Black Atlantic cultural project.

For Gilroy (1993), the global cultural exchange in the Black Atlantic has four nodals: the Caribbean, the United States, Europe, and Africa. What is missing from Gilroy's "Black Atlantic," significantly, is Black Canada. There are, therefore, five, or maybe six nodals if Central/South America is also added to the equation. Invisibility does not mean absence, and the invisibility of Black Canada in Gilroy's articulation speaks loudly to the power of iteration of Black America and its seductive and hegemonic nature. Speaking about Black Britain, Gilroy (1991, p. 154) writes:

> Black Britain defines itself crucially as part of a diaspora. Its unique cultures draw inspiration from those developed by black populations elsewhere. In particular, the culture and politics of black America and the Caribbean have become raw materials for creative processes which redefine what it means to be black, adapting to distinctively British experiences and meanings.

Given the history of the Caribbean and American presence in Canada, Black Canada is no different from Black Britain when it comes to its relation to the hybrid Black Atlantic cultural project. Indeed, they are identical. The cultural influence of Black America in Canada is significantly palpable for three reasons: the history of the runaway slaves who fled to Canada from the United States (Hill, 2007; Walker, 1997), the close proximity of the two nations, and the global dominance of the United States.

This hybrid Black Atlantic cultural project creates a process, a language, if you like, that involves and invokes Black styles, music, body, dress/fashion, dance, and fashion and, in turn, affirms while it protests. It affirms the mongrel nature of Black styles: Not only are they African, but Africa itself has been metamorphosed through the experience of displacement, slavery, and migration. Africa is now mediated by the present postmodern social, historical, cultural, geographical, and linguistic conditions of the diaspora. In the diaspora, Africa becomes a site of desire, memory, and remembrance; the name of the missing term, the great aporia, which lies at the center of its cultural identity (Love, 2012; Osumare, 2012). Afrika Bambaata and Jah Shaka are two leading Hip-Hop and reggae performers who are named for African chiefs distinguished in anticolonial struggle (Asante, 2012; Dei, 2009). This creates, in turn, an intimate portrait of bonding wherein Africans in the diaspora and on the continent understand what it means to be enslaved and living under abject colonial, dehumanizing conditions. It is in and through this common language of experience, Gilroy (1991) explains, that the soul singers of the Afro-Americas have been able to send a message to their brothers and sisters in Africa and elsewhere. For my research participants, the colonial legacy in Africa is a play and they know the script quite well: They are its products, they speak its languages, French and English. As Gilroy (1991) put it, "It may be that a common experience of powerlessness somehow transcending history and experience in *racial* categories; in the antagonism between white and black...[and] European and African is enough to secure affinity between [the] divergent patterns of subordination" (p. 158).

But *there is no easy return of or to history*. Africa and its cultural expressions are already *in* Europe, and vice versa. The outcome of this interstitial and synchronized "event" is linguistic innovation in rhetorical stylization of the body, forms of occupying an alien social space, heightened expressions, hairstyles, ways of walking, standing, and talking, and a means of constituting and sustaining camaraderie and community (H. Wright, 2004). The effects of these heightened expressions are experienced not only by Black people but also, and more significantly, by White people. Kobena Mercer (1994) has shown in his discussion of the Black hairstyle that "it is white people who have been doing a great deal of the imitating while black people have done much of the innovating" (p. 114). Out of this came the story of "Black innovation/White imitation." This is well documented, in the "zoot suit,"[12] jazz, reggae, Hip-Hop, dreadlocks, and rasta; and in Elvis, the Beatles, Frank Sinatra, Eric Clapton, Vanilla Ice, Pink, the Backstreet Boys, Nelly Furtado, Lady Gaga, Madonna, and Eminem (see also Mercer, 2008).

However, Hall (1992) argues, the borrowing is mutual because in "Black popular culture, strictly speaking, ethnographically speaking, there are no pure forms at all" (p. 28). Rather, there is synchronization, pidginization, and creolization, wherein Black popular culture is an organic product of the West. Take jazz for instance, "where elements such as scales, harmonies or even instruments like the piano or saxophone from Western cultural tradition are radically transformed by this neo-African, improvisational approach to aesthetic and cultural production" (Mercer, 1994, p. 114). What is true for jazz is also true for other Black cultural expressions. Black (sub)cultures are thus a bricolage of (neo-)African traditions and cultures existing alongside

Western traditions, performed in the "New World." And one of its most hybrid, creolized, and synchronized forms is Hip-Hop.

Rap or Hip-Hop?

> There's no such thing as alternative hiphop because
> the only known alternative to hiphop is dead silence.
>
> (Ndegeocello, 1993, n.p.)

Contrary to Catherine Tabb Powell (1991), who sees Hip-Hop as "the beat of the music" and Rap as "the rhythmic talking over the beat" (p. 245), I make a greater distinction between Hip-Hop and Rap (I capitalize both Hip-Hop and Rap as proper names). For me, the term *Hip-Hop* "encompasses everything from music to clothing choices, attitudes, language, and an approach to culture and cultural artifacts positing and collaging them in an unsentimental fashion" (Walcott, 1995, p. 5; see also Alim, Ibrahim, & Pennycook, 2009; Dyson, 2004; Forman & Neal, 2004; Low, 2011). More skeletally, I use Hip-Hop as the name for a category that needs to be studied on its own terms and to describe a way of dressing, walking, and talking (Alim et al., 2009). The *dress* refers to the myriad shades and shapes of the latest "fly gear": bicycle shorts, high-top sneakers, chunky jewelry, baggy pants, and polka-dotted tops (Low, 2011; Rose, 1991, 1994). The hairstyles, which include high-fade designs, dreadlocks, corkscrews, and braids, are also part of this fashion. The *walk* usually means moving the fingers simultaneously with the head and the rest of the body as one is walking. The *talk* is what Alim & Smitherman (2012) refer to as "Black talk."

Some have argued that Rap (or MC-ing) stands out as one of the most identifiable elements of Hip-Hop culture (Dimitriadis, 2001; George, 1998; Huq, 2001; Low, 2011). The other elements include: DJ-ing (music), graffiti (arts), B-boying and B-girling (dance), and consciousness (knowledge). Originated in the South Bronx, New York City, in the late 1970s, Rap is a form of popular music that entails talking or "rapping" to a rhythmic musical background. Rap started when the Jamaican sound system was adapted to the experience of urban New York, and Jamaican-born Clive Campbell, aka Kool Herc, is the person most often cited as Rap's inventor (Chang, 2005; Ogg & Upshal, 2001), cutting and mixing dance hall music with James Brown's "Give It Up Or Turn It Loose" and Michael Viner's "Bongo Rock," among many others. Rap is now popularized as an urban African American youth cultural form that revels in the reduction of the music to its essential African components of rhythm, words, and voice (Chang, 2005; Forman & Neal, 2004). The Rapper, according to Powell (1991), is a "vocalist [who] tells a story set to syncopation, and a disc jockey (DJ) provides the rhythm with a drum machine or by 'scratching' on a turntable (rapidly moving a record back and forth under the needle to create rap's famous swishing sound)" (p. 245).

Rap lyric is primarily an empowered narrative that both tells and critiques the experience of dominance and marginality of people of African descent in North America and the Black Atlantic world (Dyson, 2001, 2004; George, 2004). It iterates the social, psychic, and human experience of desires, sex, sexism, racism, crime, police brutality, and politics (Alim et al., 2009; Rose, 1994; Simmons, 2001). Political figures such as Malcolm X and Dr. Martin Luther King, Jr. often feature in Rap. In spite of these specificities, according to Nelson George (1998), Rap is now produced primarily in the "hood" and sensationally consumed in unprecedented numbers by White youths in suburbia, across languages, genders, and classes in North America (see also Chang, 2005; Conyers, 2001). Like reggae, jazz, rhythm and blues (R&B), and other Black Atlantic musical forms, Rap can be heard in every area of the world, and not only in English; I have experienced Rap in French, Spanish, Greek, Korean, Italian, Arabic, Hebrew, German, Swahili, and Portuguese. This globalized phenomenon of Rap, as Gilroy (1991, p. 212) argues, would require a new articulation of race, ethnicity, and consumption, which is well documented in Alim et al. (2009) and Terkourafi (2010), and it is beyond the scope of this project. It is worth wondering, nonetheless, whether Hip-Hop culture and Rap in particular have become the new global space of intercultural communication (see Osumare, 2012) or a name for a new nation, which I referred to it elsewhere (Ibrahim, 2012) as Global Hip-Hop Nation. Rap is indeed a superlative example of how the empire strikes back, where the historically marginal is loud enough to create its own center. It is where identities, including gendered identities, are articulated.

> I've been puzzled by the fact that young black people…today are marginalized, fragmented, enfranchised, disadvantaged and dispersed. And yet, they *look* as if they own the territory. Somehow, they too, in spite of everything, are centered, in place: without much material support, it's true, but nevertheless they occupy a new kind of space at the center. (Stuart Hall, cited in Mercer, 1994, p. 19; emphasis added)

Hip-Hop and Gender Performance

Hip-Hoppers and Rappers set themselves within a discourse and a performed politics of resistance. In doing so, however, male Rappers tend to reinscribe themselves to, and bond with, the normative and normalized White heterosexual male gaze, whereby the female form becomes a highly sexualized object of desire (Love, 2012). Maleness, then, defines and shapes the meaning of resistance, community, and culture. In Rap, Love (2012) explains, gender is addressed only when women are doing the talking or when they are talked about; otherwise, the male figure—the "nigga" and his lower class status (Forman & Neal, 2004)—is left unchecked at the center. Here I do not mean to dehumanize the already abject living conditions of Black men (as if I could!), but to express a genuine desire for an empowered critique of both her absence and his centrality, visibility. Yet, as Ebron (1991, p. 25) demonstrated, any dialogue "about community resistance in which Black women are absent also has a gendered dimension" (see also Dimitriadis, 2001; Richardson, 2003). So gender encompasses men and women alike, and what is commercialized and perceived from the outside as homogeneous Hip-Hop culture is actually stratified by age, class, culture, and political agenda, and it is a product of confrontation and dialogue between Black men and women. From this perspective, women's intervention in Rap as a site of symbolic exchange is a counter act to their exclusion and silencing, and offers young Black women a small but potent culturally reflexive public space (Love, 2012; Richardson, 2003; Rose, 1994). Lil' Kim, Queen Latifah, Missy Elliot, TLC, Foxy Brown, Sister Souljah, Lauryn Hill, Salt-N-Pepa, Ms. Jade, Eve, Brianna Perry, Nicki Minaj, and Diamond, to name but a few, are female Rappers who are quite vehement in expressing their desires and positionalities and in creating their own spaces in a terrain dominated by men.

> Of course as Black men articulate the "Black experience," Black women have not remained silent; they have taken exception to these narrow representations of womanhood and Blackness and have called for inclusion in both male and female projects. The interventions by African American women have challenged an almost exclusively male domain of rappers. Women rappers like Queen Latifah, among others, respond to sexism and contest the most regressive ideas about the role of Black women in the process of cultural production. (Ebron, 1991, p. 26)

Therefore, for Rap and Hip-Hop in general to represent a relevant and new cultural politics, Rappers need to articulate the hidden complicities of a position that chooses to prioritize one issue—the "hood," the "ghetto" as a dominant metaphor of the Black lumpenproletariat—over another—gender as well as sexuality and their place in social and political struggle. This creates an exceptionally interesting yet complex situation for continental African youths. It will therefore be important to see if male students take up Hip-Hop and Rap masculine identities, and how the female students negotiate the already inscribed gendered positions. These positions will be expressed, at least in part, in and through language practice. In the following section, I conceptualize the politics of language and argue that language, especially Black English, cannot be bisected from who utters it, its cultural context, and its politics.

Linguistic or Cultural Literacy: The Politics of Language

According to Chomsky (1965), "Linguistic theory is concerned primarily with an ideal speaker-listener, in a completely homogeneous speech community, who knows its language perfectly and is unaffected by such grammatically irrelevant conditions as memory limitation, distractions, shifts of attention or interest, and errors…in applying his knowledge of the language in actual performance" (p. 3). Though it still haunts linguistic theory, Chomsky's proposition has long been questioned and challenged, firstly because this ideal speaker-listener simply would never exist. Above all, his proposition is challenged because it conceives language as an entity independent from the "laws of construction," with internal dynamics that answer only to itself, hence sidestepping "the question of the economic and social conditions of the acquisition of the legitimate competence and of the constitution of the market" in which the acquisition takes place (Bourdieu, 1991, p. 44). Simply put, within a Chomskyan framework, the speaking subject—or the language learner—is ideal *and* outside the economy and the social condition of acquisition and production.

Influenced by sociology, anthropology, philosophy, and cultural studies, inversely, language is articulated increasingly within a vocabulary of sociality, as a social phenomenon (Bourdieu, 1991; Heller, 1994, 2011; Ibrahim, 1999, 2000a, 2011; Norton & Toohey, 2004; Pennycook, 2004; Rampton, 1995). As such, it cannot be located outside the social signification and symbolic representation (Kristeva, 1989); it constitutes the social and is simultaneously constituted by it (Gumperz, 1982; Griswold, 2012). Pierre Bourdieu (1991) argues that language is a social and historical product, as well as an instrument of power, and that it has never been simply a medium of communication. This being so, then any syntactical, morphological, lexical, or phonological study has to be situated within an *economy of linguistic exchange*, which determines its production, transaction, currency, and profit. There is no ideal speaker-listener. There is, instead, a particular relation of power between a sender/producer and a receiver/consumer. Within this relation of power, which is capable of procuring a certain material and symbolic profit, "utterances are not only...signs to be understood and deciphered; they are also *signs of wealth*, intended to be evaluated and appreciated, and *signs of authority*, intended to be believed and obeyed" (Bourdieu, 1991, p. 66, original emphasis).

To speak and to be listened to, as a corollary, signify more than enciphering and deciphering a language per se. At a basic level, speaking "means to be in a position to use a certain syntax, to grasp the morphology of this or that language," Fanon (1967) contends, "but it means above all to assume a culture, to support a weight of a civilization" (p. 17). Learning Black English and taking up Hip-Hop by African youths, therefore, were acts that understood the significance of cultural and linguistic exchange among the Black Atlantic, where linguistic and cultural literacies became acts of desire, bonding, and investment. It should be noted, importantly, that learning Black Talk (Smitherman, 2000),[13] or Black English Vernacular (Labov, 1972), or African American Vernacular English (AAVE)—a creolized linguistic repertoire of English and African languages (Smitherman, 2000)—did not depend on a full mastery of the language by African youths. Rather, it banked on "ritual expressions" (Rampton, 1995).

I therefore distinguish between Black English (BE) and Black Stylized English (BSE). BE is what I referred to above as AAVE or Black Talk, which has its own grammar and syntax (Ibrahim, 2011). BSE, on the other hand, refers to ways of speaking that do not depend on a full mastery of the language. It relies on ritual expressions such as *whassup*, *whadap* (what's up), *whassup my Nigga*, and *yo, yo homeboy* (you, my cool friend), which are performed habitually and recurrently in Rap. These rituals are more an expression of politics, moments of identification, and desire than they are of language or of mastering the language. They are an expression of identity location: where African youths locate themselves and where they want to be located, which I address next.

Identity or No Identity, That Is the Question

> Identity is not as transparent or unproblematic as we think. Perhaps instead of thinking of identity as already accomplished fact...we should think, instead, of identity as a "production," which is never complete, always in process, and always constituted within, not outside, representation. (Hall, 1990, p. 222)

Recruited under the umbrella of "crisis," identities are coming back, Hall (2006) continues; they are "returning." By "returning," Hall is not suggesting that the question of identity ever went away, but that it is returning with a particular kind of force (see also Woodward, 1997). This forceful return, in my view, is linked to poststructural, postcolonial, postmodern, antiracist and feminist discourses that place identity performance in that complex intersection of multiple discourses, including discourses of difference, subjectivity, language, history, memory, and power relations (see also Althusser, 1971; du Gay et al., 2000; Griswold, 2012; Rajchman, 1995; Yon, 2000).

Identities are ongoing productions, unstable points of identification or *suture* (Silverman, 2000) that are given birth to at the borderland between the Self and the Other (Bakhtin, 2000, p. 365). It is in this dialogue with the Other that the Self knows its virtues; it is in that split that the Other enters the Self. As Hall notes,

> The critical thing about identity is that it is partly the relationship between you and the Other. Only when there is an Other can you know who you are…. And there is no identity…without the dialogic relationship to the Other. The Other is not outside, but also inside the Self, the identity. So, identity is a process, identity is split. Identity is not a fixed point but an ambivalent point. Identity is also the relationship of the Other to oneself. (1991, p. 11)

The Self, the identity, the subject is no longer found in isolation, nor is it a saturated point. On the contrary, it is a meeting point between multiple discourses, including discourses of Otherness. Hall (1990) refers to this process of identity formation as the "New identity," which he distinguishes from the "Old identity." The terms *Old* and *New identities* are used interchangeably with Old and New *ethnicities*. The discourse and the logic of the Old identity, Hall (2006) explains in another context, "contains the notion of the true self, some real self inside there, hiding inside the husks of the false selves that we present to the rest of world. It is a kind of guarantee of authenticity. Not until we get really inside…do we know what we are 'really saying'" (pp. 124–125; see also Griswold, 2012, ch. 3). It is, in short, an expression of the Cartesian stable self, where the subject is situated within thetic and static discourses of history, self, and memory.

The New identity discourse, in contrast, is more complexly different. It neglects neither history and the multiple discourses about it and the contradictory nature of these discourses, nor power relations and the politics of positioning, nor the dialogic relationship between the Self and the Other. For Bakhtin (2000), this dialogic relationship is indeed "a dialogue of social forces perceived not only in their static co-existence, but…as a dialogue of different times, epochs and days" (p. 365). It is "a dialogue that is forever dying, living, being born: co-existence and becoming are here fused into an indissoluble concrete unity that is contradictory, multi-speeched and heterogeneous" (p. 365).

This indissoluble and heteroglossic nature of the forever dying and reborn subject formation processes, according to Bakhtin (2000), is part of the ongoing processes of "ideological translation." By heteroglossia, Bakhtin refers to the notion of having more than one voice, language, style, and subjectivity *within* the Self. These poly-voices are also underscored, from a different angle, in Kristeva's (1974) notion of "transposition." For Kristeva, transposition refers to the poly- and multi-positions that the subject takes up, depending on who is speaking, to whom, and what is talked about. By introducing desire and impulse, Kristeva (1974, p. 231) concludes, the Saussurean bar of signifier/signified (*Signifiant -Sa/Signifié -Sé*) can only be taken as inauguration, *processus primaires*, and not a final product of the process of understanding of how male and female subjectivities are formed and understanding the dialectic relation that can and does exist between them. Because identity cannot be barred (either/or, *Sa/-Sé*), but dialogized; and because identity is formed within multiple yet contradictory discourses, Kristeva asserts, the *Sa/Sé* bar can only serve other objectives such as Man positioning himself as, and at, the center of the sign (see also Barthes, 1983; Griswold, 2012).

For Bakhtin (2000), these processes of transposition and heteroglossia are also true when applied to "ideological translation." When the receiver, whether a reader or listener, for example, is interpellated (Althusser, 1971)[14] by the speaking subject's language and voice, she/he is "coming to know one's own language as it is perceived in someone else's language, coming to know one's own belief system in someone else's system. There takes place…an ideological translation of another's language, and an overcoming of its otherness" (Bakhtin, 2000, p. 365). In other words, during the processes of ideological translation, the Other's language and, I add, culture, will eventually belong to the Self. But because this translation is processed mostly unconsciously (Bakhtin, 2000), the Other will also discursively become part of the Self. For me, the moment of identification in this dialectic relationship between the Self and the Other is extremely significant. It impacts and guides the shape, the form, and the intensity of the ways in which the Self translates the Other. and vice versa. De rigeur, the question of intensity is a subject of desire. As we shall see, African youths' desire and identification with Blackness has certainly influenced their translation of the new Canadian/North American context, in what they learned and how they learned it. They were interpellated by, and in turn they identified and named, somewhat unconsciously, North American Black culture and language as sites of intense investment and desire. Thus, two conclusions can be reached at this point. First, *identification is the inaugurating point of the identity formation processes* and, second, *identity is the accumulative moments of identification.* Put otherwise, when the naming, hailing, and interpellation take place, the process of ideological translation is inaugurated; the result, in the case of displaced subjects, is a third, hybrid and rhizomatic space.

Making Connections: Rhizomatic Third Space of Becoming and the Politics of Articulation

If identities should not be barred—*Sa/Sé*—how do we then think about the dash, the in-betweenness, that interstitial moment that hails, produces, and names us as subjects? In the case of African youths, what name should we give to their identities: Africans, Canadians, Africans in Canada, African Canadians, or some other unbarred combination? And what happens to the African identities once in Canada/North America? These questions necessitate the language of what I am calling *rhizomatic identity*. Very similar in its internal mechanisms and final product, this rhizomatic identity has been called the "third space" by Homi Bhabha (1990, 1994) and Edward Soja (1996). I will borrow from the language of the third space but will focus primarily on developing the language of the rhizome as I theorize the complex and complicated ways in which displaced subjects form and perform their identities, especially how they become Black.

As I outlined in the introductory chapter, I am using the rhizome as a metaphor for identity. The rhizome, Deleuze and Guattari (1987) explain, is a plant that is welcoming the sun, the snow, and the rain, but whose shape, form, thickness, and greenness is never sure or predictable. Thus, constantly one has to observe both how it receives the rain and the final product it produces. Horizontally positioned, the rhizome is not a point we reach; it is a way of becoming that is always in "a middle (*milieu*) from which it grows and which it overspills" (p. 21) and which we are forever struggling to attain.

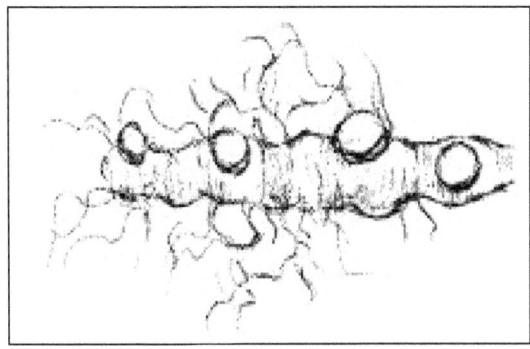

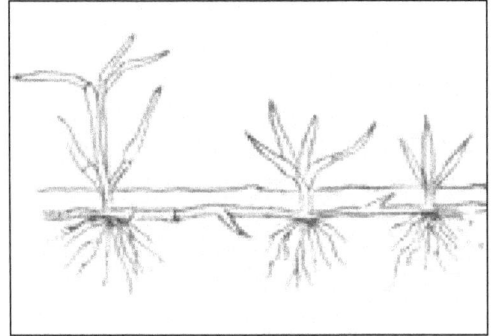

Figure 1. The Rhizome: A Web-like figuration of identity.
Source: 1) www.living-foods.com/ 2) www.ipm.ucdavis.edu

As such, the rhizome resists verticality and chronological lines of flight, where its growth is conceived in a nonlinear, nonarborescent, and unsystematic line. Radically conceived, almost anarchist in nature, the goal of the rhizome is "[t]o reach, not the point where one no longer says I, but the point where it is no longer of any importance whether one says I" (Deleuze & Guattari, 1987, p. 3). The rhizome, then, is a metaphor for identity that is invoked here for three reasons: (1) to join Stuart Hall (1991) in questioning the logic of the Old identity, Old ethnicity, where the self is stable and its formation is linear, arborescent, and systematic; (2) to question the verticality of power relation as it currently exists in society; and (3) to indicate the multiple, multiplying, complex, complicated, fluid, and infinite lines of flight and possibilities of identities and becomings.

In sum, *rhizomatic identity* is an "interbeing, intermezzo" (Deleuze & Guattari, 1987, p. 7). It is an *assemblage*: an existential place of consciousness where we-subjects, owning our own subjectivity, practice constant "experimentation" and "nomadism." It is a line of flight that is welcoming sociality, with everything that it brings (the good and the ugly), as I already have argued, but offers no guarantees as to what its final product might look like or what maze it has to go through to get there. As such, rhizomatic identity finds itself in a constant state of flow, de-/reterritorialization, and multiplicity.

It is worth noting that Deleuze and Guattari (1987) do not use the term *identity*. They prefer *assemblage*, as a formation that captures the duality of identity: that is, we assemble ourselves (owning our own subjectivity), but because we do not do it in total freedom, we are also assembled (falling within the apparatus, gaze, or discourse of power). Assemblage is for Deleuze and Guattari what identity is for me. Both, according to Deleuze and Guattari (1987), are found in a constant move between two spaces: *striated* and *smooth*. The former is used to refer to the power that controls, sedates, imposes, and limits, whereas the latter is a welcoming space where people are free to become themselves and to assemble themselves and with others as they desire. In the smooth space, Deleuze and Guattari explain, we become nomads. We do not walk around aimlessly, they remind us, but really we do not know or cannot fully predict the storm that is coming our way. So, we find ourselves in a constant vigilant move between smooth and striated spaces. It is in this intermezzo between the smooth and the striated that I am situating the *rhizomatic process of becoming Black*: this complex, complicated and forever becoming process. The rhizomatic process of becoming Black, in toto, is an identity formation process that is an infinitely deterritorialized (passive process of being assembled) and reterritorialized (active process of assembling) sense of self and subjectivity.

In a classic article, Stuart Hall (1986) refers to this constant move between smooth and striated spaces as "articulation." For Hall, articulation is an expression of the *politics of tension* between *making* and *being made*: that organic supplement that is dealing with two or more different elements that "can, but need not necessarily, be connected to one another" (p. 46) such as a lorry which has a cab and a trailer. When continental African youths, as we shall see, speak Somali *and* Black Stylized English and dress in Hip-Hop *and* traditional national dress, ethnographically speaking, these are performative acts of this politics of articulation, and thus they create a rhizomatic and, in the words of Homi Bhabha (1990), new "hybrid third space."

The language of the third space complements the rhizomatic framework in that it brings to the forefront and centralizes the question of culture. Similar to rhizomatic identity, the third space is about living the politics of tension, constantly moving between striated and smooth spaces. In discussing this tension, Homi Bhabha (1990) advanced three notions that are relevant to my research and my conceptualization of rhizomatic identity and the rhizomatic process of becoming Black. The first distinguishes between what Bhabha calls "a creation of cultural diversity" and "a containment of cultural difference." Bhabha (1990) argues that within the West's cultural tradition, "although there is always an entertainment and encouragement of cultural diversity, there is always a corresponding containment of it" (p. 208). This containment is an event taking place in subtlety and through processes of normalization whereby the dominant culture becomes the ubiquitous normalized gaze. In other words, "a transparent norm is constituted, a norm given by the host society or dominant culture, which says that 'these other cultures are fine, but we must be able to locate them within our grid'" (Bhabha, 1990, p. 208).

Unsatisfied with this liberal distinction, Bhabha proposed a different turn, his second notion: *cultural translation*. It argues that "no culture is plainly plenitudinous, not only because there are other cultures which contradict its authority, but also because its own symbol-forming activity, its own interpellation in the process of representation, language, signification and meaning-making, always underscores the claim to an originary, holistic, organic identity" (1990, p. 210) Cultural translation, then, is:

> a way of imitating, but in a mischievous, displacing sense—imitating an original in such a way that the priority of the original is not reinforced but by the very fact that it can be simulated, copied, transferred, transformed, made into a simulacrum and so on: the "original" is never finished or complete in itself. The "originary" is always open to translation so that it can never be said to have a totalised prior moment of being or meaning—an essence. What this really means is that cultures are only constituted in relation to that otherness internal to their own symbol-forming activity which makes them decentered structures. (Bhabha, 1990, p. 210)

Similar to rhizomatic identity, where there are no facile roots and origins, cultural translation therefore does not allow for the essentialization of the so-called original or originary culture, for the latter itself is, and always has been, open to and for translation. It is only original in the sense of being anterior, Bhabha argues. Thus, third and finally, he convincingly concludes that all forms of culture are "continually in a process of hybridity" (p. 211). However, Bhabha emphasizes, "the importance of hybridity is not to be able to trace two original moments from which the third emerges, rather *hybridity...is the 'third space'*" (p. 211, emphasis added). Hybridity here is equated with the rhizome, which then produces: *rhizomatic third space*. This is an extremely hybrid product of intermezzo, of in-between spaces. In my research, the challenge is to ethnographically "see" what this synthesis of cultures and languages, this rhizomatic third space, this hybridization project might look like. If the Old and the New are now rhizomatically metamorphosed into a hybrid third space, one might argue, the final product would look fully like neither the former nor the latter, but the two: the Old *and* the New.

Here, the Bakhtinian (2000) ideological translation might prove to be useful in ethnographically researching this rhizomatic project of hybridization. For Bakhtin (2000), the result of cultural and ideological translation wherein two linguistic, ideological, and cultural systems are to be mixed is to give birth to an organic worldview that, in turn, will be performed in New linguistic and cultural practices. The product of this mixture is or can be hybrid, and for me it is sociolinguistically detectable and ethnographically observable. "It is of course true that even historical, organic hybridity is not only two languages but also two socio-linguistic (thus organic) world views that are mixed with each other," Bakhtin (2000) asserts, "but in such situations, the mixture remains mute and opaque, never making use of conscious contrasts and oppositions" (p. 360). He then adds,

> It must be pointed out however that while it is true the mixture of linguistic world views in organic hybrids remains mute and opaque, such unconscious hybrids have been at the same time profoundly productive historically: they are pregnant with potential for new world views, with new "internal forms" for perceiving the world in words. (Bakhtin, 2000, p. 360)

This new rhizomatic third space is organic precisely because it is historically situated and partially unconsciously executed. It is an indissoluble mixture of two or more linguistic, ideological, cultural, and belief systems. It finds itself in the *inter* of (the first and the second) geographies, cultures, languages, and memories. It is where the first and the second are produced in the same sentence, in the same syntax, in the same grammar, in the same garment, at the same time. In the case of African students, as we shall see, the product of the ideological translation of the Canadian context that synchronously starts at the moment of identifying and naming Black North America as a site of investment by African students is a rhizomatic third space. In other words, the third space for African youths is an upshot of the language, experience, culture, and memory they bring with them into Canada and what they negotiate and translate as to what it means to be Canadian. They seem to identify with a Canada that is Black, hence the saliency of race. This identification is a complex, multilayered, and rhizomatic process, and it takes place mostly subconsciously.

For Bhabha (1990), this rhizomatic third space "enables other positions to emerge….[It] displaces the histories that constitute it, and sets up new structures of authority, new political initiatives, which are inadequately understood through received wisdom" (p. 211). These emerging positions are unrecognizable because they are the product of that luminal space where the Old is already in the New and the different. And both are born out of longitudinal *negotiation* and *translation*. Bhabha (1990) refers to this negotiation as "the process of cultural hybridity" that "gives rise to something different, something new and unrecognisable, a new area of negotiation of meaning and representation" (p. 211).

It is the understanding of this new area of negotiation of meaning that might better illuminate our conceptualization of the rhizomatic identities, especially those of displaced subjects: immigrants and refugees. My experience as a refugee from Africa now living in Canada tells me that displaced subjects find themselves at the border post, at the frontier of two or more cultures, languages, and belief systems. In the process of understanding and translating the New context, displaced subjects also understand and translate the Old. We are located, I argue, in the interstice between the Old—which is part of us—and the New—which is becoming part of us. It is not a curse, but we are in a *permanent exile*. Even when I "went home," desperate to blend in, I was reminded of how differently I started to talk or dress. I felt homeless at home. In-betweenness becomes an identity in itself, creating a rhizomatic third space.

To avoid relativism, however, I would like to see these processes of linguistic and cultural translation and negotiation taking place within a sociohistorical and political space. The episteme of hybridity, rhizome, and third space, more importantly, has to be positioned within *relations of power* that place students in certain relations, including unequal power relations (see also Pascale, 2012). Generally, the notions of rhizome and third space—like Giroux's (2005) "border crossing," in which pedagogues, cultural workers, and students are asked to be border crossers and facilitators of border crossing—raise fundamental questions about who is (always-already) asked to be a border crosser and who is asked to be hybrid. Hybridity, rhizome, and third space therefore are not abstract but contextually specific categories, and should be engaged as such.

The next chapter will set the stage with an exploration of students' and one teacher's narratives of their social and racial experiences at the school. As we shall see, identities are "barred" here, and the bar is dazzlingly clear: Black or White. The former becomes the umbrella under which African youths find their identities circulating. They find themselves in a Weltanschauung of recognizable Otherness; not a subject of *différance*, a subject formed in another place and at another time, but an object of *idée fixe*, a simulacrum that is already signified, imagined, and displaced: of Blackness.[15]

Notes

1   "In hip hop," writes Kuoch (2013), "when something is worth a closer inspection, examination or consideration, one calls attention to it by saying, 'we got a situation herre'" (p. 67).

2   I use the term *race* without quotation marks, and, candidly, I do not think the case has been made to do otherwise. From the outset, I see race as socially constructed and historically specific, but so are class, gender, sexuality, and so on. None of these require quotation marks to emphasize their nonessentialized nature. Biologically speaking, as we already know, race does not exist (Back & Solomos, 2000; Dei, 1996; Essed & Goldberg, 2002). Yet, using a Lacanian language (see Woodward, 1997), its "hoax" and "bogus" biological existence does not exclude its social existence. I agree with Winant (2004, p. 37) that North Americans' "ability to recognize race is so finely tuned, so ingrained, that it has become a 'second nature.'" So, he adds, "with the development of this ability comes a *naturalization* of race itself: if racial identity is so recognizable, so palpable, so immediately obvious, then in practical terms…it becomes 'real'" (original emphasis). Indeed, it has been argued, to be without a racial identity in North America is to have no identity at all (Anthias & Yuval-Davis, 1992; Dei, 1996; Ibrahim, 2000b; Omi & Winant, 1994).

3   Presently, I teach classes that are 90% composed of White students. As their first assignment, I usually ask them to reflect on McIntosh (1998) and Frankenberg (1993), who offer deconstructions of the ubiquitous White and male privilege. Unanimously, students indicate that they have never thought of themselves or their bodies as either racialized or classed. Clearly, the danger of privilege here, as McIntosh shows, is its misrecognition: I could live my whole life without ever feeling the need to think about my body. Privilege is when one finds oneself in a position of advantage by virtue of "being," without uttering a word. It is, for McIntosh (1998), when one is carefully taught not to recognize one's own advantage.

4   According to Eagleton (2000), the closing of meaning is a function of power. The object, for Eagleton, is a free-floating signifier whose meaning lies not in and within it, but at the borderline between the object and the meaning maker. And over time, the meaning maker usually has the upper hand in how the object is signified, which is also historically and socially constructed.

5   See, for example, the debate on and about the theory proposed by the *Bell Curve Wars* by Herrnstein and Murray (1995), linking race, biology, and intelligence. Only White people are assumed capable of doing intellectual work, and if people of color are to do them, they have to "act White" to do them (Ogbu & Fordham, 1986).

6   As George Dei (1996, p. 25) argues, acts, gestures, and utterances are deemed racist not by their intentions but rather by their effects. And language is in no way racist in its structure, but only in its application (Rothenberg, 1998).

7   My conceptualization in this section is indebted to Judith Butler (1999). Although her focus is on gender, I found both her language and conceptual framework extremely helpful in my understanding of race as a performative category. One critique I level against her idea of the subject, however, is that she borrows extensively from the French feminist school. Here, we know that *je* in French—the "I"—is always already masculine and refers to "him," and I do not think it works the same way in the English language. I agree with her that the deep structure of the latter is still very masculine, but there is a need to acknowledge that in French, the very use of she as a subject-in-language is at the heart of French feminism, whereas in English this has become a fait accompli, at least in large measure.

8   For Lopez and Espiritu (1990), Asian or Black Canadian/American, for example, which are multiethnic, multicultural, and multilingual categories, are treated like Italian, Polish, or Greek Canadian/American. This construction has a long history. Up until the civil rights movements in the 1960s, the notion of "unmeltable" European (read White) ethnic groups existed (Novak, 1972; Kailin, 2002). Afterwards, Italians who came from the different parts of Italy, for example, all melted into Whiteness, which was a step "towards assimilation" (Lopez & Espiritu, 1990, p. 200). However, the situation is different when it comes to people of color: the *really* unmeltable groups. Thus, Lopez and Espiritu (1990, p. 220) concluded that panethnicity "may not be generalizable to sets of panethnic subgroups that are not racially distinct." The question of ethnicity, therefore, is increasingly "a question of race. And those well-established 'ethnic' groups that are still most excluded…are racial minorities. For Italians and other whites, panethnicity may indeed have been a step towards assimilation and 'Anglo-conformity.' But…no non-white ethnic group has ever fully assimilated [sic] in American [and Canadian] society" (Lopez & Espiritu, 1990, p. 220; see Dei, 1996; James & Shadd, 2001; Solomon, 1992; Lee, 1994 for the Canadian context).

9   Traditionally, "high" culture is judged as cultivated, important, elitist, and legitimate, and hence needs to be studied, whereas "popular" culture represents the layperson, the leftover, and is too ordinary to be worthy of theorizing (Eagleton, 2000; Bourdieu, 1991).

10 When it comes to race, see Hall (2002). Here, Hall explains that throughout history hegemony has been vital to the process of racialization and hence racism. Hegemony can only be maintained, Hall argues, as long as the dominant blocs "succeed in framing all competing definitions within their range." It is not, Hall maintains, "universal and 'given' to the continuing rule of a particular class. It has to be won, reproduced, sustained. Hegemony is, as Gramsci said, a 'moving equilibrium' containing relations of forces favorable or unfavorable to this or that tendency" (cited in Hebdige, 1979, p. 16).

11 Danesi (2009, p. 6) distinguishes between adolescence and teenagehood. Adolescence or young adult, for Danesi, "refers to the psychosocial behaviors that are characteristic of all

primates at puberty...[I]t designates the behaviors set in motion by the onset of the reproductive capacity. Teenagehood, on the other hand, refers to a socially constructed category superimposed on the life continuum by modern consumeristic culture."

12 The zoot suit, together with the conk, constituted "the *de rigueur* hepcat look in the black male 'hustler' lifestyle of 1940s ghettos" (Mercer, 1994, p. 120). The zoot suit, a bricolage of a Western style refashioned in a neo-African format, signified and projected stature, dignity, and presence for the Black man, demonstrating that he was important in his own domain. Interestingly, by 1948 the American fashion industry toned it down as the new "bold look" was marketed to the mainstream White male (Mercer, 1994, ch. 4).

13 Black Talk has other equivalent terms: African American Vernacular English, Black or African American Language, Black English, Black Dialect, Ghetto Speech, Street Talk, and Ebonics (see Alim & Smitherman, 2012; Smitherman, 2000).

14 For Althusser (1971), we become who we are, and we occupy our subject positions, through processes of "recruitment" and ideological "hailing." We are recruited or interpellated when we recognize ourselves in the representations before us (p. 172), as if these representations are saying, "Hey, you there!" and we respond by saying, "Yes, that's me." So, interpellation is an unconscious (ideological) process that both names and positions the subject who is thus recognized and produced through symbolic processes and practices (see also Woodward, 1997).

15 For an extensive review of the literature and a thorough discussion of the history of Blacks in Canada, with an emphasis on French and Black Franco-Ontarians, refer to Ibrahim (2011) and Heller (2011).

CHAPTER TWO

"Wallahi, ils sont tous des racistes!"[1]

Striated Racialization and the Rhizomatic Process of Becoming Black

"You have no idea what I have lived through. Every waking moment is a nightmare for the captives you hold right now, on the other side of these stone walls. You have no idea what they endure, if they will even survive in the ships, no idea of the thousands of humiliations and horrors waiting at their destinations."

"Some things are better not to think about," he said.

"Tell that to your captives," I said. (Hill, 2007, p. 422)

The aim in this chapter is to set the stage where African students' subjectivities are *made* and *being made*. It is a stage on which they are expected to perform and painfully experience the theater of schooling in Canada. This colorful—or I should say, wanting to be color-less (Stanley, 2011)—stage is set with the hypothesis that African students enter, so to speak, a *social imaginary*—a discursive space where they are already imagined, constructed, and thus treated as "Blacks" by hegemonic discourses and groups, and hence asked to racially fit somewhere. This is done through complex and mostly subconscious processes of racialization. A significant part of these processes is the experience of racism, and as will become clear, students' narratives show the differential treatments they have received in the academic and non-academic spheres. Their narratives also show that, while confronting and combating racism, students ally themselves with North American Blackness and thus become aware of the history of racism, discrimination, and dehumanization of Blackness within the Euro-Canadian and American contexts. In the process of comprehending their own plight as "Black" subjects in Canada, they become Black, which has a sharp political edge (see Fisher & Model, 2012).

To reiterate, *becoming Black* is the building of memories and experiences that help African youths translate and bear witness to the sociocultural environment that surrounds them, whereas *being Black* indicates the presence of these historical memories and experiences. Put otherwise, when continental African youths experience both the physical and the psychological pain of differential treatment, they comprehend that this treatment has a long history. In fact, their experiences are only one line in a long script of what it means to be Black in North America. Before discussing these experiences, however, I want to introduce two contrasting cases, one of a teacher and the other of a vice principal. The case of the teacher shows the agony of finding one's self within the striated space of blunt forms of racism. The vignette of the vice principal makes the case for what Charles Taylor (1994) calls the "politics of recognition": One needs to recognize one's self in the school, teaching staff, and material taught.

Behind the Scene I: A Teacher's Agony

His name was Aristide (pseudonym) and he was the only Black teacher at Marie-Victorin (MV), and had been for two years prior to my study in 1996. Aristide is Canadian of Haitian descent, and moved to Ontario from Quebec where he had taught since 1970 in a large metropolitan city and in First Nations reservations in Quebec. He had two masters degrees, and at the time of the interview, he was enrolled in a Ph.D. program. In early 2012, I was in communication with Aristide. He told me that he had moved back to Quebec and obtained his Ph.D. in 2005. But because he could not land a job at a university, he was teaching at a high school in eastern Quebec. When I asked him about the stories he had told me in 1996, he confirmed that the problems had continued to the end of the school year and through summer 1996, when he decided to move back to Quebec to teach and continue his graduate studies. Unfortunately, he added, what he had told me in 1996 also summed up his workplace situation in 2012 in Quebec where he continued to be treated unfairly, snubbed by colleagues and not offered a lengthy contract despite his Ph.D..

In the text that follows, Aristide describes his experiences at MV in an extract of a two-hour interview in which he discussed, in particular, how the other teachers did not want him there, and his superior qualifications for the job. The latter issue became a particular sore point, and as he put it,

> People did not want to see me at the school and since I arrived, the principal[2] told me that. He told me, "Be careful!" because the teachers did not want to see me. I said, but I noticed that there is a lot of, I told him that I noticed that there were a lot of suspicious looks towards me. But what did I do to them? Because I knew that I had to continue to live with them! And I knew that these heads of divisions are the ones I am going to meet in the interviews. Because they called me for one [interview] every three months when my contract ended. That was their politics [with me]. If they had to give me another contract it is because they didn't find anyone else. I had to fill out an application, and then pass another interview. Then, they had to call the places where I had worked before. It was always the same places. But every time they had to call them to tell them, "We are going to offer a position to Aristide, what do you think of him?"...I was there with the most experience of all of

the teachers. I was the teacher who had the most recognized experience....And I am more or less certain that in terms of diplomas and qualifications, I had superior qualifications. (individual interview, French)

This is how striated spaces are encountered and experienced. The minoritarian body, it seems, is controlled through contract: Aristide had to apply every three months even though he was more qualified than the other teachers. Aristide was brought into the school because more than 65 percent of the school population was Black. But being the "token Black," however, "is not fun," as Seegars (2007) put it. The token Black is not supposed to "slip up in front of white people. He feels as if he can't make certain mistakes because he represents the entire race. One mistake will set black people back 100 years—and no one wants to be 'that negro,'" Seegars concludes (n.p.). Being the token Black was neither flattering nor experienced without difficulty.

Aristide discussed how certain rules and regulations (some made up) that dealt with seniority, contractual agreement, or unwritten ordinances were used to exclude him. The worst part of the narrative is when Aristide is told by less qualified teachers that they do not trust him, that he is sneaky, and that he does not know what he is doing. For those of us who have been public school teachers, we know that one needs to exert one's authority in the classroom; otherwise, one is destined to be disrespected as a teacher. How can one teach when one's authority is undermined in front of students by other colleagues and teachers? His story is very disturbing, and it is worth quoting at length:

> Aristide: I put my trust in them [White teachers]. I asked the head, the [teachers'] union representative, who is called, how is he called, Pierre [pseudonym]. He told me "I don't see you here next year." But, I did not understand what he wanted to tell me by that. By the way, previously, he had told me, "You don't have the right to fill out an application." I didn't understand that either. He told me, "You don't have the right to fill out an application, you have to wait, there are two openings, but you, you don't have the right to fill out an application. You have to wait for the teachers who are there before you to be hired. And when [we] have nobody to hire, then the Board will send you an outsider form [*formulaire extérieur*] because you, you are supposed to be in the outside list [*tu supposais d'être à l'extérieur*]." They will take care of those in the inside before everyone else. And I waited and it never came. [...] But it had been two years and I was still waiting. I arrived the following year; there were openings. I was always there [at the school]. The positions were empty. They called the

	others, they called the candidates, but they didn't want to, they didn't want to hire me.
Awad:	Why?
Aristide:	They told me that they have to be careful with me because I was the spy [*espion*] of the principal, the spy of the Board.
Awad:	But no! but no! [*mais non! mais non*!]. You didn't hear it like this? You were told, right?
Aristide:	No, it is not that I overheard it. It was not someone who was talking to someone else and I overheard. These were people who told it to me to my face. And [these were the] people, for example, who were hired after me, who are now tenured teachers [*professeurs permanents*]. At one point, the principal called me to tell me, "They don't like you."
Awad:	Completely [*carrément*]!
Aristide:	What did I do to them? Yes, completely! I have seen enough in this school [*J'en ai connu dans cette école*]. I was humiliated. What happened was that when the principal told it to me, all the students already saw that I was weak at the school. And this made me sick because we were all teachers at the same level. And moreover I was the most experienced among them, more qualified than the others. But we are all in this together [*Mais on est dans le milieu*]. Everyone looked down on me as inferior, and consequently I felt inferior. I had accepted this because I was telling myself that "after three years, five years, it is going to be all right. I have just arrived [to the school]." One time I was in my classroom. There were two people, the head of the division who was all the time in front of my classroom door to assess the students, to see what they were doing in my class, and then another person, a special education teacher [*éducatrice spécialisée*]. Her name is Simona [pseudonym], I think. Every time these two people come to the door, this female student tells me, "Monsieur, look at the door, you are being assessed."
Awad:	Ohhh!
Aristide:	"OK," I told myself, "it is not too bad. I have my work to do and time has its own."

But this hopeful statement turned into a fatal destiny, a dream that turned into one nightmare after another. Aristide experienced this nightmare from men and women, teachers and students, young and old. Dehumanization, it seems, does not break the spirit of the dehumanized; instead, its repetition makes the process of dehumanization more vicious. While working at the library, Aristide told me, he was not given the computer password to do computerized library search. So whenever students asked him for something, he had to ask another colleague, with lower experience, to write the password. This was done as the students were watching:

> Aristide: This was how the teachers who worked with me at the library treated me. There was this computer which needed a password. All the teachers had the password except me. If a student came up to me and he wanted to do some work, he addressed me, and I in turn had to ask another teacher to go write the password. In one incident, there was a student who found the password; this guy Pierre [the teacher in charge of the library] called me. He said to me that it was me who gave the password. I found the student who had the password; the student said "Monsieur Pierre, it was not Monsieur Aristide who gave me the password. It is another teacher who wrote it and I was watching him and I saw the password." Another time, I saw Pierre going out. There was another woman [teacher] who came in with me. A student came asking for a diskette, I went into the office to give him the diskette. This woman got into the office [after me]. She said, "go ahead, go ahead!" I said, "Why this 'go ahead?'" She said, "I see you were sneaking and busy doing something in Pierre's office, and once you saw me, you stopped. I said you can continue and it doesn't bother me."

Another abject horror that made me wonder how Aristide was emotionally and psychologically able to handle all of these situations:

> Aristide: One time, two days after [the above incident], I was at the library with my class. We worked in the library because we were doing research. But, the classroom where I worked, I shared it with two other teachers. The youngest teacher her name is Hélène [all names are pseudonym]. She, I am telling you, is a racist to the maximum and it is her husband that was kicked out of school because he insulted a student by calling him "nigger" and so on. And so Hélène comes in and tells me, "Aristide, I went to the class and there were a number of bad words like [in English] *fuck you*, which were written on the board. I know they are not the students of Armand [the other teacher who shares the same classroom] who wrote them. They are not my students either, they have to be your students." I said, "Me! It's impossible!" But I was calm. I said, "There is one thing, check on the notebook, you will see that it has been two days that I didn't go to the class with my students because we are working at the library, since we are doing a research project." There are plenty of these happenings which really, I don't know what to say, in any case, I had enough.

What is significant to remember in Aristide's retelling is the fact that these are the same teachers that African students encounter every day in their schooling processes and their identity formation. *Students are ethnographers,* as we shall see later, and as such, they observe, take thorough notes, and interpret what is *coming into being* around them, and they are intelligently receptive, perceptive, and conscious of the messages they receive from what they see around them. This receptivity is more heightened and pronounced in the case of displaced students and those who come from minoritized groups (see also Garcia, 2005).

In my 2007 and 2011 studies, I did not see this racism. In fact, the opposite is true. At both Sunnyside and Maxwell High, there is an overt discourse of social justice and antiracist politics. Yet, having such diverse student population with very few teaching personnel and staff of color triggers a flashback to Marie-Victorin. Moreover, having Ali at Sunnyside and Dave at Maxwell High can only bring to mind Aristide. Ali is Canadian of Somali origin. He was hired at Sunnyside as a community liaison, bridging community and school, teachers and students, parents and administration; and often he acts as an interpreter. Ali has a Ph.D. with a background in physics and math. While the school needed a physics teacher, Ali was never offered a full time job as a physics teacher. However, he was asked by school administration "to help" (as he put it) students (minoritarian or majoritarian) in physics and math. On the other side of town, having Dave at Maxwell High is also incongruous, if not cynical. Dave has a masters degree in education and is qualified to teach at least three subjects. In my interview with him, he explained that he was told that the reason he was not offered full-time employment was budgetary. But, he added, two teachers were hired in the last two years while he was at the school. Whether intentional or not, the effects of being in a striated space are felt by both Ali and Dave. Indeed, George Dei (2007) argues, intentions matter only in their final effects.

Behind the Scene II: A Vice Principal of Color and the Politics of Recognition

In the midst of it all, there was Brian. Brian is a fairly young (mid-thirties) vice principal at Maxwell High. À la Obama, he was hired as part of a new administration team that is trying to "fix" (Giroux, 2012) the school. Most of what I am addressing in this section comes from a journal entry dated June 5, 2011, that provides a glimpse into the daily life of a dynamic vice principal whose life and background is in many ways relevant and important to his current position at Maxwell High. He is an African Canadian of Caribbean background who absolutely loves teaching and who has long experience in different provinces and (mostly affluent) schools. His presence at the school hints at new lines of flight and possibilities forward.

As I always do, I am waiting with the students outside Brian's office. He has a rainbow sticker on his door, which is supposed to symbolize safety for students of any sexual orientation. Brian is always busy, and now he has someone (a student in trouble?) in his office. I am sitting beside Ginette, a grade 10 student who came to Maxwell High two years ago. "Thank God Mr. Brian is here; he helps a LOT," she says emphatically. This is not the first time she has said this, and all the African students say the same thing. She is part of the informal group of continental African students that I work with at the school. While keen to tell me how much she loves Mr. Brian, she is worried. A few weeks previously, the province of Ontario required that all students provide evidence of immunizations, and Ginette does not have that record. "I don't want to go home," she tells me, but she thinks that will happen because she was not able to get her medical records. Her older brother has not come home from college, and she needs to see if he has the papers or if he can take her to the clinic. He is her guardian and she lives with him, his young daughter, and three other siblings. I ask her who does all the cooking for such a big group. "I do," she says with a look of assurance.

During our conversation, Brian emerges from his office and asks me to come in. As I do, he speaks to Sherifa, a girl of Somali origin, who is standing just outside his office. She, too, is part of the group of students I work with. She is missing her paperwork too, and he tells her, like the others, that she will have to go home or go to the quarantine room. She explains that she has had her shots but does not have the confirmation slips, and begins to cry. With incredible care, respect, and concern, Brian takes her into his office and calls her father. Her father explains that he was told that he would receive the record in the mail but never received it. Brian accepts the explanation and asks Sherifa to go back to the library, where he will later come to fetch her. It is the end of the year and exams are days away. Moreover, the new school administration, including Brian, have decided to do away with suspension. No student will be sent home or suspended. Brian did suspend students, as we shall see soon, but it was extremely rare. What I am addressing here are Brian's high ethics and cultural sensitivity as well as the spirit of the law itself, which puts him in a difficult situation.

Brian came to Maxwell High in 2010 as part of an administration team that included a White principal exceptionally committed to social justice. Together, they hosted a school community potluck where all students, along with their parents and siblings, brought food and shared it with everyone else. That evening I watched their speeches, dances, theater performances, First Nations ceremonies, and poem recitations, and sampled lots and lots of dishes from around the globe. The intent behind this annual evening, as

Brian explained it to me, is to bring the "whole community" into the school and to make the school a "community hub": a crucial part of the larger community, where "good things are happening."

As he reflects on his first year at the school, the biggest difference he sees between Maxwell High and the "affluent schools" where he has taught is that "parents do not complain here." He wants that to change, especially with immigrant parents, who constitute "the majority of the students' parents here," and "who think we know what we are doing." Clearly, Brian is not disputing the "good things" that the school is doing, but as he put it, "I am looking for discord." Immigrant or not, he continues,

> I want parents to be indignant if they do not receive information about their child. There is not enough indignation on the part of the school over these issues. If there are 25 percent or more students failing or at risk of failing in a class, the teacher needs to have a conversation with the administration. The teacher needs to contact parents. There should never be a surprise on the report card—it should be transparent.

While we are talking, Brian takes a call from an immigrant parent and learns that many of the parents have been able to contact public health. He is ecstatic because it means that parents are "advocating for their kids" and because public health is "giving them a week of grace." Brian contends that, for him, "parental involvement is engagement." He wants parents to ask their children, "Did you eat your breakfast?"

There is a persistent knocking on the door: a student (of Somali origin?) is asking for bus tickets. Brian explains that he has to go to transportation. Maxwell High "needs more bus tickets for students," Brian contends, which is one of the school's biggest expenses. Some students are eligible for free bussing because of their family income, but many fall into a gray area and depend on the school. Brian smiles and says that he likes the challenge: There's "never a dull moment in this school."

We get talking about what he calls "the pulse of the school." For him, the pulse of the school—that is, "what makes the school unique"—is its diversity: having so many peoples, cultures, and languages in one place,

> At the present time, it is obvious that our main purpose is not the moral one of producing caring people but, instead, a relentless—and, as it turns out, hapless—drive for academic adequacy. I am certainly not going to argue for academic inadequacy, but I will try to [argue] that a reordering of priorities is essential. All children must learn to care for other human beings, and all must find an ultimate concern in some center of care. (Noddings, 1992, p. xii)

and the challenge as well as the triumph of making it work. One challenge he had faced that morning was to suspend a student. "A very rare occasion, and it happened only three times this whole year," he explains. He had to call the parents, only to realize they spoke only Vietnamese and they had no one at home to translate. With sincerity and a smile, he says, "that's my easy day!"

"We have to care! Isn't that what Nel Noddings says: Pedagogy of care?" Brian continues, "We must care for each other, for the environment, for everything that is around us." Without a pause, he explains, "I get it from my parents and from my upbringing." Brian grew up with Caribbean immigrant parents who worked two or three jobs, but "there was always a caring adult. That was what I knew, care! We didn't have much by way of material possessions, but we had love and care." He sees himself in these kids, he explains. When his parents separated, he tells me, the situation at home got so bad that he had to stay in a shelter. This affected his brother, who was "genius, absolutely brilliant," and who now, unfortunately, suffers from mental health issues. "So, I have seen the good and the bad," he concludes.

"I know what these kids are going through," he adds, "what I want to get across is that suffering and struggle don't have to be the end of their story, just like they were not the end of mine. I want students to learn how to survive an arrest, God forbid. How do you do it? I tell all students: 'If you're angry, the most important thing is you. You can always get the cop's badge number later.'" As teachers, Brian contends, we have to prepare our students "for the real world."

Brian brings up "the idea of being bicultural and how language and culture plays into this." He talks to kids on their way to college or university. He tells them that "they are going to meet kids just like them except for their ethnicity, i.e., they may know what a Danish or nachos are." He tells me that when he went off to school he knew what Kraft singles were, and cheddar and maybe Swiss cheese, but the rest were not part of his family culture. He wants kids to be ready to know "how to act and eat when they get to a job site so they are not afraid and end up declining." He says we need to be explicit with youths so they can function in the dominant culture, telling me, "I spoke with a [Caribbean] accent until grade 3. A teacher sent my brother and me to a speech therapist to get rid of our accent." That was not long ago. Today, he asks how schools can do this, yet he says that this opened up the possibility of him being here

> [T]he first job of the schools is to care for our children. We should educate all our children not only for competence but also for caring. Our aim should be to encourage the growth of competence, caring, loving and lovable people. (Noddings, 1992, p. xiv)

right now in this very office, and now he can work with other students to help them. He says his life would have been very different without this transformation.

If Aristide's story is a demonstration of the ugly face of the striated space, making him a *persona non grata*, Brian's is a hopeful line of flight, an expression of a smooth space. Both cases, however, show what takes place behind the scenes, and especially the burden of carrying such a heavy weight as Brian does. According to Annette Henry (2012), Brian's case is only too common among minority teachers, whether they teach in elementary, secondary, or higher education. No one person can or should do as much as he does. It is physically and emotionally taxing. Yet his commitment, it must be noted, is very much appreciated by students, especially African students. Ginette's comment was echoed by many other students. As I said before, students, especially displaced students, are the best ethnographers: They "ethnographically read" their teachers (Brian included) and recognize whether these teachers are genuine or not. This is a contention worthy of further explanation and exploration.

Displaced Subjects as Ethnographers

Understanding a new social context is always-already an arduous and significantly formidable task. It is formidable because it works both at the conscious and the subconscious levels. In trying to understand a new social context, I am contending, displaced subjects become ethnographers. We look around for the familiar and the foreign, we identify with that which we know, and try to make sense of that which we do not know. When I first went to Marie-Victorin (1996), Sunnyside (2007), and Maxwell High (2011) with the intention of understanding the plight of African students and "hunting" (Noddings, 1992) for patterns of social life, I found that for African students, their first arrival to Canada and their first arrival to the schools were not that different. They went through similar rapid processes of *translating* the new Canadian and school contexts. The nature of these processes is best captured by Amani (MV, F, 17, Somalia) in an individual interview. In recounting her first day experience at Marie-Victorin, she said:

> *No, I mean,* it's like, for me, the situation was new, new school, new country, new society, *new everything is new.* […] So, I found myself in a situation where I was mainly observing. I didn't talk in class. I didn't saying anything, I was there just to observe because there were lots of things to observe, right [*n'est-ce pas*]? So, I did. The things that disturb me ah, in class, it was the way, the relationships between students and teachers. I was surprised especially when they said the word *tu.* (individual interview, French)

It is obvious that during the first few days and months, Amani was the ethnographer, whether in the classroom, the school, or the larger society. One of the first things she observed at the level of teacher-students relationship was the use of the pronoun *tu*. It was one of her early "cultural shocks," if you like. *Tu* in French is used among close friends and peers, for children, or pejoratively for an unknown person or an interlocutor we mean to disparage. For Amani, using *tu* for a teacher is a sign of disrespect. This reading is demarcated and influenced by Amani's memory—what John Ogbu (1983, 1990) calls "comparative system"—of the teacher-students relationship in Africa, which is based on respect, authority, and, significantly, discipline, which is performed in the use of *vous* instead of *tu*.

In a similar example, the ethnographer and participant-observer Amani "took note of" the reasons why continental students did not have a sense of belonging, or of being integrated or welcomed in the school. Her ethnographic gaze is reflected in this same individual interview when she compares MV with James High School, another French-language high school in the same metropolitan where there is no streaming—all students are in the college-bound advanced level. She continues,

> But one of the features of, *sorry*, one feature here at the school that I was able to take note of [*j'ai pu remarquer*], compared to probably James or things like that, is that here at Marie-Victorin you will not really have students who are really all integrated in the same activity or something like that. But that is explainable *you know*, there is a history to this. When [continental African] students came here [to the school], they feel, they felt marginalized [*égaré*]. So, when you feel marginalized, you stay marginalized, right? *Not dig in*. (individual interview, French)

On the same topic of entering a striated space and not being welcomed, and in turn not being able to engage with the school curriculum and extracurriculur activities, Amani again has *taken note of* this:

> You see, Awad, here's the situation at Marie-Victorin. It is easy to understand, you know. You came to almost all the organizations, the activities which we had for a year now; and you were able to film or even ask questions. It is easy when you really *observe*, and then you try to evaluate the situation here at Marie-Victorin, you notice that the [African/Black] students are only involved in Black History Month [*le mois de patrimoin africain*]. It is very rare *to see* a student of color taking part in some stupid activities [*des actvités bêtes*] they put in place at the school. It's really ridiculous. There isn't anything that was put in place which interests us. It is only things that interest a Canadian [read White] student or I don't know what. And I, I am not interested, *I won't go to some shit like ah like ah...* [the name of a student organization that totally excludes African students, they have no representation in it at

all—see chapter 5] *or whatever. It doesn't interest me, you know.* (individual interview, French; emphasis added)

To *see* and to *observe* what is happening in the school, on the school board, and in the larger society is an ethnographic attempt to make sense of that which is around us—a form of what Homi Bhabha (1994) calls "cultural translation." Here, Amani is expressing what every immigrant and displaced subject has to go through: scrutinizing a new sociocultural context, their new "home." This scrutiny determines how one reacts to and interacts within this new context. It is important to remember that most of this scrutiny takes place at a subconscious level. In the following section, which discusses the students' accounts of their racial experiences at the schools, this will become more evident.

On Stage: African Students and the Experience of Racism

As I have noted, the experience of African students should be read as part of the process of becoming Black, as part of building memory of what it means to be Black and where they fit racially. Continental African students show an understanding of race through the retelling of their racial experiences. These racial experiences, by and large, meant racism. Their understanding of what constitutes racism varies from one student to the next. However, there are three threads and streams of thought.

(1) Racism as an offered positionality: This is when the dominant group restricts one's choices and possibilities. Omer (MV, M, 19, Ethiopia), who came to Canada by himself when he was fifteen years old, exemplifies this situation. Omer was living in a shelter at the time of the interview, yet he was longing and enthusiastically planning to go to Laurentian University. In Althusserian (1971) terms, Omer conceives this restricted positionality as interpellation: "Hello there! You are Black, you can't do anything. Muslims, you can do nothing. This is what is astonishing to me. It is already seen [that is, what Blacks and Muslims can or cannot do]" (individual interview, French).

(2) Undemocratic decisions: This is when students feel they are not consulted on matters related to their lives, and the decisions then are perceived as racist or discriminatory. For instance, because all school teachers and personnel are White and Christian (except for one Jewish female teacher), when the school decided that it was no longer permissible to do midday Muslim prayer, the decision was read in multiple ways, including as racist. Aziza (MV, F, 18, Somalia) put it thus:

> So now there is this new rule. They met, the personnel of the school, they met. They agreed, like we were nothing at all. They said "Oh, who cares!" you see. We have to

just tell them not leave the class, because our class is more important than their prayer. [...] So, there wasn't, I am sure there wasn't even one teacher who opposed that. They all agreed. (group interview, French)

Although students finally agreed with the school decision, obviously they needed to feel they were participating in the decision-making process. To soften the situation, the school brought in a Moroccan teacher from James High School, the other French-language high school in the city, who explained to students that midday prayer did not have a specific hour but an extended period from 12 noon to 3 p.m.

Here, one is reminded of George Dei's (2007) contention that intentions matter mostly (if not only) in their final effects, that is, in how they make people feel. The intentions of the teachers did matter crucially, but their undemocratic action of stopping midday prayer without consulting students spoke for itself. This action "told" the students that, first, being a Black and a Muslim is a double curse and, second, they "can do nothing" (as Omer put it above).

When it comes to action, in my experience, MV stands in sharp contrast to Sunnyside and Maxwell High. When the Muslim students at Sunnyside decided they needed a prayer room, they had their room in two days; indeed, the decision was so quickly made that it created rumors of favoritism and special treatment. In Maxwell High, this went even further. Led by a White teacher, students built their own prayer room, with the help of the larger Muslim community. Now the prayer room is used by the Maxwell High students and the Language Instruction for Newcomers to Canada (or LINC) adults who come to receive ESL instruction in the school.

(3) The minute and the trivial: This is the third and final way in which racism is seen as the accumulative memory of small details which, when put together, tend to leave students with clear messages that they are not trusted and wanted, and that they are deviant or divergent. Listen to Aziza again as she explains that even our names become a burden, when having to repeat how they should be pronounced becomes a marker that sets us apart:

I am going to give you an example. A female teacher always gives the absence sheet [*la feuille d'absence*], always to White students. They are moreover going to know the names...a teacher is supposed to know the names of all the students. He is going to know more the names of the White students than the names of Black students. "What's your name again? Bûralé? How do you want to me to pronounce that, Bûrralé, Boralé?" You see things like that. It's a bit, it gives you pain here [pointing to her chest]. This is like, these things are small, but they can be big, which can also be something catastrophic you see. And you, you have to live with this every day, you see.

Following the same line of the everyday, the case of Aaliyah (F, 16, Kenya) at Sunnyside is particularly interesting. She was sent to a co-op program along with a White female student, but her host (a White businessman) was so "uncomfortable" around her that he did not say a word to her for three days. She did not even know what was expected of her for her co-op assignment. Talking about the interaction between the White student and the co-op manager, Aaliyah told me, "I watched them every day, and they were laughing and joking all the time. It hurts [pointing to her chest]." It is the "small talk I wanted," she continues, "so I couldn't bear it and I never went back" (individual interview, English). Sunnyside and Maxwell High, it seems, are not that smooth after all, not so radically different than MV in terms of how African students experience exclusion and what Philomena Essed (1991) calls "everyday racism." The "smooth space" is filled with lots of bumps, despite schools' best intentions (Egbo, 2009).

Before proceeding to the next section, a reminder is necessary at this point. As I made clear already, my intention in this book is not to compare schools or to evaluate the progress made over the years, but to signify the process of becoming Black. Here, a complex picture is emerging thus far, one where what teachers do and decide has a direct effect on African students' positive or negative experiences of integration, schooling, and becoming. These students seem to be oscillating between smooth and striated spaces. The undemocratic decisions weigh heavily on their minds. Even though the experiences are markedly different in the three sites, as we shall see in the following chapters, the outcome is the same: a rhizomatic emergence of Blackness, Black popular culture, and Black English as sites of identification.

Racial Stratification

Marie-Victorin provides an illuminating example when it comes to racial stratification. Whatever the stream of thought and perception of racism, students here bear the experience of blunt and shocking forms of racism. The following story depicts the danger that stems from discerning and treating race in opposition to ethnicity, where the latter is imagined in cultural terms. It seemed that at Marie-Victorin, for example, once Chinese and students from the Middle East were represented in school activities, Black students[3] were stratified at the bottom and thus cut off from these activities. According to San Juan (2002), these situations produce antagonism between minoritized groups. This is Aziza again telling her story:

Aziza:	I also remember in 1994, I tried to join the volleyball team here at, at the school. And then I tried, I started when I first came here. When I first arrived like that, I started to try because I always, I was always good in volleyball. I played handball and volleyball when I was back home, which were popular especially [among] the women (*les femmes*), the girls (*les filles*); whereas soccer was only popular among the boys.
Awad:	All right.
Aziza:	OK, I always loved this sport you see. I came here, I tried to join the team, and then I was accepted the first two years. The third year, I started to, because you see why he accepted me [in the first two years] because I was the only Black.
Awad:	Aha.
Aziza:	You see, so in other words, me being accepted, it was like he was doing me a favor, you see. (…) So, after that I tried in 1994, I tried for the team, I wasn't accepted. He used to tell me at the time, "Oh, Aziza you are good." I tried for the first two years and he kept telling me, "You are good." He even asked me, "Do you want to try for the team next year?" I told him "Yes, I would love that, yes." [When] I came next year to try for the team, I was, I was not accepted.
Awad:	Why?
Aziza:	There were other students, students from other origins. There weren't only White students. There were, there was an Indian girl, there was an Arab girl, there was an Asian girl, things like that you see.
Awad:	Oh OK (*oui, d'accord*).
Aziza:	So there, they favor, you see, the people; for example he is going to favor an Asian girl over a Black girl, who comes from Africa. (group interview, French)

However, the story does not end in Aziza's ethnographic gaze and her perception of the racial and ethnic conflict. She is about to encounter another event of racism:

> So, I always came to practice. I came, I hadn't missed even one practice, and I was never late because he told us "Don't come late and don't miss the practice." Part of me, I was already, I am never [late] because it's a sport which I love, I really want to be accepted in the team. So, me who always came to practice, without delay, I was not accepted whereas few students who were accepted in the team, they missed the practice two times. […] You see always that. […] But believe me I have witnesses in the team who were not accepted like me, you see. (group interview, English)

Armed with frustration and proof, Aziza took matters into her own hands and complained to the principal, who apparently spoke to the physical education teacher, the person in charge of the volleyball team. The principal also asked Aziza to speak to the physical education teacher: "No Monsieur, I have no desire to see him," Aziza responded to the principal. But she was too angry and furious to let go of a rage that was paralyzing her. For example, the same morning when Aziza spoke to the principal, the physical education teacher called her:

> And he started to tell me "But what is your problem Aziza? Do you have a problem against me?" And me, I looked at him like that [stern face, with a look that went from top to bottom]. I have no desire to [speak to him] because I know that if I start talking, it is going to be catastrophic. All my rage, which is here [pointing to her chest] will come out. Because you know you are really, you are really angry. (…) And when I spoke to him, I told him, "Monsieur, you are a racist," and I left. "But what does this being racist mean? I was never a racist (…) I treat all students equally." I looked at him like that and I told him, "Oh really? Good." And I said, "Of course you are a racist and I have no desire to speak to you, I will be late for my class," and I left. (group interview, French)

To take this stance, Aziza had to calculate a number of things in her mind, including the fact that this was her teacher who would grade her, and that he might complain to the principal or other institutional bodies. Nevertheless, Aziza was psychologically and emotionally motivated to let her paralyzing anger out and to take a firm stance.

> I was so relieved that I told him that, because it came out of me, it is a rage. All what I had here [her chest] before, had finally come out like that. I don't want to have anything here, I want to feel comfortable, I want to breathe, I want to be set free you know. (group interview, French)

Interestingly, the incident went no further: "And you know what, nothing happened," Aziza explained. However, leaving the matter unresolved and unsolved produces two significant questions: What else can Aziza do, and where else can she go to complain about the incident? A recurrent theme I found in students' narratives is the differential power relation that positions teachers in ways that allow them to do anything they please to students, particularly Black students. In their study, Dei et al. (1997) reach similar conclusions and findings. Aziza, again: "Always teachers are protected. This means that teachers could inflict anything on us, especially they could do anything on Black students and no one is going to defend us" (group interview, English).

Justice and School Structures: Plight of Refugees

> A *caring relation* is, in its most basic form, a connection or encounter between two human beings—a carer and a recipient of care, or cared-for. In order for the relation to be properly called caring, both parties must contribute to it in characteristic ways. A failure on the part of either carer or cared-for blocks completion of caring and, although there may still be a relation—that is, an encounter or connection in which each party feels something toward the other—it is not a *caring* relation. (Noddings, 1992, p. 15; original emphasis)

Aziza is crying for help and for a caring relation. She is expressing the agony of the Black subject in Canada, and North America in general, with the word *justice*. The history of racism and racial stratification had taught Black people in the Americas that justice is neither fully implemented nor expected (Pascale, 2012; Taylor, 2004; Winant, 2004). Even in places like Sunnyside and Maxwell High, which declare antiracism as their official policy goal, it is possible to hear voices similar to Aziza's. At Sunnyside, a very politically and socially active student, Jenny (F, 16, South Sudan), told me that once she was walking by the library where a number of White teachers were laughing and chatting. Unintentionally, she overheard a female teacher saying,

Jenny: "They really lack work ethic these newcomers. I tell you what [imitating the teacher's high-pitched voice], without a Western curriculum these students will not be able to be successful."

Awad: No way?

Jenny: Yes, way! Ask, and you'll hear similar things. (individual interview, English)

So, I did. When I asked Ali, the Sunnyside multicultural liaison worker, about what Jenny overheard, he almost did not believe that I would have any doubt. "I know you are doing research, but man, our kids are suffering. You know what's worse," he adds, "this might be a very good teacher who genuinely wants to help our kids! Can you imagine those who [she] intends to hurt?" I then told him about Aziza and her experience at MV. I asked whether there is any "institutional body" students could appeal to if they have any grievance. "No, there is nowhere for them to go," he confirms. Indeed, in the case of Aziza, who mistrusts teachers, complaining about one of them would mean addressing the same individual—the same symbolic and material structure that inflicts the injustice on her and other Black students. She has a sense of not being heard, of not being listened to:

And then on top of it all, every time we go to make a complaint to the office and all that, we were ignored. We weren't taken seriously. We weren't taken seriously at all. What pisses me off (*ce qui m'enerve*), if you think about it, this discourages us because every time we try to talk to them, to talk to them, "no Monsieur, listen we have a problem," they ignore us, you see. And we become all discouraged and despair because nobody is willing to hear us. (group interview, French)

Aside from the language of "us" and "them" in Aziza's speech, which I will discuss later, what is significant about this is that it seems that the school system does not have internal mechanisms to handle the influx of refugees and displaced students. As Brian (Maxwell High vice principal) noted, "Literally, wherever there is a war or a conflict around the world, you will see an increase in the school population [from that part of the world]. Now, the Syrians have started to come" (Brian is talking about Syrians fleeing civil unrest stemming from attempts to topple the Bashar al-Assad regime.) School structures and personnel are not accustomed to the particularity and peculiarity of refugee students and refugee situations. The school system is not used to situations such as Ginette's example, which I discussed above. Ginette is a sixteen-year-old girl from Bénin who came to Maxwell High in 2009 speaking not a word of English. Her older brother (twenty-one years old), who is at college, is her guardian, and he has a three-year-old daughter. Ginette lives with him, his daughter, and her three younger siblings in a two-bedroomed apartment. She is the "mother of them all," as she put it smilingly. "I cook, clean, help them in their homework and make sure they sleep. When they sleep, I do my homework."

For many teachers, an underage student (under sixteen years old) in the school with no parental support is aberrant. At MV in particular, and to a lesser degree at Sunnyside and Maxwell High, even those who are over sixteen feel the burden of representing themselves before a structure that they know does not recognize their plight, is incapable of listening, and can offer very little support. During my focus-group interview with the boys at MV, Musa (M, 19, Djibouti) talked about the agonizing feeling of fending for oneself before such a structure, where justice is almost always unexpected. Musa lives with three other students from the same school, and it is in their house that I conducted the group interview. In the school, importantly, Musa plays the role of the "African elder" (as he called it), one who is there to help younger students with their academic and social problems. For example, he explains, "I noticed that all African students were taking general-level [that is, non-university-bound] courses." In an effort to support especially the younger students, he pushed them to take advanced-level and university-bound courses:

But the majority of the [African] students who are at Marie-Victorin, every time I see them, they take general-level courses, I don't know why. "Why are you taking a general-level course?" [explaining how he talks to other younger students] "It's Madame Robert [the principal] who gave it to me." "But, *gee* Madame Robert, [let her] go to hell, and take an advanced-level course," I said. (group interview, French)

In my field notes I wrote, "Musa came to me requesting if I can offer an English-language tutoring course because he thinks that African students have problems with English." What is significant in all of this is that unselfishly, in the tradition of the elder, Musa is looking after other younger African students, something that is culturally specific and may be foreign to mainstream Canadians. His personal, social, and academic experience is his guide here:

Musa: The African students, they have a lot of problems. Here, the Canadians don't have problems, they have their parents, there is that. We, we have problems. You, you are late, she [the principal] sends you home. You go home for three or four days. We, we can't afford that because there is the immigration that calls us: "you have to come to see me today." You have to sign your check, things like that. There is back and forth. So, you have to go to the immigration, you have to go with, your, how do you call it, counselor?

A male voice: Social worker.

Musa: No no, there you go! You have to speak with your social worker. If not, you don't receive your [social assistance] check. You can't live [without the social assistance check], you know! This is the problem; she [the principal] doesn't try to understand the problems. For example, the Canadians who were born here, they don't have these problems. They have their parents, they bring them to school. They feel comfortable, he will not be late, unless he is sick. He can't be late, he can't be absent. But us we have nothing. There isn't, our parents don't live here. I live by myself, he lives by himself, he lives by himself, he lives by himself [pointing to at least four students who live alone]. (group interview, French)

Living on one's own often requires developing everyday survival mechanisms. Students have to sort out their refugee or immigration papers by themselves, pay their own bills, and see their social workers for their social assistance. Social assistance for these students is their only source of income. However, as Musa hints at, school rules and regulations are incongruent with these lived experiences. According to these rules and regulations, no one may be late or absent as often as these students, despite their legitimate reasons, without being suspended. This feeds into the stereotype that

African/Black students are always late (Pascale, 2012), and as a result, as we see next, African students at Marie-Victorin are guilty of lateness unless proven otherwise. *We cannot conceive and talk about what we do not know*: Clearly, the school administration and personnel have no knowledge of the students' everyday lives, nor are they (cap)able to listen and hear the students' stories:

> Musa: The other day, I was absent the first period. I came in the second period. And that day, I didn't even see her [the principal]. I came the following day and I told her "Yesterday, I was absent." "All day? You were absent because you had problems." I had problems with *Hydro*, [city name], *Hydro*. I told her that I was going there; if not, they were going to cut off my electricity. So, I would not, I would not have electricity. So, I told her that I had this problem, I went to see them to pay the bill, and once and for all solve this problem. She said, "No no, that doesn't concern me. That is your problem. If you have to solve that, use your holiday time." But holiday times, they are closed. Saturday and Sunday, *Hydro* is not open. So, I have to go, I have to miss a class in order to go there and solve my problems. She didn't even listen, she said "You were absent all day." "But Madame, how do you want me to, I was absent the first period." I didn't even finish, she said "No no, you were absent all day for *Hydro*, to solve this problem." I told her "Madame, try to listen, try to hear me, leave me finish first." And I told her that I was only absent the first period. "Ah," she said, "you were only absent the first period, I am sorry. Then, I give a paper to [the administration?] this time, but don't be late." But that is me, I told her straight, "That is your problem, you don't try to listen to the African students. You only scream. That is your problem, and you have to change this character." I told her, straight, I told her that. (group interview, French)

In Musa's case, intentions matter only in their final effects, and they are not the most appreciated in this episode. That is, no matter what intention the principal had, as the helm of the school, she left Musa and other African students with the impression that they were guilty unless proven otherwise. This in turn creates a situation where the Black body is either completely obliterated from public spaces and activities, or it falls under strict, microscopic surveillance.

Thankfully, there are Brian (vice principal) and Dave (teacher assistant) at Maxwell High and Ali (multicultural liaison) at Sunnyside, among others, who are responding to Musa and Aziza's call with exceptional care. As Dave put it, "I wish I could shelter and protect these students from the alienation and discrimination I had to experience in the school system." Seeing himself in the students, Dave remembers: "coming into the school every morning is a reminder of my own alienation and exclusion; me being on a temporary contract; I can be let go any minute. Do we really have to repeat history again and again?"

Excluding and Surveying the Black Body

As social and psychic events, *racialized experiences* take different forms and shapes. In addition to the examples cited above that speak to and about the upper echelon of the school, I will discuss two more incidents in this section. Both are from Marie-Victorin. The first is related to the exclusion of African students from school activities and the second has to do with the Black body falling under a strict code of behavior and hence receiving special surveillance. In my field notes, I wrote about an event that was organized in the foyer of the school by the student council. It was a theatrical competition between male and female students. In the play, the actors presented their best performances, which then were judged by how loudly spectators applauded and screamed. Shah (the president of the student council, originally from Iran) was the judge. The event was poorly attended, in part because there was a total absence of Black students either as spectators or participants. "This," my notes read, "was a common pattern that was also confirmed time and again in African student narratives." They confirmed their own sense of alienation or "*non-appartenance*" (as one student, Najat, called it).

In remembering one general school assembly, Najat (F, 15, Djibouti) describes this sense of *non-appartenance*. Najat had been in Marie-Victorin since grade 7 and she disliked the school precisely because she felt disengaged from school activities, academic or otherwise. She was otherwise exceptionally energetic and humorous, especially with this researcher. Below she describes an activity where male and female students were auctioned before the school general assembly. The student in question comes onstage and the auctioneer starts a price and it is up to the students to add to it or not. The student from the assembly who pays the most "gets" the auctioned student.[4] The activity seems to have two objectives: The first is sexual and the second a test of students' popularity. Being sexual is always juxtaposed with gender in that it is the female body that is highly prized, and it is the "stud" (as one student calls it), the most attractive and popular boy, who is the most expensive. Nevertheless, there is no actual money involved.

Najat: You know, and I go all the, all the guys were there [including] the council members. I was like, "They not worth it." I was like, "Hold on, how come there is no like, you know, how come there is no like Black guys coming, you know." Goes you know, I be like, "Oh my God you know, I got like 100 dollars on me." [laugh] I feel like keeping that 100 dollars.

Awad: There wasn't any Black person over there?

Najat: There wasn't. I was like, all last, 'am like [pause]; so I just left. Because I got a practice, I just left "Oh wo, bye." Everybody is like left, there wasn't any Black person, and we suppose to be like all White. (individual interview, English)

In cases like these, I noted that African students use several strategies to deal with their sense of alienation. The first is to play the role of the present-absent, that is to say, being physically present but mentally somewhere else; second, they converse among themselves during the course of the activity about something of relevance to them. They also, third, listen to music on their personal headsets, and finally, leave the whole event. This sense of *non-appartenance* serves as a significant reminder of African students' Blackness. In other words, it is part of their process of becoming Black, and it is a reminder, at least to those who are not yet aware, of their Blackness.

The second form of continental African students' racialized experience is related to the Black body, when this body is turned into a site of surveillance and restriction. Listen to Najat recounting her story about an incident in one of her classes. Although she is not doing anything that other students are not doing, she, along with other Black bodies, receives special attention:

Najat: Madame, me and my friend used to, the course is so boring like nobody actually cares about the course, you know. We like, sitting in a class, you know, it's a drama class. Sitting in a class and then we do whatever we want, we eat and then, when she talks, we ignore her. We like, "Madame bye" [laughs]. OK I was OK, this what happened. Once there was a party from the other class, from Khadija right? So then after that they invited us to come with them. But then the stupid teacher comes and says "*vous devez pas aller*" [you should not go]. And then, and I start; me and my friend start running ah, and then she is like "*reviens*" and tha was like; so I came back you know. And then she comes "go to the *bureau!*" [pronounced in French]. It's only me, she goes "go to the *bureau.*" She hates me and my friend, she hates us. Always our names, always our names. She doesn't care about the rest of us, there is always our names Najat, Amina, Sara you know, Alia you know. "You guys have zero," you know. And my friend comes and says, what's call ahm, "Madame you racist you know, because."

Awad: Why?

Najat:	You just look, because it's always like us. It's always like, you have to be like most important people you know. Whereas you know she doesn't see others, you know, the other people in fact.
Awad:	Do they do this thing or, or you guys kina, ahm, does the rest of the class do what you do?
Najat:	Oh yah. The rest of them kina so bad you know. They like jumping around and everything. And sometimes, we just go you know, OK we have to have some respect for the teacher. So we just get quiet. And then she didn't even see what the rest of them are like doing that jumping around, looking at everything. And then she is like, "Oh no it doesn't have to be them." And this guy call her a bitch, you know, and she didn't do nothing.
Awad:	He did?
Najat:	And then we like you know, we like, "Oh my God," and...
Awad:	And what did she do?
Najat:	She doesn't do anything and she always looks at us. We didn't curse, you know. We start like tha tha day I got mad. Me and my friend we got mad, and then I was like stuffed. We ran to her and I was like, "Madam you so racist." You dat dat and dat, you know, my friend goes, "You need a man." I go, "You need a mental hospital" [laugh]. "You need help, you need" [laugh]. No it's true because we like so mad. (individual interview, English)

It is obvious that, for this teacher, chatting away and jumping around is more absurd and problematic than the sexist name-calling ("bitch"). Interestingly, nothing happened to the boy who did the name-calling, but when Najat decided to go with the other class, she received a warning by being sent to the *bureau*, which usually means the principal's office where she would be disciplined, and maybe warned or even dismissed. This differential treatment, again focusing strictly on MV, is a recurrent theme found in almost every student narrative, especially those of the boys, and it takes three forms: (1) differential treatment by the school administration and personnel (including the principal), (2) differential treatment because of their age, and (3) *le contrat*. I will discuss each of these forms respectively.

Being Spoken To

African students sense these differential treatments first and above all in language, in how they are talked to or addressed. They are talked to in a patronizing and accusatory tone, where they are guilty till proven otherwise. Sam

(M, 19, Djibouti) and Mukhi (M, 18, Djibouti) explain the nature of these differential treatments:

Sam: OK, this woman there [the principal], *you know*, she came from this school there, what is it called? Lionel-Giroule [an elementary school], you know. *She knows you know*, she learned how to speak to kids *you know*, the kids and all that, the small kids [*les petits gamins*] there. *You know she learns how to, you know*, how to speak with kids. You go to the office, you know, you see, you know, only the Africans there. But, you see a difference in how she speaks to African students and the students, how do I say it, with other students there. There is a big difference.

Mukhi: But she doesn't know anything. She comes from an elementary school, she treats us like kids. You know, the way she talks to us, she talks like a baby, *man* [laughs]. *Wallahi* [swear to Allah], like a kid, but really sometimes she gives me, I have a desire to put a bomb to blow her out. (group interview, French)

The consequence of these phonological and lexical usages by the principal—that is, how she talks to these students—is what Feagin et al. (1996) call the *unconscious accumulation*, whereby one just *knows* that one is being treated differently. The lexical usage, however, has the potential to turn into psychically abusive language. For example,

Sam: *Wallahi bellahi* [in the name of Allah], *sometimes, you know*, she [the principal] said to me, she didn't say, *she didn't say nothing about that, but* I overheard the guy who spoke with her and she told him, how do I say it, "You, at this age," *you know*, "you are still here," *you know, you know!* "You are never going to finish your studies?" *You know!* "You don't have anything to do or what!" I don't know, she doesn't know why you are at the school, yah? (group interview, French)

Some of these students are refugees and, as such, their studies have been interrupted (see Harushimana & Awokoya, 2011, for further discussion of this point). So it is possible to have an older student in a lower grade. Given the school's evaluation of their scholastic level, students do not have a choice about where they are placed (I will come back to this point later in the chapter). Nonetheless, the use of this infantile language, one may conclude, aggravates African students' sense of *non-appartenance*. The situation is aggravated further when that language is used by an unauthorized person, the school secretary, which happened so often that one student asked me to go talk to her. Pierre Bourdieu (1991) shows that when an unauthorized speaker uses an authorized language, usually they are trying to place themselves above their addressee. We already know what the principal told the student above, but when the school secretary takes on the language and the role of the principal in relation to African students, it should not surprise us that the latter feel out of place in the school:

> Sam: OK, it was an African student who arrived late. Me, I was there. Me, I wanted to speak with Madame Robert and whatnot; I had an appointment with her. So, this student comes in late, so he says "Madame, I am late." You know, the secretary, the secretary of the office, it is her who starts with him. She says to him, "Why are you late? You, you always late." She doesn't even know the guy, this student. She doesn't know. It is not, it is not her job to question him, she is not the principal or what. She, she is there. The secretary, she has nothing to do with that. (group interview, English)

Age, Displacement, and Interruption of Schooling

When the principal says "You, at this age," she is indeed pointing to the obvious, that African students are often older than their Canadian-born counterparts. This is a well-known phenomenon in refugee and immigration studies (cf. Harushimana & Awokoya, 2011). At Sunnyside and Maxwell High, but particularly at MV, this is connected to displacement from civil wars—particularly of Somalia (MV), Sudan (Sunnyside), and Iraq and Syria (Maxwell High) and the refugee experience, and the years lost between countries and schools. Nonetheless, the principal's insensitivity and incapacity to seriously take into account these experiences make her reading of the age question problematic, at the least, and discouraging to students. To the extent that African students feel alienated at Marie-Victorin, for example, the school thus becomes "her school": it belongs to someone else, not to the students:

> Sam: Things like that [including what the principal said], that discourages you, really *wallahi* [swear to Allah].
>
> Mukhi: I had some problems last semester, so like I couldn't come to school [for] a month. So, I had a lot of absences, so this semester she asked me, ahm, why instead of coming to **their** school, why don't I go to another school. Like, she wanted that I leave, I go from **her** school and I go somewhere else. She didn't want me back. (group interview, English, emphasis added)

Even if one reads in Mukhi's comments a simple reference to the possessive ("her school"), he is being sent a message that his presence in the school is not desired. I will show later that the students who receive this type of message tend to have a stronger identification with the political agenda of Blackness and find their desire and identity reflected more within Black popular culture.

Le Contrat: **Dropped Out or Pushed Out?**

In their study of the "drop out" phenomenon, Dei et al. (1997) observe that in most cases students do not voluntarily drop out; they are "pushed out" through very complex mechanisms. These include pedagogy, curriculum, classroom and school climate, language, and teachers' attitudes and expectations, among others. These are factors at Marie-Victorin. In Sam's narratives, above, ageism was turned into a mechanism to push students out of school. In this section, I will put the emphasis on *le contrat*, a phenomenon very specific to Marie-Victorin; I did not find this at Sunnyside or Maxwell High. In fact, when I asked about whether they had a similar policy, Brian (Maxwell High vice principal) first could not believe such a policy existed, second, questioned the objective and the ethics behind it as discriminatory, and, third, explained that Maxwell has a policy that is the total opposite. At Maxwell High, the policy is "no suspension no matter what students do" (as Brian put it). As already indicated, Brian is speaking about the spirit of the law, which is there to be broken, since he suspended at least three students that I am aware of. Nonetheless, for Brian, the school is better off dealing with the students inside the school instead of sending them to cause more problems outside the school. "Moreover," Brian continues,

> where do I send Brent? Two days ago, I came to know that Brent [a grade 11 White student] was evicted out of his apartment. If I suspend him, where do I send him? Doesn't it make more sense for me to keep Brent in the school? If I suspend him, it may be easier for the school and the teachers, but am I not causing a bigger problem to send him…I don't really know where?

Le contrat is a contractual agreement that all students at MV must sign that stipulates that if a student is absent or late a fixed number of times, she/he is asked to leave the school. It was introduced by the White female principal, who saw that students were chronically late and sometimes absent. I noticed all through the narrative around *le contrat* that it is a male narrative, cited only by male students; it is non-issue for female students. This supports an established body of literature that shows that Black men receive a higher level of scrutiny, surveillance, and punishment (cf. Emdin, 2012). As I shall discuss later, in chapter 4, even the girls noticed how differently the boys were treated, and they had very strong reflections on the implications of this differential treatment.

I have outlined already the particularity and peculiarity of the situation with African students—including often having no parental support, and living and surviving on their own, having to fend for themselves. So, in essence, the category "student" that *le contrat* stipulates seems to equate to, in all but a few cases, continental Africans. Furthermore, because of institutional lack of support and the total absence of the Black body among the school administration, African students felt the burden of being attacked and the burden of defending themselves. Although students can be criticized for being late and absent, one has to consider the source of the problem, not just its surface, before making so harsh a decision as pushing students out of school. The following exchange in my focus group interview is illustrative:

> A male voice: She [the principal] knows that we [African students] will be absent or late because we have problems. She knows that, this is why they have the new law, which states that if you are absent one day, you are screwed, you understand!
>
> Sam: All those who are in *le contrat* are African students, how do I say it, it is the African students who have problems and all that.
>
> A male voice: I didn't see any White there [signing *le contrat*].
>
> Musa: There had White students who signed *le contrat*, but the majority, the majority were Africans. But you know why the majority are Africans? Because White students at Marie-Victorin don't have problems. They have, they have their parents.
>
> Sam: But then, if we make the defense, we, we are on our own, by ourselves. It is us who take notes for ourselves. You know, we have to defend ourselves, but they have their parents. You know, their mother who comes to the school who says, "Why this law? I don't see that in the book," you know! So, they have their parents that are defending them, but us? (group interview, French)

Because of his age (over sixteen), Mukhi in the following episode is caught between a rock and a hard place: either sign *le contrat* or leave the school. In the same episode, another male student's chance to correct his mistakes no longer exists thanks to *le contrat*, which stipulates that once a student reaches his/her quota of absences, this nullifies his/her chances of remaining at or returning to school:

Mukhi: If your age is over sixteen, you are not obliged to go to school. So, this is the only reason why she [the principal] gave me, what did she say before, she said "Sign or leave, sign or leave" [*signe ou va t'en*]. Me, I don't have the choice, I don't have any choice. Sign or leave! If I leave, I don't have anywhere to go. Like I don't have any school to go to, like, and [...] so I don't have the choice.

One male voice: Listen, I had some problems before that, two years before. I wanted to come back this year, this semester, they told me, "You had a lot of absences two years ago." I said, "That was two years ago. What do you think of me now, if I will, because I will study hard to pass my test." She said to me, "You had too many absences before." She doesn't even know if I changed and all that, she said to me, "No, you had absences before, you can't enter the school." (group interview, French)

Incidentally, during my focus group interview with the boys, a student from Senegal (Hamidou) was present. Hamidou was not a participant in my research, yet he offered the story of his experience with *le contrat,* which was both interesting and illustrative. In view of his age, he signed *le contrat* himself, with no parental consent. He was then dismissed from the school for once being late by 5 minutes. He was staying in Musa's house to avoid the wrath of his parents, who had not yet been told about his dismissal from the school. He was dismissed even though all his courses were grade 12 advanced-level courses. I asked him,

Awad: Why did you leave [*quitter*] the school?

Hamidou: I didn't leave voluntarily [*de ma propre volonté*]. I was kicked out through the door. It is because of the principal who said to me, it was because I was very very late. I think it was because I signed *le contrat*. I was in *le contrat* like all the old [students who are asked] to sign the contract, because of absences. This is why she kicked me out. But, this is why, because I was only late, that's why she kicked me out, it is because I had signed *le contrat*. Yes, that's it. (group interview, French)

One may detect a hint as to why the number of African students in MV dropped so drastically in a short time, and the kind of structural pedagogy, teachers, and personnel that African students have to encounter on a daily basis. Age is a crucial factor in pushing African students out of school, and as we shall see in the next section, language is another. Although African students possess highly valuable linguistic capital, they are streamed into lower-level courses in substantial numbers.

Before proceeding to the next section, however, it is worth noting that the situation was different at Sunnyside and Maxwell High. It is summarized best by Jean-Yves (JY), a grade 10 Congolese student at Maxwell High, who switched from a French-language high school to Maxwell High. In my interview with him, he put it thus:

JY: Man, I am glad to make the switch.

Awad: Why?

JY: In the French school, you feel like you don't belong. It is "their school" [making air quotes]. Here [at Maxwell High] you feel you belong even if you don't speak English. Everybody is so welcoming, and whassup with their French, man [the Franco-Ontarian variety of French]? I don't understand most of it, yo yo yo y'knanhmsayin' prof?

Awad: I guess I do [laughter]. (individual interview, English)

Language, Race, and Streaming

Among the three research sites, Blackness in MV is experienced differently by various students, and with variable degrees of emotional intensity. For this reason, in the following sections I concentrate exclusively on MV, because its students' experience with Blackness is particularly illuminating, especially as far as language is concerned. Given their postcolonial education, by and large, African students arrive to school fluent in and armed with highly valuable symbolic capital: *le français parisien*, Parisian French. Interestingly, the mandate of the French-language schools in Ontario is to introduce students to this variety as well as to the variety spoken by the middle-class Franco-Ontarians (Heller et al., 1999). However, when African students come to school with this capital, there is astonishment on the part of teachers and school counselors. In the words of Ben Rampton (1995), their language is *deceptively fluent*. They cannot be so fluent and speak the language with such mastery! This scepticism stems from the fact that, as Bourdieu (1991) would have said, the "legitimate" language is spoken by an "illegitimate" speaker: a refugee who is imagined to be, at least in the dominant mediatic representations, a source of pity, and astonishment and envy. This mistrust of the linguistic capital that African students possess has led to a patronizing attitude that is easily opened to a racialized/racist reading. In the following excerpt, female students reflect on this situation:

Amani: The teacher could not stop to thank me every time, and tells me "Here, your French, you can, it is different than the others. How did that happen, where did you learn that? Are you sure that you are not in the wrong

	stream [this was a general-level course]?" You know, things like that. And then, she was really surprised, you know. I told her, "No, I know what I have to know for my level, my my…" [interrupted]
Aziza:	And then she was very impressed when we said that we learn our French in our country. And then things like that, and then she said, "Really, in your country, there is really this system?"
Samira:	"Are there professors who speak French like that? But my God you have *l'accent français*!" But of course we have *l'accent français*, there were teachers that taught us, no? And then this: "You are coming from Somalia oh, we never heard that in Somalia people speak French with…" [interrupted]
Aziza:	"Really in Somalia you have this system?" You know, **they don't accept that**. (group interview, French, emphasis added)

In my individual interview with Aziza, she expands on how teachers' disbelief is patronizing and grossly disturbing, especially given the racial connotation:

> The first day when I wrote my [evaluation] test, of my French level, he [the counselor] was really surprised because I spoke an excellent French. The good and rich French; you know when you live in Africa? He was really surprised, you see. "You have an excellent French," you see! Because that is new you see, **an African who speaks a good French, better than they do**. It is a bit [too much? unbelievable?] you see. And also there is a teacher who said to me, "Where did you learn your French? Your French is good." And then I said that I learned there where I came from, in Africa. And then she said, she could not believe, you see. You see, she said that all the time. (individual interview, French, emphasis added).

In spite of their "good," "rich," and "excellent" French, continental African students are disproportionately streamed into the general, non–college-bound level. Apparently, the good, the rich, and the excellent is not good enough for advanced or university-bound–level courses. This disproportionate number is noted by the students themselves. Using his ethnographic gaze, Musa (M, 19, Djibouti) observed that "the majority of African students who are in Marie-Victorin take general-level courses." Although not all African students are in the general level, it is noteworthy that Musa introduced this observation unsolicited to the discussion during my focus group interview with the boys, which itself is an indication that it was a burning issue for him at the time.

Building on their memory of how schools functioned in Africa, African students were not fully aware of the difference between fundamental-, general-, and advanced-level courses. In Africa, all students go to the same class to perform the same academic task:

> A male voice: When you come, when you first arrive in the school, you don't know what general, advanced, fundamental courses mean. It is them [counselors and school administration] who give you your courses. You just want to go to school to study. They force you to take general courses [telephone rings]. You don't know what a general course means.
>
> Musa: With general courses you can't go too far. (group interview, French)

On the other hand, disturbingly but not surprisingly, most African students are pushed towards sports. Many studies have arrived at this conclusion (Dei et al., 2000; James & Shadd, 2001; Mensah, 2002; Neslon & Nelson, 2004; Yon, 2000).

> Mukhi: But still, there is Monsieur Raymond [a counselor] who even if you took five physical education [courses], he is going to give you a sixth.
>
> A male voice: Yah, I don't know why.
>
> Mukhi: I don't know why, like, to make you waste time or something. (group interview, French)

Using their ethnographic gaze, the girls seem to believe that boys are more often streamed into the lower levels; but because of lack of statistical information, I cannot confirm or comment on this observation. Nonetheless, I made the same ethnographic observation. The girls believe that this has to do with the boys' exclusivism between sports and academic performance. Always, according to the girls, becoming a successful athlete for the boys is seen in opposition to doing well academically. When one is doing one's homework successfully, one is seen as a "nerd," a term connected to what Ogbu and Fordham (1986) call "acting white." The girls have seen these boys "back home," where they were "first-class" students. Something has happened that caused them to see academics in opposition to athleticism.

> Awad: I have noticed that at the school, especially there is a very very strong majority [of the African students] who are in the general level.
>
> Asma: That I know why. You know why?
>
> Awad: Why?
>
> Asma: The majority are boys. The majority are boys, they want *basketball*. *Dream Team*, I love the *basketball* [a girl talking].

Ossi: Yah, what does that mean?

Awad: Yes, yes, what does that mean?

Asma: They really want, they really could, I know these boys. They are really good. I remember in my country, they were really intelligent students.

Aziza: First class.

Asma: Yes, they know, they know. They know their academics, they know how to do this, how to do that. The problem is that if I start doing my homework, and I am a boy, this means I am a nerd. (group interview, French)

If the boys were doing well back home, then what is reflected in their behavior, tentatively analyzed, is a sense of alienation whereby becoming Black is equated with playing basketball. For them, becoming Black means entering the arena of exclusivism: basketball versus academics. Not surprising, the girls, by and large, tend to do a lot better academically. Lois Weis and Michelle Fine's (2005) study showed a similar conclusion. Whether in the classroom or on the basketball court, in the hallways or the cafeteria, by boys or girls, African students are in the process of creating new social boundaries.

Language, Demarcation, and Social Boundaries

These social boundaries are demarcated by culture, ethnicity, language, and race. They are also geographical and spatial, and best captured in Beverly Daniel Tatum's (1997) book title, *Why Are All the Black Kids Sitting Together in the Cafeteria?* As displaced subjects, African students' sense of *appartenance* or belonging was made worse by how they were welcomed at the school. In the African tradition, when a visitor or a new person moves into a neighborhood, the neighbors are supposed to bring their food or whatever they can afford and share it with the guest as a welcoming gesture. This did not happen at Marie-Victorin. On the contrary, African students receive a message of rejection: "We were rejected even by the students," as one female student explained to me.

This rejection, according to African students, is articulated in and through language, the space where social boundaries are first demarcated. For example, when African students first encountered the phono-syntactical structure of the French language spoken by Franco-Ontarians, they had some difficulty understanding it, especially given its particular phonetic structure (see Heller et al., 1999). And because Franco-Ontarians use the English language extensively in their everyday interactions, African students find themselves at a loss. Not only did they not understand the *franglais* (a speech act combining French and English) that the Franco-Ontarian students were speaking, but the extensive use of the English language, with which they were not previously familiar, added to their sense of alienation. They found themselves thus doubly erased. To counter this erasure, African students reverted to either French or their mother tongues. Yet, whenever they spoke their native languages, they were looked at suspiciously. The girls explain the interplay of languages in the building of social boundaries in this way:

Asma: And the way they spoke French, I understood nothing.

Aziza: That's true.

Asma: They spoke to me, and [when] they spoke to me, I could see them but I couldn't hear them. And then, little by little I learned very well and very quickly how they spoke.

Ossi: We were rejected even by the students. So, [interrupted]

Awad: Oh yah, it's interesting.

Asma: We had a debate in grade 8, because of the fight we had with the students. But, it's not really a fight, it's a dispute.

Aziza: Could you elaborate to him more Asma?

Samira: [Samira and Asma are in the same class] It is that, we were in our corner as Somali girls, as persons who did not speak English. We could not have spoken to them though. We felt, they felt more that every time we spoke our mother tongue, we were seen as if we were speaking about them.

A female voice: We were insulting them.

Samira: Or we were looking down at them. But, by the way, each in her corner because we were all lost in, ah, in a new school, a new world, a new country, all is new, a new quarter, the snow, all new. We were scared even of ourselves. And we were like, "Oh my God, what are we going to do in this, this school?" In classes, everyone has been in their small corners. If you trace a line, only us, the others, the rest of the class is them. So, we felt rejected, and they were scared of us. (group interview, French)

Clearly, language separated the two sides in ways that made intercultural dialogue hard if not impossible, and created a context where mistrust is possible if not inevitable. In the following extract, Musa (M, 19, Djibouti) sees language as a poignant marker that goes beyond race. According to him, given their knowledge of the English language, Canadian-born Black students would feel more "comfortable" with White students than with Africans whose knowledge of English is limited:

There was always the separation between the Black students and White students. There are Canadian-born Black students who would feel comfortable with Canadians, I mean Whites. They sit with them, they speak, they communicate with them. We, we are born in Africa. We came to Marie-Victorin and we feel comfortable with the people who speak the same language as us. If you go, me I came to Marie-Victorin in 1993, it was my first year. I knew, I knew nothing in English, I knew not [even] one word of English. So, I could not go and sit in an anglophone milieu where everyone speaks English. I had to speak in French or in Somali with my people. So, I sat with him, with him [pointing to another student] to feel comfortable with them. (group interview, French)

Hassan (M, 18), who lived in Somalia, Djibouti, and Ethiopia, has a different and more philosophical take on these demarcated social boundaries. As he sees them, these boundaries are a reflection of the modernist notion of individualism, which is contrary to the previously delineated notion of African individualism. In the latter notion of individualism, the self is always situated within a community: The self is there for and thanks to the community (see also Dei, 2009; Ibrahim, 2005), whereas in the Western modernist liberal discourse, the self is marked before everything. Social cohesion and economic advancement are measured in individual terms—how much social progress and how much money one can make. The underside of this philosophy is that one takes care of oneself first (see Foucault, 1980). Hassan gives the example of the bus, where people could care less if one says hello or not, and definitely would not give up their seats, even, sometimes, to elders. Carelessness, for Hassan, should not be taken as a performance of maliciousness; it is a cultural expression:

> Hassan: This [separation between groups in the school] is not a fault of one group or the other. I am going to tell you one small thing, and it is related to the bus. When you enter and sit on the bus, everyone does what he has to do. Everyone looks at the ads on the wall. Nobody says good morning to another person, you see.
>
> Awad: Yah.
>
> Hassan: Even if you see this person every morning on the bus, what happens is that nobody speaks and asks the other person *"bonjour, comment ça va?"* He has to wait for the other person. The other person does the same thing [laugh]. There is no tension, there is no maliciousness in this, so we find ourselves with the most close [to us], who are the most close to us. This means that they find themselves with the persons who are closer to their culture [...]. So, this is why we find Somalis here, Iranians there, and all that. (individual interview, French)

For Hassan, opening channels of communication will be the best means of breaking down these barriers, which will enable people to intermingle between cultural, linguistic, and social borders (see also Giroux, 1992):

> But me, if you see me in the afternoon, I sit in every chair. There is nobody who tells me, "*Yo*, I don't like you, get out of here!" Everyone, I have this character, it is a character that I cultivate: speak with people, become friends with them. They will accept you. (individual interview, French)

In spite of its simplicity and although it does not adddress the systemic (race, gender, class, and sexual) ways that people are perceived and thus treated, Hassan's philosophy not only won him the presidency of the student council in 1994 to 1995, but also made him the most popular student in the school across races, ages, and genders. Yet it is precisely because of these systemic ways of being that some other students felt the need to create new spaces and markets.

Black Noise and the Creation of New Markets: The Strike

In his autobiography Malcolm X (1965) argued that for Black people to be heard, they have to make loud noises. For McLaren (2005), this is related to the shortsightedness and muted nature of Malcolm X's White interlocutors. It seems that African students heeded Malcolm X's advice, especially when they felt denigrated by teachers in such obvious ways as name-calling. During my research at MV, students told me that a male physical education teacher (Monsieur Duras) was brought to the school from an elementary school. He was the coach of the soccer team even though he did not know much about soccer, which, besides basketball, was the only sport in the school accessible to African students. The other available sports were hockey and volleyball, both of which were played almost exclusively by White students. A few White students were also oin the soccer team, and although they missed some of the pregame training, they were always chosen for the team whenever MV played other schools. This was done in spite of the fact that some of the best African players were kept in reserve:

> Hassan: You see, there were Black and White students. The White students don't know soccer, it isn't a volleyball business, you see. So, Monsieur Duras made the White students play, but not the best players, who were Black. He made the students play, I mean the White students who were absent. Because, how? Absent and you, you play? [If you don't] train, you're no longer on the team. But the African students who did the same were ex-

cluded, but he left White students to play [even when they didn't show up for practice]. (individual interview, French)

Concerning the name-calling, Hassan cited that Monsieur Duras used to call African students not by their names but as "you the Black": "And you the Black, you see. And so pass it to the Black there, without calling the White student the same way" (individual interview, French). In my individual interview with Aziza, she confirmed this name-calling phenomenon. Although the teacher did not use terms like *petit nègre* (Fanon, 1967), Monsieur Duras spoke of their way of playing as *sauvage*: "*Vous jouez d'une façon sauvage*" [you play in a savage way], Aziza recalled (individual interview, French). In both *Orientalism* (1978) and *Culture and Imperialism* (1994), the late Edward Said exposed the history behind this term. It is a term that connotes the mythical, the mystic, the abject, and absolute Otherness: "you the Black," which needs a form of *mission civilisatrice*. Teaching here takes on a missionary role of civilizing those who so desperately need to be civilized.

The African students decided they would not have Monsieur Duras as their coach, and out of desperation they wrote to the principal citing the verbal abuse they had received from him as their reason. The principal did not take any action. One day, I was told, the African students on the soccer team announced that the next day they were going to boycott classes, and they then sought the support of other students. They distributed flyers to every student, and particularly White students. As Aziza remembers it, "They even gave flyers to White students. The White students didn't want anything to do with it [*ils veulent rien savoir*]. In the morning, they went to their classes, you see. So, in other words they don't care" (individual interview, French). For the record, there was one White female student who supported this cause; she boycotted classes as well.

Though "the strike" (*la grève*) was about African boys, the African girls were emphatic not only in organizing the strike, but also in seeking the support of *all* Black students. Thus the strike became an issue for all the Black students, whether Haitian, Canadian-born, or African:

Aziza: Because the boys were few, all the Black girls there left the school. They didn't go to their classes. And those who were in their classes, we went looking for them. Because we wanted to show them that this problem is a serious problem, a grave problem, and if you don't do anything about it, we will leave the school, we will go to court. We will go and tell your shame to the newspaper and we will air your shameful behavior on TV, things like that, you see. So, that day there were journalists who came, they interviewed us and we told them everything. They took notes and then we told them all the shames of the French-Language Board of Education. (individual interview, French)

As a result of the strike, Aziza explained, "all worked well, you see. The teachers became more friendly, they heard us more, you see, and Monsieur Armond arrived, a new principal" (individual interview, French.) The French-Language Board of Education brought in a new principal, Monsieur Armond, a French White male who had lived in Africa for a long period of time and who situated his administrative policy within an antiracism praxis. For the African students, Monsieur Armond, like Vice Principal Brian at Maxwell High or Ali at Sunnyside, represents a fine human connection with the school that was missing before. If there are no Black teachers, there is at least someone who understands African students and their particular experience of displacement. "For me," Mukhi explains, "Monsieur Armond, how do I say it, he has direct experiences with Africans." He was liked by African students precisely because of what he said and what he did:

Aziza: All of a sudden [after the strike], a new, a super principal arrived, he gave us things, ideas. He told us, "Why don't you start celebrating the month Black History Month?" It was him who gave us the idea. A number of African students came into the school after his arrival, because they were told this school is superb, the principal is superb. And you know what happened, he left, he was fired [after a year of being in the school], and after he left the school, I started to hate the school again, because all which was there had fallen apart. (individual interview, French)

For me, the strike is a significant turning point in the process of becoming Black for three reasons. First, this incident makes explicit the language of Black and White, which itself is indicative of a level of maturity of identity formation, namely in becoming Black. That is to say, the strike is a demonstrative moment of the African students becoming wide awake not only in terms of their own bodies and how they are perceived and treated, but also in their agentive response—their ability to "fight the power," as one female student put it. Second, its significance stems from the fact that the strike joins a long history of protest by Black peoples in the diaspora, from movements for civil rights to voting rights to equal access to education and resources. It is also significant, thirdly and extremely importantly, because it shifted the dominant centers, spaces, and markets in the school. It is no longer volleyball that occupies the center of the gymnasium, both literally and metaphorically, but basketball. I contend that, although it does not reflect the actualized power relation (Deleueze & Guattari, 1987), the metaphor of moving volleyball to the margin of the gymnasium is indeed a reflection, at least momentarily, of the decentering of power (of Whiteness?).

In other words, the centering of basketball in the gymnasium should not obscure the power relation: It is White teachers, administrators, personnel, and students who hold power within and outside school structures. This is true in all three sites of this research, but most pronounced at MV. Nevertheless, from that point, basketball became the most popular sport in the school. For me, this shift to "Black" sports indicates that the markets and spaces where African students participate in the school culture were relocated from White-dominated markets and spaces to Black-dominated markets and spaces. Put otherwise, instead of participating in the same pre-existing markets and structures of the school, African students created their own, which may include basketball, soccer, and Hip-Hop.

Conclusion: Gimme the Low Down[5]

In this chapter I laid out some of the narratives that express the striated racialized experiences of African students, which is done with the implicit understanding that these racialized experiences of becoming Black are significant because they shed light on the students' sense of identity, and thus raise the essential question of where they see themselves reflected and with whom they identify. Students have different understandings of what constitutes racism: (1) as a positionality, offered by the dominant hegemonic discourses and groups, that restricts one's choices; (2) as undemocratic decisions taken by the school that impact students' everyday lives; and (3) as an *accumulative memory* of minute details that, when put together, tend to leave students with clear messages that they are not trusted or wanted, and thus are subjects without subjectivities. It should not be surprising, therefore, that African youths would look for alternative identities and representations, particularly in Black popular cultural forms, as we shall see. Language, streaming, and *le contrat* were subtle but evident means by which racialization is experienced by African students. I cited some blunt forms of racism experienced by Black students as well as by the only Black teacher at MV. However, students were not silent in their rage and concerns. The strike was a case in point. Besides being a breaking point in their process of becoming Black, for African students the strike was also a moment of disruption and decentering of the school's dominant, legitimizing, and authorized capitals, spaces, and markets. Finally, we know that memory cheats us all the time; nothing is remembered as it happened. To avoid this pitfall, I am making sure that no single narrative is presented alone. I am interested in patterns, the *accumulative memory*: that which is narrated time and again by different people. The triangulation and cross-referencing here is significant. When that is done, in this and other chapters, one has a clear picture of the processes of becoming Black.

Notes

1 Mukhi (M, 18, Djibouti) contended, "I swear in the name of Allah, they are all racist" (group interview, French). Throughout the book, each research participant is identified by age, gender (F=Female, M=Male), and country of origin; and for each extract I identify the type of interview (individual or group) and the language in which it was conducted. See Appendix I for transcription conventions and Appendix II for biographical details of research participants.

2 The principal at that time was an Africanist White man from France. He had a Ph.D. and he had lived in Africa, where he had taught for many years in different parts of the continent. He did not hide his admiration for Africa and Africans, and had a solid antiracism discourse and praxis and was exceptionally well liked by students, particularly African students. Interestingly, he was so disliked by the staff and teachers as a result of warmth towards African students that he was fired and replaced by a very timid, extremely shy White woman. She hardly ever left her office. I should note, I have no knowledge of the actual legal bases for his dismissal.

3 Throughout, I use "Black students" interchangeably with "African students," "continental African students," and "Africans," because the population I was working with referred to themselves as both "Africans" and "Blacks." In Marie-Victorin, in particular, except for a few, all the Black students were African. Hence, in all three research sites, unless otherwise indicated, Black students are African students. This is the reason why Aziza used "Black students" interchangeably with "Africans."

4 This activity conjured up in my mind the abject horror of the slave trade, except disguised in gendered and sexual performances.

5 "When one says, 'Gimme the low down,'" Kuoch (2013) explains, "one is essentially requesting the most essential details of a particular situations or asking someone to sum up something that is relatively complex or lengthy. This expression is also used when one wants to 'get up to speed' with what has already transpired" (p. 37).

CHAPTER THREE

"*Si tu allais faire un sondage, ça vient souvent de l'orientation ou des personnels*"[1]

Teachers, Curriculum, and Pedagogy

In my MV field notes diary, I wrote:

> I still remember, on my first day at the school, while standing in the middle of the foyer, the fifteen-year-old girl Najat came running to embrace me in a manner of a lost old friend. She then wondered in French if I was coming to school to teach. "Non," I said in French, but I was also curious why she wanted me at the school. "Just because there is nothing Black in this school. All you see is white, white, white," she responded in English.

The absence of Black teachers, and the absence of Black/African peoples[2] from the history books, are two of the themes I discuss in this chapter. The narrative of African students concerning the culture of schooling is introduced to argue for what Ogbu (1990) might have called a *comparative system*. In this system, immigrants and, I add, all displaced subjects compare their schooling experiences in their new homes with what they knew and experienced in their homelands. I am using "displaced subjects" to refer to the ensemble of individuals, such as immigrants, exiles, and refugees, who are relocated or relocate themselves to a new geocultural place. Certainly, they have accumulative memories of the schools and the learning cultures in their homelands. It is upon these memories that they base their judgments of the school cultures in the new contexts. Again focusing primarily on MV, I show in this chapter that African students' racial experiences, discussed in chapter 2, continue when they encounter school counselors and teachers; indeed, this chapter should be read as a continuation of chapter 2 and thus as a further delineation of the (striated) processes of becoming Black, particularly at MV. I conclude the chapter on a hopeful note. In reference to Maxwell High and Sunnyside, I show that there is a (smooth) process of becoming Black, which is less antagonistic and confrontational and more hospitable. Again, this is not meant to compare the schools, but to offer a different configuration to/on the *rhizomatic process of becoming Black*.

Articulating a Comparative System: The Teacher-Students Relationship

As part of their translation of the new Canadian context, when African students first encountered the culture of schooling at Marie-Victorin, they were culturally dismayed by what they saw as "undisciplined" ways of interacting between teacher and students. Some went so far as thinking that students had more power than teachers, which is a costly and false misconception. This reading is done by comparing the school systems they were accustomed to in their homelands, where teachers are never called by their first names, always addressed as *vous*, *Madame*, or *Monsieur*, and respected for what they know, and their relationship with their students is sharply formal and disciplined. In my focus group interview with the girls, Amani (F, 17, Somalia), using her ethnographic gaze, noted that:

> I was there [in the classroom] observing. [...] So, in classes, it was the way that, I observed the relationship between teachers and students. I was surprised, especially when they say the word *tu*. I was like, that is the discipline, which was completely lacking here. And then for you, a person who really had a strong discipline in **the school where we were before**, you find this as a shock, wouldn't you? (group interview, French, emphasis added)

In Canada, the notion of discipline is signified differently than in African students' homelands. Being friendly does not mean giving up power, a not-so-recognizable notion that caused African students more harm than good. Yet, as Aziza (F, 18, Somalia) notes, giving students more than one chance to redo a course or a year is an invitation to "laziness"—*paresse*:

> The first days when I arrived in the school, those were difficult days because we, first of all, teachers were not similar because I got used to teachers in my country who were teachers, very tough, a strict system, you can't say *tu* (*tutoyer*) to a teacher. In other words, the teacher is superior in relation to the students. Here, it is the opposite, it is the student who is superior in relation to the teacher, which means that the student can do anything he wants onto the teacher. You see, there is no respect, you see. Whereas for us it was like that [respect, formality, and discipline]. Here, it is completely the opposite. There is no respect, there is no discipline. You see, here you are given a lot of chances. If you fail, if you fail a course, you restart. You fail, you restart it, whereas there [in my country] you fail it once, you are screwed. You see what I mean? Whereas here, you are given a number of chances, you are given chance chance chance. You will become lazy, it is laziness. I think it's good to give them one or two chances, but more than that, I think it's too much, you see. (individual group, French)

To offset what seems like a naïve understanding of an extremely complex cultural phenomenon, one must note that African students' reading of the more open and interactive relationship between teachers and students as a lack of discipline stems from what they see as a false liberatory practice in which teachers seem to be equalized with, and equalizing themselves to, students. Yet, we know that the power of grading and streaming is in the teachers' hands. It is precisely the perceived inauthentic relationship between students and teachers—where each is "playing a role" and playing the system to get what they want—that makes African students cynical. For them, this inauthentic relationship is performed at several levels: personnel, counseling, curriculum, and their relationships with White teachers.

Who Is Teaching What, and From Whose Perspective?

African students are unapologetic in their observations about the absence of Black teachers. This absence, they argue, is morally discouraging, and expresses the lack of desire for pedagogical and curriculum changes on the part of the school system. In their narratives, they speak of the lack of "role models" and their need for academic help, which they rarely receive from White teachers. The politics of identification—where one empathizes with the implicit cultural nuances of what people go through—is crucial here. For African students, this was not readily available with White teachers and personnel. This is not to suggest that all teachers were unempathetic, but African students were searching for *safe spaces* and individuals (such as Brian and David in Maxwell High and Ali in Sunnyside) with whom they can share their anger and their problems, and to whom they can complain when they face racism or other social problems. In my focus group interview, the boys were quite emphatic:

> Mukhi: It is really like somewhat morally discouraging whenever I see a White teacher who doesn't even understand you, and who wants to judge you, who is going to give your grades, and who doesn't even know you. It is really discouraging, they have a new physical education teacher, they can't even find a Black teacher who teaches us, ah, sports. It is somewhat discouraging.
>
> A male voice: I was going to say that there has to be a teacher there to defend the cause of, our causes. Like me [who is kicked out of school] because of *le contrat* business, there is nobody who defends us. (group interview, French)

Students also expressed the need for role models because, they explained, in a school where two-thirds of its population are students of color, it is unacceptable to not have at least one teacher of color. In my focus group interview with the girls, they were similarly compelling in describing the abject condition of having no role model:

Aziza: The student needs a role model. When you see a teacher of color, he is going to say "Oh, yes, there is a teacher of color," you see. He, he [the student] does more to liberate himself and say to himself "Me, I am going to do all that is possible to really be like this professor [...]." But if the student doesn't see any teacher of color, if all of his teachers are Whites, the majority are Whites, he feels somewhat pushed out. (group interview, French)

In contrast, students spoke highly of their experiences with Black teachers. This included Aristide, who used to be at the school and was liked even by students who did not have him as a teacher. "He was cool. I didn't have him for a class, but he was cool," Najat (F, 15, Djibouti) contended in English. Omer (M, 19, Ethiopia) had sentiments similar to Najat's, and appreciated that Monsieur Aristide stayed after school; he was the only teacher to do so. Omer compared Aristide to a White teacher who came to Marie-Victorin from James High School[3] to teach what Aristide was capable of teaching, science:

Omer: There is this [White] teacher, but he stays to the second period, then he leaves.

Awad: He only teaches two periods?

Omer: And then he goes to James.

Awad: Ah he comes from James, oh it is, I don't know, he teaches history?

Omer: Science. Because really, you know, Aristide, he wanted to always stay after school sometimes. Helping students, oh, he wanted to stay. Now, there is nobody who you can ask [for help]. (individual interview, French)

On a similar note, Sam (M, 19, Djibouti) "couldn't believe" that there are teachers with whom one can have a human as well as an academic rapport, connection, and relationship. He took a course at Marie-Victorin one summer with a Black teacher who taught in James High School, and upon remembering how he related to teachers of color, he contended (in English) that "they [teachers of color], they know where we from, they know our values, they know our morals and they know our background. So, we can relate to them, you know" (individual interview, English). Sam continued to talk about his experience with one of these teachers:

'Cause I had one teacher from James, that was a summer school, I couldn't believe they had this kind of teacher out there. 'Cause he was a nice teacher and everything, you know! He knew what the deal was, he knows the problems that we have, he knows what we go through every day. (individual interview, English)

As demonstrated by these narrated memories and experiences, White teachers are not expected to be in alliance with Black students, to do favors for them, spend time with them, or provide academic help. The example cited in chapter 2 of the undemocratic decision taken by the MV school administration and teachers whereby African students were no longer permitted to do midday Muslim prayer is a case in point. But the decision and how it was understood should not be read separately; instead, both should be conceived together as part of African students' accumulative memory of how they were treated before and after this incident:

Aziza: They met, the personnel of the school, they met. They agreed, like we were nothing at all. They said, "Oh, who cares!" you see. We have to just tell them not to leave the class, because our class is more important than their praying. [...] So, there wasn't, I am sure there wasn't even one teacher who was opposed to that. They all agreed. (group interview, French)

Whether there was opposition to the decision among the staff is irrelevant here. The importance of this incident lies in how it is read. Students have accumulated enough memories and experiences that prompt them to read the incident not in isolation, but in cynical terms, as part of a larger tableau that is getting clearer and clearer. Framed as a racialized and panethnic experience, the incident creates despair in the students, which does harm to their academic futures. The incident exposes the lack of role models and the need for safe zones, by which I mean individuals as well as actual geographical spaces where students have a sense of comfort, of not being surveyed. To whom would African students talk in case of a problem? That was a question that did not have an answer in MV. They had Brian (vice principal) and Dave (teacher assistant) at Maxwell High, and Ali (multicultural liaison) at Sunnyside.

If Canada is to be truly multicultural, students argue, actions and action-oriented policies are what is needed, not rhetoric and tokenism. Multiculturalism has to critically approach the question of representation and power more seriously. It has to address the racial, gender, class, and sexual differences among the personnel and teachers of the school. In addressing the absence of Black teachers and other multicultural representation both at the school and in the larger Canadian society, I had this conversation with Omer (M, 19, Ethiopia):

Omer: It is not, it is not only the fact that there is not even one Black teacher in Marie-Victorin, there are not enough Black teachers in the Ontarian and Canadian schools. That frustrates me in Marie-Victorin, that frustrates me, there are no Black teachers in Canadian schools. It is like, on the one hand, they talk about multiculturalism, but there is no multiculturalism.

Awad: Ah no?

Omer: There is no multiculturalism.

Awad: How is that?

Omer: To be multicultural, it has to be multicultural at all levels. In the ministry, deputies, it has to be integral, you see. Look, if you walk around in places like Toronto, for example, you see one Canadian out of five, who are they? They are the refugees, the immigrants [...]; you go in factories, you see a lot of immigrants. You go to school, you see a lot of ethnic groups, you see. At work you see a lot of immigrants. And you look on top you see only Whites, always the head is a White man [*un blanc*]. Vice president, you see a vice president, an assistant, I don't know, but you never see, very very very rarely you see a head, a head of a department or a male director [*directeur*] or a female director [*directrice*] who is immigrant, you see. It is very rare. Wherever you go, always the head is a White man. Look at the government, look everywhere [it is always the same]. This bloody idiot came to Marie-Victorin one day but he said, "I am an immigrant." I know that, but your race!

Awad: Who who?

Omer: Colenette, David Colenette [the former Minister of Foreign Affairs for the Liberal federal government]. Because they are selling themselves, "I am an immigrant." He is an immigrant, but your race, what is your skin. So, don't tell me. (individual interview, French)

Omer offers a complex and brilliant intersectional analysis, where the discourse of being an immigrant is espoused alongside an intersection of racial, gender, class, and sexual social difference. The expression "bloody idiot" should not be taken as an offensive term here; it is simply an expression of rage. For Omer, the essential question is: How can Colenette declare his immigrant status, yet be blind to the omnipresence of privilege thanks to race and other social differences? In pronouncing "So, don't tell me," Omer is saying, "I know you are an immigrant, and so are all Canadians except for our First Nations, but you are also White. And, by virtue of being White, you are in a position of power without needing to pronounce a word" (see also McIntosh, 1998In short, Omer is calling for what McLaren and Farahmandpur (2005) call "radical, revolutionary multiculturalism," where power relations, performed through gendered, sexualized, and racial identities, have to be critically centralized, represented, and critiqued. Significantly, this entails a mass representation of these identities in the school structure, including teachers and counselors.

Teachers, Counselors, and the Trauma of Being Spoken To

It is worth remembering that, at the time of this research at MV, Aristide was painfully finishing his year, and the Africanist principal, Monsieur Armond, was replaced by Madame Robert, a timid White female principal who was extremely nonresponsive and, in the words of one student, "always hiding in her office." African students were traumatized by how they were talked to patronizingly and treated badly. When one's back is against the wall, one does not have much to lose, so it is not surprising that they took action with the strike. In response to the strike, the school board decided to bring in a Black counselor for a year-long contract, but no one counselor could change the negative memory that the students had accumulated. Their relationship with Madame Robert contrasted sharply with that with Monsieur Armond—a progressive, Africanist[4] principal who was discharged by the school board because White teachers could stomach neither his character nor his progressive and antiracist praxis,[5] which most of the time sided with the students and not the teachers. As noted earlier, I have no knowledge of the actual legal bases of his dismissal, but it became clear to the student that the teachers, along with the school board, pushed Monsieur Armond out.

> Mukhi: For me, Monsieur Armond, how do I say it? He has direct experiences with Africans. He lived in Burkina Faso [as well as Chad, Senegal, and Sudan]. So, he has, he has knowledge, he knows how we are, how we react, how we live. And then how we are here. But, she [Madame Robert] doesn't know anything. She comes from an elementary school, she treats us like kids. You know, the way she talks to us, she talks like a baby *man* [laugh]. (group interview, French)

This example shows that, first, students urgently need safer zones to succeed as human and intellectual beings, and second, that these zones can be created by progressive White teachers, school boards, and principals. Yet, because these zones do not exist in the school, especially after the dismissal of Monsieur Armond, African students always-already have the feeling of being personally attacked by the school authority and of having no academic or social support. With MonsieurArmond, African students realized that their schooling experience could be more hospitable, welcoming, productive, and humane, and extremely successful. After his dismissal, unsurprisingly, they called their teachers "hypocrites" and "disgusting." They teach subjects they are not even qualified to teach, according to the students. In my interview with Aristide, he contended that although there were teachers of color qualified to teach particular subjects, they were passed over in favor of unqualified White teachers. The following conversation is from my focus group interview with the girls:

Asma: It is disgusting, they are disgusting. I can count the teachers I like, I can count on one hand, my five fingers. I assure you. Now, the teachers here are hypocrites, they hate me. One woman [another voice interrupts: who judges us], I can't say her name. I hate, I hate her like you would not believe. She is going to listen to that ah?

Awad: No, no nobody is going to listen.

Asma: Hélène [the same Hélène that Aristide talked about when discussing his incident at the library], Hélène [laughs]. Excuse me [laughs]. No, really I swear. She is really a hypocrite like you would not believe. The way she speaks to me, I am sorry, the way she speaks to me it's like I am stupid, mentally challenged, who understands nothing.

Ossi: Ah, she has favorites. In fact, like how can she have favorites in class? All the students [inaudible]. No, it is no good.

Asma: [inaudible] discriminations, she has favorites, she discriminates. […]

Amani: How are you going to judge this when you have some teachers, especially there are a lot of teachers who should not even occupy the position they are occupying? There are many teachers who had never taught a course. Do you know what they do? They going to pass him a dossier, and tell him, "Just study this in the summer and then next year you gonna teach the other kids." What happened after? Who pays the price?

Ossi: A music teacher.

Amani: He now teaches computer; ouhahah. Frankly, do you know who pays the price? Who is going to pay the price? This teacher gets paid. (group interview, French)

Without dissembling, who pays the price? The answer must be the students. At the time of this research, students were being pushed out of MV in record numbers: "We had 400 or 500 students, now we aren't even 300," Samira (F, 16, Djibouti) observed. "Who pays the price?" is a candid question that implicates not only the principal and teachers but also the French-Language Board of Education. Amani (F, 17, Somalia) contended:

> If the top [i.e., the school board] is malfunctioning, do not expect the bottom of the pyramid to hold and really be strong. In the end, it can hold but it is really disgusting. Here, when the system is malfunctioning, you know what is happening in the French Board? They didn't want to pay a lot of teachers, first they don't look for teachers who are from different races. OK, so, that does not interest them; put race to the side! (group interview, French)

However, it is not all trauma when it comes to interaction between White teachers and Black students. Some White teachers understood empowering pedagogical tools that took into account students' desires, interests, and histories. This was the case with one geography teacher, Monsieur Laurence. After the Africanist principal Monsieur Armond, who is eulogized by a number of students, Monsieur Laurence is the next best thing; he is described as "cool" and "wicked." (In Black English, "wicked" and "bad" are used to commend something or someone who is exceptionally good.) In describing how "boring" and disengaging her classes were, so much so that she slept in one of them, Najat (F, 15, Djibouti) contrasted her geography teacher and his class with other teachers and their classes:

> Najat: I don't, ahm, the school sucks, boring; and every day, I'm like damn [and] I fell asleep in a class. It was so boring.
>
> Awad: You did?
>
> Najat: Yes, everybody is like sleeping in the class because we got so bored, except my geography class [with Monsieur Laurence].
>
> Awad: You actually slept in class?
>
> Najat: No, I didn't sleep in my geography, I'm like so happy, you know. "Hi Mr." He is so happy you know, it's like a friend, "Hi Monsieur." And then he is like, ahm Christmas before [inaudible], I was like saying, "Monsieur, I hope you can buy your wife a [gift?]." "Where?" "At Eaton's." And then he goes "OK, I'm gonna do that" [laughs]. He is so cool, he is so wicked. (individual interview, English)

In a different context, Aziza (F, 18, Somalia) has similar sentiments about Monsieur Laurence. She compared him to other White teachers:

> But I am telling you, all the teachers in this school, they are all racists, except Monsieur Laurence, who is a geography teacher. He is very friendly. It is the first teacher I always liked. I had him for geography, physical geography, especially geography;

and then he is super good, he is very friendly with every student, no matter who the student is—white, red, yellow. He is super good. (individual interview, French)

George Dei et al. (1997) show that teachers' expectations play a central role in students' successes. This is also true at MV. Unfortunately, as Amani noted, "If the top is malfunctioning, do not expect the bottom of the pyramid to hold and really be strong." The top is the school board, and it is interested in rearticulating and reproducing the "French language and culture"—here, clearly at the expense of students (Heller, 2011; Ibrahim, 2011). In so doing, it is reproducing a problematic status quo, where teachers and counselors are two of the major "technologies of control" (Foucault, 1977). In the case of African students, teachers were discouraging, disengaged, and had low expectations, and played with the students' insecurities. Listen to what these students have to say:

Asma: Yes, the teachers discourage us.

Amani: If somebody, if somebody [the teacher in this case] tells you, "Are you sure you didn't make the wrong choice [by taking an advanced-level course]?"

Asma: That's exactly what they say.

Amani: "Are you sure you're in the right place? Maybe you should go, maybe you should go and check with the orientation."

Asma: OK, *I remember in my country*, if you wanted to do something, the teachers encourage you. They say to you, "Do that! You can do it." My mother wasn't good in math, her teacher encouraged her to do it. Now she is really good. Me, I am not good in math. The teachers [in this school], whoever they are, if you have a test of 50 percent, let's say, he is going to say, "There are some individuals in this class who did not do well. Go, let's go [i.e., leave the class to take a general-level class] instead of making an idiot of yourself." You see? You have 50 percent, make an effort, you have to do your math. You have to do that, don't go back to general level. But, instead of saying that, to really encourage you to go to advanced level, he tells you, "You know, there is a better [and easier?] course than this."

Amani: They generalize, discourage.

Asma: General.

Aziza: "For people like you!"

Asma: Yes, exactly. Wait please, there is something I want to tell you. We enter in class, we have the course syllabus, it is the first day of the school.

	They're going to tell you what we are going to do. We're going to do these tasks, tatata. They are going to tell you the plan of the class and what we are going to do, during the semester.
Awad:	Yah.
Asma:	"The persons who cannot be in this class, go to general!" I have even, I haven't even, I have no homework, I don't know how the teacher is like, I didn't have any test, I don't know if I am good. They are going to really intimidate you that you are going to say, "He is right? This teacher is right. May be I am not comfortable, that I am not too good because I am not Canadian. I am not like them, it is possible that I [should] go to general level, I am going to." Our French class of the second year, there were a lot of students, we were almost thirty, now there are only twenty. (group interview, French)

At its height, the state of doubt is unpleasantly deployed by teachers to tell students, through exceedingly complex language, that they are capable of nothing but general-level courses. The teachers seem to believe that being Canadian, which is defined in a narrow way, plays a role in the students' academic abilities. Clearly, the above excerpt is a testimony to the power of teacher expectations, which can be either positive or negative. Another factor that influences students' senses of self and their abilities to perform is *l'orientation,* or counseling. African students reported that counselors pushed them to take general-level courses time and again, and in some cases made decisions on their behalf by placing them in courses they had not chosen. Moreover, counselors did not provide the right information, were hasty in making decisions, and too old generationally to know and define, let alone identify with, African students' needs. Finally, counselors discourage Black students in general from going to universities by arguing that they are too expensive for them to afford. In short, in spite of its importance in their lives, counseling was another unsafe space in the school for African students.

Amani:	I assure you we have to also take note of, even when you go to orientation, when you are busy making your course choice, you are called so frequently, OK, especially the general-level students. They are called, and then instead of seeing what the problem or the difficulty is, they are so set in their minds that they make [snaps her fingers] decisions very quickly. And then we wonder why the foreign-born students find themselves in the general level. You know, we wonder why. It could be for a number of reasons. I don't say there is no laziness on the part of students, it can be because students are lazy and do not work hard, eh? But, but the percentage of these students there really [unbelievably] high. If you conduct a poll, it

[the source of most of Black students' problems] will be either within counseling or the personnel. (individual interview, French)

In the end, being *spoken to* is not just a linguistic act but a mindset, where the speaker transforms his/her institutional power (e.g., as a counselor or teacher at MV) into technologies of control, thus leaving the interlocutors (African students, in this case) disgusted, dismayed, disoriented, paralyzed, and betrayed. They have nowhere to go and no one to talk to in confidence. For all of us, this is or should be an unacceptable situation in a system that is built on meritocracy and equal opportunity. "If you conduct a poll," Amani concludes, "it [the source of most of Black students' problems] will be either within counseling or the personnel"—that is a damning statement. At MV, as we see next, it does not stop there.

Colonized Curriculum, Language, and Representational History

The prominent curriculum theorist William Pinar (2004) sees curriculum, or *currere*, as a landscape, an interdisciplinary approach to the conceptualization of educational experience, an experience that involves culture, schooling process, pedagogy, language, and identity. Curriculum, for Pinar, should meditatively imagine the future; it "promises no quick fixes" (2004, p. 4), focuses on critical self-understanding, and sees a direct link between school life, including what is taught inside the classroom, and the larger society. Unfortunately, what African students encountered at MV is what Pinar (2004) calls a "nightmare," where the school is turned into a skill-and-knowledge factory and teachers into colonizers who hardly question what they teach or how they teach it.

Besides having limited course choices and no night classes, African students complained about the curriculum being too Eurocentric. It focuses, they argue, almost exclusively on Canada, the United States, and, "don't forget," as one female student reminded me, "the European countries." In doing so, the school curriculum functions to exclude the Other: the so-called Third World, people of color, and First Nations. Sam (M, 19, Djibouti) is vehement: "In the books, they don't even teach you about Black people, that's one thing. They teach you about White people, and they teach you about what White people used to do and what Whites, you know, do, did before, you know" (group interview, English). In my focus group interview, the girls eloquently summarize this exclusion of the Other this way:

Aziza: You know the students, especially Whites, are not educated to learn what is Africa, how many countries are there in Africa, how do Africans live; even other countries in Asia. We hear all the time....

Asma: Canada, Canada, Canada.

Aziza: Exactly, Canada, don't forget the European countries also. This is what they know.

Asma: Listen, when I came to Canada, we learned the history of Canada: grades 7, 8, 9, 10. I continue, Canada, Canada.

Aziza: It's true.

Asma: I assure you. I wanted to have the history of Africa, but they say there aren't enough students who want [a course on Africa]. I am sorry, but there were hundreds of students of our school who want to learn the history of Africa. But they don't even offer it in this case.

Samira: The history of the world is in, in Canada and the United States. We have enough of that, the United States and Canada.

Ossi: No, it is good to know your country.

Aziza: It is good, I don't, it is really good. It is really good to know, but to a certain point. The only countries they know more about are the European countries. After that they don't know any other countries. They don't think there are other existing countries. Like us when we told them that we came from Somalia, the first days…[interrupted]

Ossi: Nobody knew, nobody.

Aziza: Nobody knew what is Somalia or, except…[interrupted]

Ossi: The war, the poverty, starvation. (group interview, French)

This excerpt attests to two phenomena of great significance. The first has to do with the observation that at Marie-Victorin, the history classes seem to repeat the same content grade after grade; this repetition centralizes a Eurocentric version of history. Second, with this neglect, history can only serve nationalist, racist, and colonialist agenda. Timothy Stanley (2011) reached the same conclusion in his documentation of the Chinese history in British Columbia (BC). Despite their long presence here, Chinese are made absent from the BC history books. When students know only European histories and European countries, both Stanley and the students in my study contend, this in itself is a statement about the Other. Pushing the Other off the curriculum indicates, always implicitly, the Other's insignificance. In fact, the Other is so insignificant, the implicit argument goes, that its history, identity, culture, geography, and memory are not worthy of study. This hidden curriculum usually results in colonizing the imaginary of both the learner (especially if he or she is from the majoritarian group) and the Other. As a result, the only other imaginary available to the learner is the mediatic and narrow representation, especially of Africa, where the Other can only be conjured in the metaphor of the four horsemen of apocalypse: plague, famine, war, and death. This notion is discussed further in the next chapter.

It is worth remembering that it is not only African/Black peoples who are excluded from popular memory, representation, and curriculum discussion; First Nations also live the horror and the consequence of absence, exclusion, and misrepresentation. African students were cognizant of this history of misrepresentation. Their acquaintance with First Nations histories stems in part from their own marginal position. and also from critically deconstructing the racist and colonialist representations found in Western popular culture, especially the "cowboy movies" that students used to watch in their homelands. In these popular culture representations, "savageness" is a nominal signifier equated to First Nations. For African students, the uncritical approach to the study of First Nations, not to say their exclusion, meant a centering of the self—French and English—as the founding nations of Canada. That is to say, the French and English became the founding nations of Canada by excluding First Nations.

> Reaching again into the Guinea portfolio, I pulled out a piece of paper with flowery handwriting: "Copied from *On Poetry: A Rhapsody*, by Jonathan Swift, 1733." And then I found the lines:
> *So geographers, in Afric-maps,*
> *With savage–pictures fill their gaps;*
> *An o'er unhabitable downs*
> *Place elephants for want of towns.*
> (Hill, 2007, p. 368)

Amani: What does the history of Canada mean? It is like either anglophone or francophone, and that's what you basically learn in the history class. How am I to know the Canadian history if I am not learning Native history? This is the Natives' land, the land they burned, the land they stole.

Asma: You know, before when I was a kid, I used to watch western movies. And I saw the Apache and the cowboys, and I am like, "Go cowboys, go cowboys!" I didn't know what these people are all about. Then I grew up and I am saying, "*Fucking cowboys* [laugh], *I hate you*." 'Cause I know the real facts now. I know they were fighting for their lands. You know why they are called savage? Because they…[interrupted]

Samira: They're different, they're different, they're different.

Amani: Exactly, if you like them, if you like the way they are, then you not savage anymore and not at all. (group interview, English)

Amani's remembrance speaks to the issue of representation and to the way in which representation creates, not simply reflects, reality (see Hall,

1997). It raises the following questions: Who has the power to represent? What do these representations look like? And who benefits from them? Significantly, what is represented—no matter what reality is, given its authority, perpetuation, and repetition—eventually ends up constructing reality. The savageness of the First Nations and Africans, on the one hand, and the "violent nature" of Blackness in North America, on the other, are all mediatic representations (hooks, 1992). They lock the everyday reality of minoritarian, colonized, and dehumanized groups of people into repeatable, recognizable, and stylized representations. So, when a member from these groups is met, what is invoked in the mind is not the individual person, but the (re)stored representations of how and who this person "should be." He or she is already known. To decolonize these representations, therefore, I introduce in the concluding chapter of this book what I call *pedagogy of the imaginary*.

For their part, the girls started to introduce in their classes a form of this critical pedagogy that challenged these colonized and colonizing representations. In doing so, however, they were seen as fanning the flames, not so much by fellow classmates, but by their teachers. One particular female teacher utterly denied the history of suffering that the First Nations had to endure, and continue to endure, when they first encountered Europeans. The students who raised First Nations' issues in this particular (law) class were called "romantics" who "read too many novels" from First Nations' perspectives. For me, this points to the validity of the question I started with: Who teaches what, how, and from whose perspective?

Samira: In the law class, Ossi and Aziza were doing…[interrupted]

A female voice: A composition.

Samira: The Native, the law, and all that. And we were speaking, we were speaking [on issues that bring painful memories and touch some nerves], and everyone was telling [us] it is their fault [i.e., First Nations'] and all that [girls talking in Somali]. In reality, it is not their fault. They were rejected by the society [girls continue talking in Somali]. The female teacher told us, "You read too many novels, books of love concerning, on Natives." "No, Madame it is the reality, it is the fact." No, no, we were completely, as students, we were shocked. She said that, "You are dreamers, you know. The Natives completely brainwash you; really they did." "No, Madame, these are the facts that Natives were rejected by the society." Even I know that.

Asma: You know, truth hurts, that's what they say. The TRUTH [high pitch] hurts, it gets right to the skin. (group interview, English)

Becoming wide awake, it seems, is arduous and requires intellectual labor; these girls needed to make mental connections between disparate facts and histories and draw from their experiential knowledge with colonialism and exclusion to challenge the teacher. In doing so, they become conscious of the similarities and differences between African colonialism and First Nations genocide and their lasting effects in terms of culture, geography, language, and identity.

The Need for Change: Curriculum and Language

When denied, truth does hurt. Its denial is reflected in many shapes, forms and places, and two of these places are language and curriculum. To state the obvious, curriculum is represented, conceived, and taught through language, and to know and possess the language of the curriculum is to enter the domain of power (Foucault, 1980). French-language schools in Ontario, Heller (2011) argues, use the English language as a supportive medium of instruction that can be referred to and used whenever necessary in the classroom. Outside the classroom, in the corridors and hallways of Marie-Victorin, for example, it is indeed more English than French that is spoken by students. So, when continental African students first arrived to Marie-Victorin, they realized their limited knowledge—in most cases, their zero knowledge—of the English language. This worked against them as the teachers continued to use their bilingual English/French repertoire to teach and talk about academic subjects. Introducing English to newly arrived students from *la francophonie internationale* is an erroneous pedagogical assumption according to African students. In their first days in the school, these students were supposed to decipher not only the Franco-Ontarians linguistic repertoire and the English language, but also the language of schooling:

Amani: You know what is really bothersome? Ahh when you don't know either English or how the system works. In class, in grades 8 and 9, they are going to show you videos.

Asma: Yes, documentaries.

Amani: Which are documentaries in English. Well, then, you are asked questions. How am I supposed to understand this? Then they are going to judge you on that. There wasn't really any consideration to our situation. There are immigrants here, in this school, in this country, OK. And the 1990s, it is in the beginning of the 1990s when minority students from other places came especially to French-language system and schools; never did they try to introduce new programs to help these students or welcome them. (group interview, French)

At stake in Amani's last sentence is the notion that newly arrived students are not welcome in French-language schools. Her point is that if teachers continue their business as usual of using English, the burden of translating and deciphering too many languages all at once can be extremely daunting, discouraging, and tiresome for students. In their narratives, African students often referred to the need for moral, academic, and social supports in their process of integration.

> Amani: You know, it is easy, it is easy for a person to immigrate to another country, but he has to be supported. This person has to be supported in order not to get lost in the system. Because I had to pose a question to the teacher in the early days about the use of English in class, and she, she had so much anger, she was so annoyed that really she didn't want to respond. So how am I supposed to integrate myself and make myself, you know, like the others? You know it's hard to do it by yourself. (group interview, French)

Even though it was natural for African students to have a limited knowledge of the English language given their limited exposure to it, students were looked down upon and in many instances patronized. This created an urge in them to learn English posthaste, and when this materialized, they were greatly pleased. Listen to Asma (F, 16, Djibouti):

> If you don't speak English, like me in grade 7, "Oh, she doesn't speak English! Oh, we are sorry. Can you explain to her, she doesn't understand English, *la petite*, can you?" They think that we are really stupid, that we are mentally challenged, that we don't understand the language. Now that I know English, shsh I speak it all the time. I show them that I do understand English [laughs], I show them that I do English. And the girls [inaudible]. *Oh I got it, it gives me great pleasure.* (group interview, French; emphasis added)

La petite is an incredibly patronizing term that is used to belittle someone and position oneself with the upper hand. While Asma may have got her pleasure in the citation above, others' dreams and desires are taken away: They are left in the cold, alone, with their agony.

The Agony of Education:[6] Who Pays the Price?

The following final sections of this chapter still focus on MV youngsters who see their dreams and desires drifting away; they can resist, to resuscitate their dreams, but it is not painless. As one female student put it, teachers "are getting paid," getting their paychecks, but who is paying the price? To succeed academically, African students have to block out White teachers, counselors, and the school system in general from their everyday consciousness. When this happens, it seems, one becomes a guest, a passerby, no longer a permanent resident at the school; just attending school because one has to. This exchange is worth quoting at length, and it certainly does not need an introduction:

> Amani: 'Am the one who is paying the price.
>
> Asma: They say…
>
> Amani: What is happening with them teachers? He gets his check. But 'am the one who is paying the price, you know.
>
> Ossi: The big percentage of people in this school are Somalis.
>
> Awad: Ohm.
>
> Ossi: You are told, "University is expensive."
>
> A female voice: And expensive, and expensive.
>
> Ossi: And very expensive. [girls talking] School is very good, go there; the Somalis, well, they think that they are saying *la vérité* [the truth]. They are the counselors [*des orienteurs et des orientrices*], of course you know.
>
> Amani: No wonder you see a student playing basketball instead of going or doing his homework, because he thinks school is for nothing.
>
> Asma: Exactly!
>
> Amani: He used to love, he used to have beautiful dreams, but what happened to them? They are taken away from him. Because the school is telling him "No it's not like this, it's not like this," you know?
>
> Aziza: Exactly!
>
> Ossi: A guy who comes from Africa, OK, who comes, a person, a Somali; I take the example of the Somali case. A Somali who comes to Canada, OK. And OK, who, who, OK, for example Somalis when they finish school and all that, they go to France to do university studies.[7]
>
> Awad: Yes, yes!
>
> Ossi: Here, they don't want to even finish high school. Why? You know!
>
> Asma: Because there is no encouragement.
>
> Amani: I realized, it's also happening to me right now, you know. That, that, you know how every kid has a dream. The dream of becoming this, I will be helping my mom.[8]
>
> Asma: You can do it if you don't listen to the assholes.

Amani: [inaudible] you know, but you know what happens, you know? It's easy to be influenced when you shouldn't.

Aziza: It's real easy.

Amani: Especially when you are in the school. From one level to another, you go from one level to another, and when you are moving up, you notice that things get harder, eh? They are no longer like before, you know. The courses become more and more difficult. So, what is happening with these people who are busy always influencing you in a negative way, what happens? Little by little [*Petit à petit*], without you noticing it, you back off; from your dreams, the dreams you have. You think you are not able anymore. You think.

Aziza: Intimidation.

Asma: Yah, it happened to me.

Amani: You know [*hélas?*], it happened to me.

Awad: Ah yes?

Asma: Yah.

Amani: I tried so hard to stay awake. To stay awake and never let go [people talking]. It's like a plant, you know? It is like the candles, you know how the candles? How the candles, a small plant?

Awad: Yes.

Amani: If, if you protect her up front, it is going to stay.

Awad: Yes, yes [girls talking in Somali].

Amani: So, it's like a dream. If you don't keep your dream alive, you know, and you don't really let anything happen between, or get between you and your dream [girls continue talking in Somali].

Awad: Ohm.

Amani: It's gonna stay alive [girls continue talking in Somali].

Awad: OK.

Amani: But you know what happened? I realized I tried so hard to stay awake or not be influenced by these people. But believe me, there are times I cried so much and I said…[interrupted]

Aziza: it's not easy, it's not easy.

Amani: "You know what, may be they are right, I will be backing off." There are times it happened to me, but I tried so hard, I tried so hard, you know, stay on course. I tried so hard, so hard to be awake and to still have my same goal. you know. Still reach whatever I wonna reach. But, with people like that, especially in elementary schools.

Aziza: It's not easy.

Amani: Because it's really disgusting. I wish I can make a report in a newspaper when I leave the school. But I also have a reputation to say IT [high pitch] you know. It's like I can't do it, there are limitations to my actions, you know.

Samira: Actions for me have no limits.

Amani: So, it's disgusting. I mean if I really say something about the whole system, IT IS DISGUSTING. [girls talking in Somali] (group interview, French)

For Amani, a dream is a rhizomatic plant that needs sunlight, warmth, air, nourishment, and protection to blossom. If it is not easy to do this, it is because the adverse and the ugly metamorphosed social forces are too strong. The beautiful plants and dreams are not only taken away from some students, but also from their parents. Indeed, part of African students' agony is the humiliation they have seen their parents go though in their everyday survival strategies. Again, it seems, history repeats itself: The place that is called heaven is turning into a "nightmare" (Pinar, 2004). Their parents were asked by Mike Harris—the Conservative premier of Ontario at the time, who introduced work-based social welfare reforms whereby social assistance recipients have to work to receive social assistance—to work in menial jobs that, at some level, turned into indentured labor. Because most of MV students' parents were recent immigrants, with little if any knowledge of the English language, these reforms were painfully lived. These parents had no choice but to work if they wanted to keep roofs over their kids' heads and food on the table. It is terrible to see what had happened to Amani and Aziza's family. This was a single mother household with ten children. The mother cannot speak—let alone master—the English language. To ask her to work is to ask her to leave her three-year-old boy at home. One must ask: With whom would she leave him, and who would pay the babysitter? Even if the mother decided to work, jobs were scarce given the recession in Ontario at the time of this research. This is how heaven is no longer imagined, but lived as a nightmare (Jaleh, 2012).

Samira: I have a question to [Mike] Harris: "You said that there is a new law now, this very month. Everyone who is immigrant or refugee to Canada, and who doesn't work, he should go to school, your mother, my mother, they have education, your father, everybody." They can't, even in Canada, though they have education and some speak French or English, but they can't find jobs. What are they going to do? Social assistance is all what we have. You know what they are going to do? They are going to wash toilets. If he is told to wash the toilet, he has to do it. If they don't do it, sorry, but they risk that social assistance might be cut off. But, they don't know that we also have our dignity, we have a memory, a beautiful life back home where we were. The government is taking away our dreams of a dignified life.

Amani: It's like, this is the thing. If you want me to give you the best job you wonna have, you got to be sacrificing and trying to be like me [Mike Harris]. You know? But, if you really know who you are, deep inside, and try not to lose who you are, then you get to the point, you wonna get to the point you wonna get to, without losing your dreams and yourself. (group interview, French)

This is an utterance of the different ways in which students understand and translate the social forces under which they live, and which are beyond their control. It is an understanding that extends beyond themselves to the larger social structure. This understanding is significant in the students' schooling process; it becomes part of who they are, their identities and subjectivities; it influences how they understand the society around them, what they learn, and how they learn it. It also enlightens our understanding, as antiracist workers, of where students stand politically, racially, and socially. Based on these arguments, one may conclude that students are wide awake, enlightened, and reflexive subjects with full agencies, desires, and dreams, which can be violently encroached on and profaned, but can never be fully taken away.

Parental Involvement

In most postcolonial educational contexts in Africa, parental involvement is minimal. Building on my own experience as an African who went through schooling in Africa, parents are always present in one's education, but parental involvement as it is understood in the West is a relatively foreign concept. The idea that parents can object to their kid's final grade is anathema (Dei, 2009). This is not to suggest that this is true across the continent, or that things are not changing. On the contrary, it is accented to highlight the fact that, in the African educational philosophy, teachers represent the mythical figure of the elder who "knows" what is best for students, and they will do their absolute best in order for students to succeed. If a student fails, teachers and schools take the responsibility for that failure, because any failure is understood to be the responsibility of the community, which includes parents, teachers, principals, the school system, etc. In this philosophy, teachers are authorized by virtue of being members of the community to take on the role of parents, and parenthood is understood as a way of making emotional and intellectual investments in the well-being of the child. It is no wonder that it takes a village to raise a child. This sense of community does not juxtapose evenly with the philosophy of education in North America, where parents are part of the decision-making body, at least as far as the law is concerned.

In the African students' narratives, the African philosophy seems eminent. Parents have no participation in the school, and when students are called for meetings with teachers and other school authorities, parents are absent. They may follow their daughters' and sons' progress through the report cards, but that is it. Also, in some cases, they experience a linguistic barrier by not being able to speak the "language" of the school, both in its linguistic and semiotic sense—that is, understanding the system, its rules and regulations. I asked Najat (F, 15, Djibouti):

Awad: Yah, yah, what does your mom say about the school?

Najat: The school?

Awad: She, she comes to school?

Najat: She doesn't come. First of all, you know, we have *réunion* [meeting], like anything *réunion* and everything. My mom doesn't show up.

Awad: No?

Najat: No, she just goes, you know, "Do good in your courses." She's just, when the report comes she say blablabla. But she doesn't come, she doesn't call, she doesn't do anything. (individual interview, English)

Some students, as I indicated, have no parental support. This absence is due, by and large, to forced displacement, which is connected to civil wars and political instability in Africa, which pressure and even compel African students to leave not only their belongings, but also their sisters, brothers, aunts, cousins, and even parents. Speaking about the civil war in Somalia, this is what Aziza had to say:

You know, when the war broke out in Somalia, everybody disengaged from everything and everyone, in all corners, you know. The war broke out, you don't think about your aunts and your cousin. You think about getting your kids away from harm's way, from military troops. You see, the war had come. You think about leaving, you don't think of your uncle, of even your mother sometimes. It is when you come here, when the tension has calmed, then you say, "What happened to my aunt? Where is my aunt?" They are already here in Canada and you don't even know, you see. When there is a war, all what you think about is, *getta out here, getta out here, we goda getta out here*, you see. (individual interview, French)

Thus, a number of these students, as young as fifteen and sixteen years old, found themselves living in Canada alone. And given the unfamiliarity of the school system, in situations such as these where there are no parents, let alone parental involvement, African students are left in the cold to feel personal attacks whenever the school introduces new rules. *Le contrat* is a case in point. As Sam and Musa put it in chapter 2, "We don't have parents to defend us, we are by ourselves. We have to defend ourselves."

Dreams From My Mother: A Pedagogy of Care

In *Dreams from My Father*, President Barack Obama (1995) tells a story of hope. As someone who grew up in a contrapuntal space where cultures, geographies, races, languages, and voices collide, he urges us to live not as strangers to each other, but as empathetic human beings who are guided by integrity, humility, justice, and equality. I had the pleasure of witnessing something close to that at Maxwell High and Sunnyside. A few examples may illustrate what Nel Noddings (1992) and I call *pedagogy of care.*

One of the places where I "hung out" at Maxwell High was the English as a Second Language (ESL) classroom, where a good number of the students were continental Africans. I saw how much Nicholas, a White ESL teacher, cared for his students. "He is the best," as Phil (M, 17) put it. When asked about his philosophy and his approach to teaching, Nicholas said,

> It is all about care. I have to. Three days ago, I had a student who came from Somalia through the UN refugee resettlement program. He doesn't know where his parents are. In the chaos of a refugee camp he simply lost them. I saw him yesterday in class. While looking at me with his eyes wide open, he started crying without realizing it. He didn't even realize who he was looking at; I had to tap him in the shoulder. I stopped teaching, and simply sat beside him to comfort him. How can you teach present tense in moments like these?

A frustration shared by Nicholas and Brian (the vice principal) is that all grade 10 students across the province of Ontario have to take the Grade Ten Literacy test. Even students who came to the school three days ago with very limited or no English have to write it. Given this Somali student's fragile psychological state, however, Brian had to ask the Ministry of Education for an exemption for him. The students take the test once, but if they just missed a passing grade, they are forced to do it again. During this research, the results of the test came back, and according to Brian, "we did well [as a school], but we need to improve." I asked Nicholas what he thought about the test, and he said:

> Yesterday I worked with grade 9 students on writing news reports. I kept thinking that this was crazy, as the Ministry could end up changing the format of the test, and here I am asking these ESL students to create these fictions that mean little to them...these kids' needs go way beyond reading and writing—they have no parents at home.

I raised this concern in all my interviews and conversations with African students at Maxwell High and Sunnyside. Unanimously, students shared Nicholas's concerns, especially about the pressure they feel to perform well on the test. Brian (Maxwell High vice principal) summed up their feeling thus: "You can feel the stress around this test. It is palpable. The students act like hard boiled eggs, but they are not." I noted that in both schools teachers tried to find ways to prevent students from losing confidence after taking the standardized tests. One White female teacher from Sunnyside had her students writing sonnets the day after the exam. After class, she whispered in my ear, "They did it, and wrote great ones." Her eyes and her smile were full of care. Clearly, her statement underlines her care and concern for providing students with opportunities to experience success, so that they can imagine the possibility of always doing better. Phil (M, 17, Nigeria) argued, "Even though none of us is an ESL student, we know what ESL students are going though. Man, that's a hard exam. No wonder lots of them graduate high school late, but they have good teachers" (individual interview, English).

One female ESL student summed up this pedagogy of care by describing how ESL teachers practice it: "They develop their books here [she holds a book of ESL units that is developed by her teachers]. They put you in a good level for you. They start teaching you from the beginning." It is worth noting that the ESL program at Maxwell High is exemplary in its programmatic activities and care. All ESL classes are locally developed by a team of teachers who have been working collaboratively for almost ten years; and the English Language Development classes, a level higher than ESL, do highly engaging social justice projects that interest students.

The last example I want to explore is that of Adonis, an exceptionally engaged teacher of Lebanese descent at Sunnyside. He works the hardest to break down certain cultural stereotypes, especially in his area of teaching: trades. Sunnyside focuses on the construction trade with electrical and plumbing. Adonis is highly accomplished in the trades and he has a "hands-on" approach to teaching. He explains that while many of the students show clear ability and enjoy the different trade fields, there is a perception that construction is a low-paying job. This assumption often comes from student's experience with how people in the trades are paid and treated in the countries from which they or their parents have immigrated. As Adonis notes,

> I try to show them the salary scales and the hourly wages to convince them that it is a high-paying job in Canada, but it is a real cultural struggle with parents who refuse it for their children, and many of these students see the young guys dressed in suits selling cell phones in the mall and they think that is a good career. You know how our people are [addressing me; laughter].

This type of care eases African students' integration into the school. The rhizome of Blackness receives enough sun, water, and care that it blossoms and sees multiple possibilities and a better future. It is no surprise that Jean-Yves concluded, "Man, I am glad to make the switch [from French-language schools to Maxwell High]." Later on in my conversation with him, he said, "I want to do well in school. I don't want to disappoint my mother; she is working hard and taking care of us" (individual interview, English). I guess if Obama's dream is from his father, Jean-Yves's dream is from his mother.

Conclusion: Gimme the Low Down

> People can, collectively, generate the kind of power that can be earth shaking, that can change societies. People need to know that, particularly in the twenty-first century, it is important, even under a Black President, to bring the kind of pressure, to force the kind of issues that would allow us to imagine a future without war, without racism, without prison. (Angela Davis in Olsson, 2011)

This chapter is an extension to chapter 2. In it, we saw, again, the structures that supported students' ongoing racialized and discriminatory experiences at MV. Student narratives showed how White teachers, personnel, and counselors treated them differently. On the other side, I discussed the pleasant encounters African students had with Black teachers and other teachers of color. This raised questions about role models and the need for a critical multicultural representation that would necessarily question the structured hegemonic power relations. Students need moments of recognition, where they see themselves mirrored. The issues concerning the curriculum were also addressed. These included history, language, and the need to ask who is teaching what, and from whose perspectives. I concluded by addressing parental involvement. I narrated students' agony in translating the processes of schooling and understanding the new Canadian social context. In this context, students understood that the racialized, gendered, and immigrant status were of great significance in their accumulative memory of becoming Black and in choosing to whom they should ally themselves. African students' experiences with the rhizomatic process of becoming Black at MV are antagonistic and striated, while they are more smooth, productive, and multiple at Sunnyside and Maxwell High.

Notes

1   Amani: "If you conduct a poll, it [the source of most of Black students' problems] will be either within counseling or the personnel" (individual interview, French).

2   I use the *Black/African* couplet to signify diasporic Africans and continental Africans, respectively.

3   James High School is a French-language school with a high representation of people of color in the teaching, personnel, and student bodies. Sam had spent a short time there, and these are his reflections on that experience: "[in] James there is no general, no lower-level classes, everything is advanced [level]. Africans or whatever, Chinese, Japanese, or whatever the hell you from you know, it don't matter, you go to that school. And the principal, he is from where? Morocco, Egypt? Yah you know! And there is a lot of international, you know, teachers and stuff like that. So, you feel comfortable and stuff like that" (individual interview, English).

4   The term *Africanist* is used in analogy to and with *orientalist*, which was introduced by the late Edward Said in his classic study *Orientalism* (1978). By *Orientalism*, Said means the discourse that references the Orient. The individuals who conduct these studies are called Orientalists. I use *Africanist* in this context to refer to the individuals who live in, experience, and study Africa. These individuals can be progressive, but they can also be conservative, colonialist, and racist.

5   I am using *praxis* as defined by Paulo Freire (to whom I dedicate this chapter). Freire (1993) argued that in order for the human liberation to be complete, the word should not be put against the world, and practice should not be perceived in opposition to theory. Praxis, then, is the intersection of the word, the world, theory, and practice.

6   *The Agony of Education* is the title of a seminal work by Feagin et al. (1996) in which the unpleasant experience of African American students who go to predominantly White colleges was exposed.

7   This is to argue that in Africa, these same boys work hard to go to university, even if this means making sacrifices to go abroad, to France, for example. This sacrifice is primarily financial.

8   Her mother is the single head of a household with ten kids, four of whom are at Marie-Victorin. Two of her sisters and brothers went to two different French-language or bilingual universities. Although all of them go or have gone to French-language schools, her baby brother goes to an English-language elementary school. I was told that this is because he was not exposed to the French language the same way they were.

INTERLUDE

Homeless Urban Dreams

Reenah L. Golden
Reprinted with permission from the author

I live for illiterate orphaned eight year olds
dangling in the space between the sky
and the clouds,
hoping their little bare feet
will never touch the ground,
wishing that birds
could accommodate passengers.
I live for
homeless mothers with
permanent addresses sheltered from the
　elements
but not their malaise,
for mindless fathers without homes
and wanderers with relations unknown.
I live for
innercity ghettos and rural island village,
where resident outlaws dance indentations
in pavement and mud,
reinventing music from bones and skulls
residing in their own nightmares
self sabotaged by their own daydreams.
We live hard and fast,
wildly swerving through reckless political
　banter
and legislation
dodging yellow tape and deep potholes
defacing the abnormally large
red and white signs—
only found in the hood
NO LOITERING
NO DRUGS
NO ASSISTANCE
NO DREAMS
NO ART
NO INVENTIONS
NO JOBS
NO EXCEPTIONS

So now we post up defiantly in suburban
　plazas
pockets full of plastic baggies
filled to the brim with ibuprofen, Excedrin
　Complete,
Rolaids and Tums and Midol
drinking Nyquil from crumpled brown paper bags.
RELIEF FOR SALE,
over-priced, over-rated, over-used
R-E-L-I-E-F RELIEF from
headaches, backaches, stomachaches,
menstrual cramps, sleepless nights,
poor diet and self abuse. If only now to live
　for medication, denial, indifference,
negligence, self indulgence.
To live pain free in my bliss filled ignorance superimposing my natural black-
　girl beauty
and healthy full figure
over skinny ass vogue models and
painted celebrity covergirls.
If only my teeth were whiter,
my lips were thinner
my hips were smaller,
my thighs were smoother,
my hair was straighter,
my skin were lighter.
If only my father or husband were somebody significant
like a Sibley, or a Rodham or Rockefeller.
If only my grandfather's father
had owned something
land, livestock, people…
I live for a forgotten past
I live for a clearly defined me,
a future not yet written,
and I write
for a life forgotten
by time.

CHAPTER FOUR

"Oh, I Got It, It Gives Me Great Pleasure!"[1]

Hip-Hop Culture and Language, Post/Coloniality, and the Imaginary

Look Son,
I would like to straighten you out
Black is beautiful
When Black is empowering
Knowledge is power
So, you can be as Black as a crow
Or you can be as White as snow
You don't know
And you ain't got no dough
You can't go
And that's fo sho

(Lewis H. Michaux in Olsson, 2011)

When it comes to the issues addressed in this chapter, Marie-Victorin (MV) yet again has proven to be a richer source than the other schools and, hence, deserves more attention. In fact, when I discussed my findings from MV with students at Maxwell High and Sunnyside, they seemed to recognize the impact of Hip-Hop culture on them, but the question of language was too fuzzy to be acknowledged as an issue. Over 90 percent of the students I was speaking to at Maxwell High and Sunnyside spoke English as a first language and described themselves as bilingual with English as the dominant language. Even in the ESL classes at Maxwell High and Sunnyside, students were expeditiously picking up English as a second language. Generally, the impact of Hip-Hop did not need to be observed in all three research sites. Because students at Maxwell High and Sunnyside had grown up with Hip-Hop, they were baffled by my question about its impact. "We are Hip-Hop," one male student contended. Hip-Hop was not an external entity they picked up and learned; they had grown with it, so they were indeed Hip-Hop.

But what are the implications of this statement for the rhizomatic process of becoming Black? This question has different implications for MV than it does for Maxwell High and Sunnyside. The rhizomatic process of becoming Black in both Maxwell High and Sunnyside is "smooth," to use the language of Deleuze and Guattari (1987; see also concluding chapter). To better understand Maxwell High and Sunnyside as "smooth spaces," I had the following conversation with Phil (M, 17, Nigeria):

Phil: My parents are Canadian, originally from Nigeria, but I was born here in this cold place [laughter]. [Name of the city], baby!

Awad: So, you are Nigerian, Canadian, Nigerian Canadian, Canadian Nigerian, which one would you choose?

Phil: All of the above [laughter; interruption].

Awad: Previously we talked about Hip-Hop. Does it have any impact on you?

Phil: I don't understand. We are Hip-Hop; I am Hip-Hop. It is what I listen to, my head is totally Hip-Hop. I grew up with it, it is all I know. I slam sometimes [he breaks into slam poetry about fighting against racism].

Awad: That's dope, son. (individual interview, English)

The situation at MV, however, was different. The students there did not grow up with Hip-Hop and the English language, and the language question was more complicated. That is to say, unlike Phil, the heads of African students at MV were not "totally Hip-Hop," and Hip-Hop was not all they knew. With no exception, all the African students at Marie-Victorin were at least bilingual in French and a mother tongue, and in many cases, they were trilingual or more. Hassan (M, 18), for example, spoke six languages—Somali, Couto (local language in Somalia), Arabic, Amharic, French, and English—with, of course, different degrees of fluency. To address this complicated picture of language and culture, I have divided this chapter into two parts. The first part addresses students' relationships with language: their memories, histories, and sites of language learning. Such sites include Black popular culture, namely Hip-Hop and Rap, as well as movies, music video clips, magazines, newspapers, etc. The second part introduces culture as found in the students' narratives. This encompasses *cultural representation* and *separatist culture*. The former speaks to how Africans and Africa are imagined in popular representation and the impact of this imaginary on the students' sense of belonging; the latter explores the boundaries of cultural zones that are demarcated by cultural practices, including language and religion.

Post/Coloniality and Language Learning at MV

In contemporary neo- and postcolonial Africa, Ngugi wa Thiong'o (1986) argues, indigenous languages are unjustifiably mortified and denigrated. They are mortified through the methods of what wa Thiong'o (1986) calls "the colonial phase of imperialism" (p. 9), where the colonial language (particularly English and French, but also Portuguese) is elevated to and equated with the "civilized," the intellectual, and the intelligentsia. African students at MV unfortunately did not escape this. French is the official language of communication and education in the home nations of all of the students, except in Somalia, where learning French is a luxury only the bourgeoisie can afford. Having French as the official language produces a situation where students' linguistic choices have already been decided by the state. In the case of Somalia, by contrast, where the official national language is the Somali language, and English and Italian are second languages, it is the students' parents—specifically, the fathers, except in the case of one female whose father had passed away when she was young—who make the decision to send their daughters and sons to French-language schools. In my interview with Aziza (F, 18, Somalia), I asked her:

Awad: But, but, how, how you ended up in a French-speaking school in Somalia?

Aziza: Yes, I went to Sisters School (*l'école des soeurs*).

Awad: Sisters?

Aziza: A religious school.

Awad: Private?

Aziza: Private, religious. Yes!

Awad: OK, OK, why a French-language school?

Aziza: Because, ahm, the choice came from my father, because he, he did his training (*stage*) in French. He went to France, his brother was living in France, you see. It is a choice he made, he said that my kids will study in French. So, it was a choice which came from my father, that we study in French, and then all the family is francophone. We also had some friends of my father who, who did the same training as my father. Because my father was in the army, he did the same training with my father. These friends there were French. And then they were living in Somalia, you see. And then they had the, the, they were opening private schools, you see. They also wanted people to speak their language. Because in Somalia we don't speak French, there was the Somali language, the Italian, and the English. The French wasn't recognized like really, like, like, like the Italian is recognized and like the English is recognized, you see. So, it is only, you see, it is only, it is only the rich people who were learning French, you see. It was the rich families who had money, who sent their kids to a private school, you see. (individual interview, French)

To call oneself francophone or anglophone in Africa is to perform the historical memory of linguistic imperialism and colonial legacy. This legacy started "when in 1884 the capitalist powers of Europe sat in Berlin and carved an entire continent with a multiplicity of peoples, cultures, and languages into different colonies" (wa Thiong'o, 1986, p. 4). The result is that, first, as colonies, and today as neo-colonies, African countries define themselves and are defined in terms of the languages of Europe: French-speaking, English-speaking, or Portuguese-speaking countries. Second, because of this multiplicity of peoples, cultures, and languages, rival peoples found themselves within the same boundaries of a nation-state after 1884, hence producing *nations* within *the nation*. Omer (M, 19, Ethiopia) is a case in point. He is a Somali speaker who lived in Ethiopia:

> Even if, even by way of colonization and things like that, you see, my languages are added to French and Arabic, while theirs [those who come from mainland Somalia]…I think that there is a difference between North and South Somalia. I think it is English, Arabic, and on the other hand Italian, you see. So, and you will have rival peoples [*des peuples concurrents*] who live together in Somalia, really pure rivals and things like that. But some don't even speak the Somali language. Yet, they say they are Somali [laughs]. Why? Because they are in the territory of Somalia. It is for that they are called Somalis. (individual interview, French)

Supporting Omer's arguments, Aziza (F, 18, Somalia) explained:

> You see, when the colonizers came to Somalia, they divided the country into two parts, you see. The English got the South and the Italians got the North. So, that is that, and then the people, the Italians were here, the English were there. It is like here [in Canada] they divided the country into two [French and English]. They said this part is mine, you, your part is there, you see. So, the people who were living there, they had to understand, they had to learn the language, you see, because they are colonized, they are conquered. So, they are obliged [to learn the language], you see! (individual interview, French)

Subversively, however, and in the face of these imperialist and colonial deportments and behaviors, indigenous languages and cultures are still the place where people's hopes, desires, and aspirations are expressed. For example, the Somali language was literally invented as a medium of instruction and schooling. Like so many other African languages, the Somali language was originally an oral language, but in 1973 the government of General Mohamed Siad Barre (who eventually turned into a dictator) decided to write the language using Latin alphabets, hence confirming the Somali language as the national language and the language of education. Before 1973, students had to study either in English or Italian.

As I experienced it myself[2] (see also Dei, 2009; wa Thiong'o, 1986; H. Wright, 2004), indigenous languages in Africa are pushed to the margin of the institutionalized processes of schooling; as a corollary, learning the official language (English or French, for instance) can turn into a painful experience where rote memorization is the only way to absorb and produce knowledge. This is because students have very little, if any, contextual communicative support to learn the language. The curriculum usually depends on materials imported from European/American contexts that, in most cases, have no relevance to the pedagogical and communicative ways of indigenous knowledge production (cf. Dei et al., 1997).

Nevertheless, neither French nor English is considered a mother tongue by African students inside or outside Africa. I therefore differentiate between *mother tongue* and *first language*. Mother tongue is the first-acquired language, whereas first language, or L1, is the language of greatest mastery. One's mother tongue can be one's L1, but it is also possible that one's L1 is not one's mother tongue. Building on this distinction, the African students all declared their indigenous languages to be their mother tongues, although some were unable to say the number 87 in their mother tongues, as was the case with one Somali-speaking boy. Hassan (M, 18, Ethiopia/Djibouti/Somalia), for instance, recognizes French as a key opener to "a world of communication" and "a world of business/jobs," but French is not his mother tongue. It is his first language, though. As he clearly indicated, he felt more comfortable in his mother tongue. In my individual interview with him, I asked him:

Awad: What does French represent to you?

Hassan: A world of communication, a world of business/jobs [*travail*] [laughs]. It is going to help me in my life, like that is going to help me to get jobs. It is going to help my mind. It is going to help me to communicate more, but I don't consider it as my mother tongue. My mother tongue is Somali. So, I consider it like that. I feel more comfortable to speak Somali. Because it is my mother tongue, I speak it at home. I speak it with my parents, I speak it with my sister, my aunt. But there are some times where I find myself, I can't find the Somali words which express something, things, let's say, modern, or things like argot. If I can't find it in Somali, I can express it in French. (individual interview, French)

What is significant in this excerpt is, first, the lack of communicative support in the process of learning French or English in Africa and, second, the question of curriculum materials. In most African contexts, English and French are seen as inorganic languages that are allied with the authority of the state and the school. They are allied, in addition, with books and not with everyday interaction. In some cases, they are spoken—usually in a highly normative lexico-semantic schema[3]—only with those who are unable to speak the indigenous languages.

> Hassan: The French language was the only mode of communication with my friends who spoke no other language but French. I had plenty of friends like that, who were always speaking French among themselves and all that. But when I find myself with other students who can speak with me, we speak Somali. (individual interview, French)

As part of the students' communicative and language learning materials, books and other curriculum materials are exiguous and scarce. Many participants have confirmed this, including Ibri (M, 19, Togo) and Hassan (M, 18, Ethiopia/Djibouti/Somalia). The official curriculum texts, they argued, are by and large the only available texts. For Hassan, for example, comic books were the only other "text" at hand outside the mandated curriculum. This raises questions about the need for a more relevant African curriculum that would have to incorporate indigenous knowledge and indigenous ways of knowledge production, and of knowing.

In the Canadian context, on the other hand, one of the recurrent themes in the student narrative is how easy it is to learn the English language. This ease of learning English in Canada is related to three threads. First, the lexicon and the grammar of the English language are easier to learn than the French language. Second, English is communicatively supported in Canada. That is, except in Quebec, Canadians dialogue in English in their everyday interactions. This presents an opportunity for students to learn new words and perform/produce new semantics every day, which, third, enables a more meaningful relationship with/to the language. As Aziza (F, 18, Somalia) put it, "I don't know how to explain really, but this is how I see it, English offers more liberty than French, you know. When I was pretty young," she continues, "we had to articulate [our French] well. **It was hell**. When you learn French, it is more difficult than when you learn English" (individual interview, English, emphasis added). Aziza is compounding all three threads in her contention, "English offers more liberty than French." This liberty, in my view, is connected to the painful memory of how African students learn the French language: uncontextually and through memorization. Focusing on the first thread, Hassan (M, 18, Ethiopia/Djibouti/Somalia) has a similar contention:

English is easy, it is more easy than French, way easy, a lot more easy than French. In English, you don't need to conjugate the verbs into masculine and feminine, put the accents where they should be [laughs], the adjectives and all that. In English, all you have is *he, she, it*. (individual interview, French)

Thus far, one can see that the process of official language learning in postcolonial Africa can turn into a process of drilling and memorization, and the so-called worthwhile knowledge becomes irrelevant to students' quotidian communicative interactions. In spite of this, as we saw in chapter 3, African students show an appreciation for the "disciplined" school system in Africa, students-teacher interactions, and the order of curriculum material and the ways in which knowledge is transmitted. In the following section, I consider language learning in Canada, discussing the sites of learning English as a second language, with special emphasis on Black popular culture. However, because African students are already at least bilingual, English can be only their third or fourth language. I conclude the section with students' reflections on the cultural representations of Africa and Africans and the impact of these representations on colonizing the imaginary of the Canadian-born students.

Becoming Tri/Multilingual: Sites/Sides of Learning English

For African students at MV, the decision to settle in an English-speaking metropolis is taken by their parents, who themselves are bound by circumstances of having relatives in the city. This was also true for the students who came to Canada by themselves. Having relatives, it seems, makes easier the integration into Canadian society in general and the school in particular. I asked Hassan (M, 18, Ethiopia/Djibouti/Somalia) why an English-speaking city might be considered a place to stay over Quebec, a French-speaking province:

First of all, we had relatives who were here. Yes, secondly, because there is French and English. It is more the relative question because, you know, when you go to a new country, there is a tendency to go towards the people you know. Because you don't want to adventure into the unknown. And you can't have, you also want to have help, all the help you can get to succeed. Canada is new, it is a new life. So, it is because of my aunt who was here, the people, the friends we knew from back home, we were able to receive the help, you can enter the larger Canadian community and settle in there. (individual interview, French)

In this contextual relationship that African students call home, the everyday language of communication is English. They have to speak in English if they are to be understood. This translates into a sine qua non situation where students have to learn English (and quickly) in order to communicate their everyday needs such as taking public transportation or getting help in their grocery shopping. Using humor, Najat (F, 15, Djibouti) illustrates this need with a story of buying a hot dog:

> I was like, what? In grade 2? I don't know. I was like, ahm, it was the hot dog guy. And then I was like, ahm, *"Excusez-moi, je veux ça!"* And then he is like, "Pardon me!" [par me] And then it was like, "Hello!" I just give attitude in French, and then it was like, "Pardon me!" [par me] And then I was like, "Dat." And then my uncles, I mean cousins, they speak English, right? And then he's like, "I wonna a hot dog." And then it was like, and he gave it to me. I was like, "Yah, *à la prochaine fois alors*" [laughs]. You know, I was like, so annoyed, I thought he kina speak French, but he's like, speaking English, you know. (individual interview, English)

The degree of the necessity to speak English is highly visible in this instance. If her cousins had not been present to help, Najat might not have had something to eat. Najat's situation is not unique, however; other narratives show the distressful extent of this sine qua non situation of learning English.[4] In two separate interviews, Aziza, followed by Hassan, narrated and reflected on their early days when their competency in the English language was limited:

> Aziza: If I want to go to the boutique, I have to speak to the monsieur in English because he doesn't speak French. If I go to the shop to buy clothes, I have to speak in English, you see. It is something that you have to, you have to force yourself. In the early days, I used to go with my sister because my sister spoke English. So, I always took her with me. Then, I had to go by myself because she was not always going to always be there beside me. I had to speak I had to learn to speak English so I can help myself and I can, you know, I can deal with anything, you see. So, in another words, you are obliged, it is something you can't escape from. Because the society is anglophone, the country is anglophone, the services are in English, you see, that's why. (individual interview, English)

Reading between the lines of what Hassan has to say, the sine qua non of English learning in this case stems from a desire to participate in the new sociocultural markets, networks, and public spaces:

> Hassan: For the first two years, it was distressing, seriously distressing. You hate that, you can't communicate with people, you can't go out by yourself, not to go to the movies [laughs]. You have to always have a translator, you can't go to buy something because you have to speak in English. You

> don't understand half of the people who are there when they speak. For the first two years, it was more than distressing. (individual interview, French)

This "distressing" situation results in an inevitable need to learn English, and to learn it expeditiously. *Popular culture, especially television, friendship,* and *peer interactive pressure* are three mechanisms that accelerate the learning. Below, I first look at some narratives concerning friendship and peer pressure. The latter is felt more in their early days in the school, when African students are denigrated for not speaking English. Franco-Ontarian students, Heller (2011) explains, use English in their everyday interactions, which means that if African students want to participate in school markets, activities in and outside the classroom, and public spaces, they have to learn English. Once students decipher the lexico-semantic structure of the English language, they have a sense of accomplishment:

> Asma[5]: If you don't speak English, like my grade 7, "Oh, she doesn't speak! Oh, we are sorry, you can explain to her, she doesn't understand English *la petite*. Can you?" They think that we are really stupid, that we are mentally challenged, that we don't understand the language. Now I know English, I speak it all the time. I show them that I understand English [laughs], I show them that I do English. *Oh, I got it, it gives me great pleasure.* (group interview, French)

Asma addresses, first, the teacher's condescending manner of speech upon realizing that Asma did not speak English. Undoubtedly, this condescension leads to more pressure on Asma, and African students in general, to learn English. Second, her narrative speaks to the threshold desire of a teenager who wants to fully participate in dominant markets and public spaces. This full participation was halted and haunted by her inability to speak English, a predicament another student, Najat, seems to echo:

> So I am like, you know, all my friends, like, this people, like friends, you know, they will be like, speaking English. So, I just, like, tryina learn one by one. you know. So, I just learn it fast. It's like, "Wa I speak English now?" (individual interview, English)

At stake in these narrated desires and memories is the emotional investment in learning a language contextually. *The more intense the emotional investment and desire, the faster one learns the language,* hence taking the feeling of performing a chore out of the language learning process. If you have, Aziza argues below, an environment where formal and informal (including human) communication is conducted in English, this may serve to connect the facility and the pleasure of learning.

> When I came here, the first days, the first months, I can only speak in French because that's what I always spoke back home and everywhere else, right? I came here, people speak in English, television is in English. Ahm, *tout à l'entour*, environment. It is all in English, so you have to adapt, right? (individual interview, English)

To conclude, like Aziza, Hassan contends that the everyday communicative support that the English language has in Canada is significant, first, in "enriching" his vocabulary, and second, in intensifying and supporting his emotional investment:

> But here you have the communication, you have TV. You have to force yourself because in order to buy something, you are obliged to speak in English. So, you have all the communication, you, you are in this surrounding which enriches you with new words and all that.

"I Just, Like, Laughing at Languages": Bilingualism and Normativity

Whether for environmental reasons or because of individual desires to participate in academic and nonacademic markets and public spaces, African students added English to their linguistic repertoires. However, their narratives show that students have a *subtractive* rather than *additive* notion of bilingualism in learning English. In cases of additive bilingualism, Lambert (1978, p. 217) explains, an individual adds a second language to her repertoire of skills; the first language is intact and not in danger of being replaced (see also Cummins, 2004). This is usually the case when the language is socially and communicatively supported, for example with an English-speaking Canadian learning French. When, on the other hand, a mother tongue is neglected or abandoned while learning a second language, the result is subtractive bilingualism (see Appel & Muysken, 1987/1990). This latter form of bilingualism is the case with Najat (F, 15, Djibouti), who argued that losing her Somali language was not her fault, and that it was socially and contextually bounded. That is, losing her Somali language was a result of, first, the social context where all her interactions were strictly in English and, second, her age. She came to Canada when she was seven years old. In reflecting on this loss, she told me:

> I like, I like, lost my Somali, you know, language. I probably, like if I go to somebody to talk, they will be like, "Oh my God! You don't know how to speak, from

what?" Oh, what 'm suppose to do, you know [laughs], like, I came here when I was seven, you know [laughs]. I just, like, **laughing at languages** (individual interview, English, emphasis added)

Losing her Somali language, as she contends, is connected to Najat's instrumental relation to language. By instrumental relation I am talking about using language as a pure medium and instrument of communication. When the Nigerian Nobel laureate Wole Soyinka, who writes almost exclusively in English, was asked how he relates to the English language, he responded that English is a language that is given and made available to him, and he is intended to use it (see wa Thiong'o, 1986). Here, one is conscious of one's own (external) relationship with and investment in the language. Najat seems to have a Soyinkan instrumental and utilitarian notion of language. She has no investment in the French-only language ideology that French-language schools seem to adopt and adapt to. French-language school officials fought, and are still fighting, against the use of English by students on school grounds (cf. Heller, 2011). This fight is based on the historical notion that students in French-language schools are expected and supposed to use French, and using English is often read as a sign of assimilation (ibid.). Put in these terms, for Najat, using English is, on the one hand, a conscious act of resisting this modernist notion of language use, which is enforced by the school authority, and, on the other hand, a performative act against the nationalist discourse that dichotomizes English and French. In many ways Najat is following the Franco-Ontarian students' dominant code-switching practice where it is English, not French, that is more often heard in public spaces, particularly in non-classroom sites such as hallways, the cafeteria, and the gymnasium. Even though Najat knew she should not be speaking English at the school, she did:

Najat: I was like, talking English, English, English, you know. Like *directrice*, the principal comes and it's like, she heard me talking. She said, "*C'est quoi ça?*" Hhh, "*le français, Madame.*"

Awad: Ya, but you are in a French school.

Najat: Oh, what am I suppose to go, "Bonjour," you know? Wa, because you know, you know it's good, it is a good language [i.e., French]. You have to know, but French with teachers and residents, no way [laughs]. (individual interview, English)

Besides showing a teenager who is resistant to the school's formal authority, this episode points to the notion that, in the Franco-Ontarian context, especially for young people, the French language is not for public consumption. For them, French is related to formal schooling and school activities.

Najat: OK, my friend is like, speaking French, you know, in a subway, I was like, "Pardon me [par me], ahm I don't know you. What was that question again?" I don't like speaking French on a subway or anything. And this guy comes, "*Parlez-vous français?*" I was like ,"No, I don't speak French." You know, when I am not in a class or anything, I just speak English, I just speak English.

Although there is little solid evidence of it, it is nevertheless worth noting the possible link between race and the use of English in public spaces. In metropolitan cities in Canada, except for within the province of Quebec, Blackness is linked to the English language. Save for some continental and diasporic francophone Africans, Black people are, by and large, English-speaking Canadians. And given my argument about how the perception of the Self by the Other influences how the Self performs itself, one may argue that this has a significant role in the process of speaking English in public spaces. That is, African students are expected to speak English in public spaces, and this may become an added pressure that might accelerate the speed of learning English, on the one hand, and keep the French language in the school and out of public spaces, on the other.

While Najat was working against the French-only language ideology, other African students disagreed with her, seeing English as a threat to their French. Clearly, for them, bilingualism is perceived in a subtractive sense, where the second threatens the first language.

Aziza: Ahm, I came here and right away I learned, I started to speak in English. I forgot my French. And then, the more and more I learn English, I learn English words, my French diminishes, diminishes, diminishes, diminishes. I learn more English, I learn a lot of English, my French diminishes, etc., you see. So, the more I learn English, the more I forget my French. You see, it is something! And when I came here, I told myself that I will never learn to speak, I will never, my French will never diminish. I am going to be good in French like I used to be before. And I will never speak in English, and you see now what I'm doing? [laughs; she realized she was speaking English to me] I told myself before, and that doesn't work or what? (individual interview, English)

Ironically, a good portion of my interview with Aziza (F, 18, Somalia) was conducted in English, a language with which she was increasingly comfortable. In fact, she was so comfortable that it seemed to be replacing her

French. In some cases, she could not find the meaning of French words she used to know: "And it happens to me that sometimes I could not find the meaning of French words that I used to know before, you know what I mean?" Other students narrated a similar feeling of losing vocabulary or their "Parisian" accents. In my focus group interview with the girls, they contended that:

Asma: We lost our accent.

Ossi: Yes, yes, completely [Amani speaks jokingly *à la québécoise*; laughs].

Asma: When they asked me a question, "*Oui Monsieur je veux dire…*" [Asma speaks *à la parisienne*]. He, he was looking at me like that [Asma make a puzzling face]. But now, "*Je veux dire ohm, Monsieur c'était vraiment oui…*" [Asma speaks with a relaxed voice]. You see, I lost my accent. And moreover people tell us that we have Parisian accent. I said, "Are you nuts [*ça va pas*]? I don't even have an accent."

Samira: Not only the accent, the French language. English, we are in an English-speaking country. Bilingual, but English dominates, you see.

Aziza: It is like you detach from your French side in speaking English. (group interview, French)

Nonetheless, not all students see bilingualism in its *subtractive* faculty. Hassan, in particular, is quite emphatic in refuting one dominant Franco-Ontarian ideology, which states that watching English-language media, especially television, and speaking English are signs of assimilation. Hassan has an *additively* pragmatic approach to language that does not fear learning new languages as long as they advance his ambitions in doing international and law studies. As he put it:

There are some people who say that "Oh, you should not lose your French. We are going to be assimilated. We should not lose. …" And I was really in agreement with this ideology two years ago. Had you asked me [two years ago], [I would have said] we should not lose our French and all that. But now I find that I am no longer agreeing with this ideology of losing one because I learned another, but I say very simply, learn this, learn the new and keep what you had before. But don't put aside other languages. Keep what you had before because it is ignorance [not to learn a new language], you understand? Seriously, there are a lot of, a lot of Franco-Ontarians who tell themselves [*qui se dissent*], who fight among themselves [*qui se battent*] to safeguard the language. "In any case, I don't watch the *Channels*, *Fox*, or I don't watch *CNN* since it's assimilation. I don't watch the televised journal. I don't want to lose my language. I want to watch my activities." This is good. This is that, but don't ignore the rest, you see. For me, it is like music. It doesn't bother me to listen to French music, Somali, Spanish or Arab music [laughs]. I am interested later in international studies, law and all that. So, I learn as much as possible.

Even though Hassan was in total disagreement with the French-only language ideology that the French-language schools have adopted, he and other African students argued that bilingualism is a necessity for francophones in Ontario and the rest of Canada. Francophones cannot escape the powerful connection in North America and around the world between economic power and the English language. It is significant to note, however, that the onus of bilingualism is put on French-speaking Canada more than English-speaking Canada. As a corollary, African students are zealously critical of the Canadian policy of bilingualism. The notion of Canada being a bilingual country is fraudulent, they argue, precisely because it does not translate into individual bilingualism.

Ossi: More and more in this country, they say it is bilingual. Me, I found that this is not the case. If it was bilingual, everyone should have been speaking French. Students here [in English-speaking parts of Canada], they don't even speak French.

Amani: Me too. Me who thought it was really bilingual, *when I was in the bus*, I was busy asking people, *"Est-ce que tu parles français? Est-ce que tu m'aidesr?"* [Do you speak French? Can you help me?] Because I didn't speak English then, right? Everybody will be looking at me like this [laugh].

Ossi: One thing which I believe is this, how can we say that Canada is bilingual while there are people who aren't?

Asma: And francophones, they have, they have two [languages]. The [francophone] teachers are bilingual. Anglophones are not bilingual. (group interview, French)

On a different note, student narratives also show a normative notion of language, a notion inherent to the French language (Bourdieu, 1991). In it, languages can be *"pauvre," "riche," "superbe,"* and *"belle."* With no specification of the rules and the rewards of the market where language is used, Bourdieu argued, the adjectives "poor," "rich," "super/incredible," and "beautiful" can perform only a value judgment of the language.

Aziza: When I first came to Canada, I had French words. In short, my French was *super bon* [incredibly good]. It was a good, a rich French, you see. When I came here, my French became poor. And when I first wrote my evaluation test for French, he [the teacher] was so surprised because I spoke *un bon français, le bon, un français riche* [a good French, the good, a rich French], you know when you live in Africa. You see, you have *un français vraiment génial* [a really awesome French], more beautiful than them. (individual interview, French)

Since there is no universally "beautiful," "rich," or "poor" language, language can be understood and evaluated only in relation to a market and within particular relations of power. English and French are "important" languages because of the symbolic and capitalist economic material capital they represent in a universe where neocolonialism, imperialism, capitalism, and exploitation are pretty much the norm (McLaren & Farahmandpur, 2005). Significantly, however, these adjectives (rich, poor, beautiful) also indicate students' awareness of the highly valued symbolic currency they possess. In a world where language is a vital key to material capital, English and French become indispensable symbolic capitals. Aziza (F, 18, Somalia) was content with learning one more universally significant language:

The English language is also a beautiful language. I learn English because, firstly, it is, I think, dominant in the world. It is a dominant language. So, of course you gonna tell yourself that "I have to also learn English." It is one more language for you. (individual interview, English)

Expressing the same contentedness, in my conversation with Hassan, he articulated how the symbolic could be converted and "translated" into material capital, that is, money and a job:

Hassan: For the time being, it is the future: French and English. **My two languages to conquer the world** [laughs]. Seriously, you've, you've English, you understand America, you understand Canada, you see! Like, it is an international language. I was really happy to have learned English. I am really happy that I have French and English; the most important two languages. And then we speak at home Somali. **I work as a translator at the school.** In the school, I do translation. It is Arabic, French, and Somali.

Awad: Wow, does it pay?

Hassan: Yah.

Awad: That's good.

Hassan: It's true. You see, *that is one of the advantages.*

Awad: Yes, absolutely. It is really marvelous. And then what does English represent to you?

> Hassan: A world of business [*un monde de travail*]; *la langue, overture, l'infini* [language, openings, limitless]. (individual interview, French, emphasis added)

For African students at MV, one has to conclude that language is not an abstract category that has no bearing on their everyday lives. On the contrary, it opens doors and brings capital and jobs. "Conquering the world" through language is neither a naïve nor a simplistic statement. Hassan has had a glimpse of what language can do and what doors it can lead him through. Some languages, however, were learned for purposes other than money and jobs. Arabic, for instance, was learned for religious and identity-formation purposes. In articulating these purposes, Aziza said, "You know we are Muslims, and because the Koran is written in Arabic, so we have to learn Arabic. Because the Koran is the book; like the Bible for Christians, Muslims' is the Koran" (individual interview, French). Besides being an international language of communication, English is a significant tool in accessing jobs and in making it possible to participate in private, regional, national, and international markets. Next, I discuss the narrative and the performance of the sites where African students learn English.

Q7 in the House: Hip-Hop Ethnography of BESL Learning

> I repeated every word that came from Georgia's mouth. After one or two months, I was accustomed to the way she spoke. As it became possible for me to follow her speech, and to talk to her, I came to see that she was teaching me two languages. It was like Maninka and Bamanankan—different languages, but related. One sounded a little like the other. There was the language that Georgia spoke when alone with the Negroes on the plantation, and she called that Gullah. And there was the way she spoke to Robinson Appleby or to other white people, and she called that English. "Bruddah tief de hog" was Gullah, and "brother done steal the hog" was the way to it to the white man. (Hill, 2007, p. 128)

To understand the different sites where African students at MV accessed and learned their English, I deployed *ethnography of performance* as a mechanism and central tenet of the hanging out methodology. Here, I juxtaposed their bodily performances—what students actually did—with their narratives—how they metacognitively understood their own performances. In doing so, popular culture (television, to be specific), and Black popular culture in particular, emerged as a central site where students learned English as a second language. By Black popular culture, I am referring specifically to music and movies. Interestingly, African students did have access to English-language popular culture in Africa, especially Hollywood and independent U.S. films:

> Aziza: You see, when you watch, when we were back home there in our country, we were watching films there. Romantic films or action films, and the actors were speaking in English. And we said, "Oh what are they saying?" And I started to imitate them [laughs]. At first, we didn't understand what they were saying, but we understood through the gestures and acts, the actions and all of that. And you dream of learning this language one day, you see. I am going to speak like this monsieur who speaks, or this madame who speaks, you see. *I wonna learn it*, you see, *I wonna learn it, English you know*. (individual interview, French)

In addition to stoking her eagerness for learning English in Africa, popular culture plays an acute, clear, and penetrating role in Aziza's life. This role becomes more pronounced once students set foot in Canada. I asked students in all of the interviews at MV, "*Où est-ce que vous avez appris votre anglais?*" [Where did you learn English?]. "*Télévision*," they all responded. However within this "*télévision*" is a particular representation—Black popular culture —that seems to interpellate (Althusser, 1971) African students' identity and identification. As Omer (M, 19, Ethiopia) argues, because the U.S. media is so prevalent, African students (and Black Canadians in general) are attracted by and emotionally invest in African American media representations. I asked Omer why African students were taking up Hip-Hop identity and speaking Black English:

> But they [African students] are influenced by the Americans. Let's speak of Canada. There is an influence of, whether White or Black youth, Canada is influenced by the American television. That means Black Canadians are influenced by the *Afro-Americans*. You watch for hours, you listen to music, if you watch a comedy with Mr. T, the *Rap City*,[6] there you will see singers who dress in particular ways. You see, so. (individual interview, French)

In amending a discursive support for Omer, Najat contended that:

> Najat: I hang out with all kina people. It could be White, it could be Chinese, it could be, anyway I do. I hang out with anybody. You see me, I hang out with White people, I hang out with Black guys.
>
> Awad: Yah, ahm, if, if I may ask you, who do you think is influencing you the most?
>
> Najat: Of course, ahh, Blacks. (individual interview, English)

The influence of popular culture, however, does not stay only at the discursive level; it occupies a central role at the performance level as well. In explaining that she "hangs out" with her "girlfriend" who is "energetic," Najat said, "hanging out with her is like so cool. She talks like Energizer, the battery never finishes." This is an illustrative example of the power and influence of popular culture in young people's imaginary, everyday speech, and conceptualization of themselves and the world around them. Energizer is a brand of battery that has an advertisement on television where a toy is charged by an Energizer battery that "keeps going and going and going," or so the advertisement says. This influence is more pronounced when it comes to Black popular culture, especially Hip-Hop and Rap music videos, television programs, and Black films. This was the response to my question about the last movies a student had seen:

Najat: I don't know, I saw *Waiting to Exhale* and I saw, what else I saw, I saw *Swimmer*, and I saw *Jumanji*; so wicked, all the movies. I went to *Waiting to Exhale* wid my boyfriend and I was like, "Men are rude" [laughs].

Awad: Oh believe me, I know, I know.

Najat: And den he [her boyfriend] was like, "Oh, women are rude." I was like, we're like fighting, you know, and joking around. I was like, and de whole time like [laughs], and den when de woman burns the car, I was like, "Go, girl!" You know, and all the women are like, "Go, girl!" you know. And den de men like, khhh. I'm like, "I'm gonna go get a popcorn" [laugh]. (individual interview, English)

Besides showing the influence of Black English in the use of "de," "den," "dat," "wid," and "wicked" as opposed to, respectively, "the," "then," "that," "with," and "really really good," Najat's answer shows that youths bring agency and social subjectivities to the reading of a text. These subjectivities, importantly, are embedded in history, culture, and memory. Two performed subjectivities that influenced Najat's reading of *Waiting to Exhale* were her race and gender identities. Najat identified with Blackness embodied in a female body; the Black/woman, in burning her husband's car and clothes, interpellates Najat.

Three things are noteworthy in Najat's example. First, the process of interpellation brings different subjectivities or subject locations within the self. That is, different representations *call upon* different subjective responses. Second, as a researcher, my access to these subjectivities is in and through linguistic performances. "Go, girl!" is indeed a gendered but also a racial performance in that it is an expression used by mostly Black women.

Thirdly, as I have argued before, gender and race are or become performative categories, performed every day in and through language. *Ritual hallooing* and *ritual expressions*, as Ben Rampton (1995) would call them, are central to this racial performance. Especially when performed by African students, expressions such as "whassup," "whadap," "whassup my Nigga," and "yo, yo homeboy" (what is up, my good friend) become more expressions of politics, moments of identification, and desire than uses of the dominant language—English—or indications of mastering the language per se. They become a way of saying, "I too am Black," or "I too desire and identify with Blackness."

Another example in a different context demonstrates the impact of Black popular culture on African students' lives and identities. Just before the focus group interview with the boys, *Electric Circus*, a local television music and dance program that plays mostly Black music (Hip-Hop, Rap, reggae, soul, and rhythm and blues) began. "Silence!" one boy requested in French. The boys started to listen attentively to the music and to look at the fashion worn by the young people on the program. After the show, the boys code-switched among French, English, and Somali as they exchanged observations on the best music, the best dance, and the cutest girl. Rap and Hip-Hop music and their fashions were of the primary interests.

The moments of identification in the above examples are significant in that they point to the process of identity formation that is implicated, in turn, in the linguistic norm to be learned. For the MV students I interviewed, Hip-Hop in general and Rap in particular were influential sites for language learning. This influence, significantly, was more prevalent in the boys' narratives than in the girls', a fact that raises the question of the role of gender in the process of identification and learning. On many occasions, the boys performed typical Gangsta Rap language and style, using language as well as movement, including name-calling. What follows are just two of the many occasions in which students articulated their identification with Black America through the use of Rap linguistic styles.

Sam: One two, one two, mic check. A'ait [aayet], a'ait, a'ait.

Juma: This is the Rapper, you know wha 'm meaning? You know wha 'm saying?

Sam: Mic mic mic; mic check. A'ait, you wonna taste it. Ah, I've to take the microphone, you know; a'ait.

Sam: [laughs] I don't rap man, c'mon give me a break. [laughs] Yo! A'ait, a'ait, you know, we just about to finish de tape and all dat. Respect to my main man [pointing to me]. So, you know, you know wha 'm mean, 'm just rep-

144   Chapter Four

> resen'in' Q7. One love to Q7, you know wha 'm mean, and all my friends back to Q7. Even though you know I haven't seen them for a long, you know. I still I got love for dem, you know what 'm mean? Stop with the tapin' boy!

A male voice: Kick the freestyle. [boys talking in Somali]

Sam: So, yo, you want me to record it again?

Awad: I don't want it, I don't want it.

Sam: Why not?

[20 minutes of Gangsta Rap music, Cool J, Boys II Men, Brandy. Jamal performs as a DJ while the song is playing, to emphasize expressions, lines, or notes.]

Jamal: Kim Juma, live! Put the lights on. Wardap. [boys talking in Somali] Peace out, wardap, where de book. Jamal am out a here.

Shapir: Yo, this is Shapir. I am tryin' to say peace to all my niggers, all my bitches from a background that everybody in the house. So, yo, chill out and this is how we gonna kick it. Bye and wid that pie. All right, peace, yo.

A male voice: Peace and one love.

Sam: A'ait, this is Sam represen'in' AQA […] where it's born, represen'in, you know wha 'm mean? I wonna say whassup to all my niggers, you know, peace and one love. You know wha 'm mean, Q7 represen'in' forever. Peace! [Rap music]

Jamal: [as a DJ] Crank it man, coming up [Rap music] (group interview, English)

Of interest in these excerpts is the use of Black stylized English, particularly the language of Rap: "Respect for my main man," "represen'in' Q7," "kick the freestyle," "peace out, wardap," "'am outa here," "I am trying to say peace to all my niggers, all my bitches," "so, yo chill out and this is how we gonna kick it," "I wonna say whassup to all my niggers," "peace and one love." When Shapir offers "peace to all [his] niggers," all his "bitches," he is, first, reappropriating the word *nigger* as an appellation that is common in Rap/Hip-Hop culture. That is, friends, especially young people, commonly call a Black friend "nigger," without its traditional racist connotation. To avoid this historical connotation, Shapir should have used the common term in Black talk, *nigga*, without the "er" (Alim & Smitherman, 2012). Second, Shapir is using the sexist language that exists in Rap (Love, 2012). These forms of sexism have been challenged by female Rappers such as Queen Latifah, Lil' Kim, Missy Elliot, and Salt-N-Pepa, among many others, and were critiqued by fellow female and male students. For example, Samira (F,

16, Djibouti) expressed her dismay at the sexist language found in some Rap circles:

> OK, *Hip-Hop*, yes I know that everyone likes *Hip-Hop*. They dress in a certain way, no? The songs go well. But, they are really, really, they have expressions like *fuck, bitches*, etc. Sorry, but there is representation. (group interview, French)

Here, Samira is addressing the impact that these expressions might have on the way society at large perceives the Black female body, which in turn influences how it is represented both in and outside Rap/Hip-Hop culture. Hassan (M, 17, Djibouti) also expressed his disapproval of this abusive language: "Occasionally, Rap has an inappropriate language for the life in which we live, a world of violence and all that" (individual interview, French).

In Rap style, one starts a performance by "checking the mic": "One two, one two, mic check." Then the Rapper either recites an already composed lyric or "kicks a freestyle," displaying the spontaneity that characterizes Rap. The Rapper begins the public performance by introducing herself or himself with a true or made-up name ("yo, this is Shapir") and thanking her or his "main man," or best friend, who often introduces the Rapper to the public. Specific to Gangsta Rap, one represents not only oneself but also a web of geophysical and metaphorical spaces and collectivities that are demarcated by people and territorial spaces: "represen'in' Q7," "a'ait, this is Sam represen'in' AQA." At the end of the performance, when the recitation or freestyle is completed, again one thanks the "main man" and gives "peace out" or a "shad out" (shout out) to the audience.

The boys were clearly influenced by Rap lyrics, syntax, and morphology (in their broader semiological sense), and especially by Gangsta Rap. In learning ESL in general and BSE in particular through music, Jamal used several strategies, including listening, reading, and repeating: He was listening to the tunes and lyrics while reading and following the written text. Acting as a DJ, he then not only repeated the performer's words and expressions but also imitated his accent.

Depending on their ages, the girls, by contrast, were ambivalent about Rap, though they used the same strategies as Jamal in learning English through music. For example, during a picnic organized by a mixed group of males and females, the females listened to music while following the written text and reciting it (complete with accents) along with the singer. The girls' choices of music (including Whitney Houston and Toni Braxton) differed in that they were softer than the music chosen by the boys and contained mostly romantic themes.

For the most part, the older females (sixteen to eighteen years old) tended to take a more eclectic approach to Hip-Hop and Rap; this was evident in how they dressed and in what language they learned. Their dress was either elegant middle class, partially Hip-Hop, or traditional, and their learned language was what Nourbese Philip (1991) calls "plain Canadian English." The younger females (twelve to fourteen years), in contrast, like the boys, dressed in Hip-Hop style and performed BSE.

In spite of their ambivalence to Rap and Hip-Hop, I detected the following three features of BE in both the older and the younger girls' speech:

(1) the absence of the auxiliary *be* (19 occasions, e.g., "they so cool" and "I just laughing," as opposed to "they are so cool" and "I am just laughing");

(2) BE negative concord (4 occasions, e.g., "all he [the teacher] cares about is his daughter, you know. If somebody just dies or if I decide to shoot somebody, you know, he is *not* doing *nothing*" [italics added]; the expression would be considered incorrect in standard English because of the double negative); and

(3) the distributive *be* (4 occasions, e.g. "I be saying dis dat, you know?" and "He be like, 'Oh, *elle va être bien*'" [she's going to be fine]).

These BE markers are expressions of the influence of Black talk on the girls' speech and performances of the girls' identity location and desire, which they apparently ally with Blackness. In reflecting on African students' desire and identification with Blackness, I had the following conversation with Omer (M, 19, Ethiopia):

Awad: Ah, OK, OK, and then, and then this basketball gang; I observed that they are very influenced by *Hip-Hop*.

Omer: Yes.

Awad: That is to say the way they dress, the English they speak.

Omer: Yes, because…

Awad: *Whassup, whassup* [I moved my head and my fingers à la Hip-Hop]

Omer: Yes, since they listen to music, Hip-Hop; since they watch Black movies; there, because you desire something. They want to have this power because they desire to become that. That is their aim. They desire to become like that. (individual interview, French)

However, not all mediatic representations are there to help identity formation. Indeed, the hegemonic and dominant media, African students argue, are there precisely to negate, castigate, and obliterate students' identities, history, language, and place of belonging—Africa. African students were dismayed by the extent of the negative representations of Africa. Africa, in these representations, is a monolithic jungle with no sense of direction, no history, no language, and thus no identity or civilization. Africa does not exist in its own respect, but always in opposition to the "civilized" Europe (see Dei, 2009). This is eighteenth- and nineteenth-century Europe representing Africa (see de B'béri, 2008; Oladipo, 1992; Said, 1993, 1978). The product of this imperialist and colonial European endowment is a contemporary colonized imaginary passed on from one generation to the next. Next, I discuss the ways in which Africa and Africans are schematically represented in the popular imagination, and African students' struggle with this imaginary.

"We Were Totally Seen": Colonization of Cultural Imagination

The Other, the so-called Third World, African students contend, is negatively represented, relegated to the margin of representation, or even completely negated. African students were already known when they first arrived at the school, and the knowledge was mediated by war, famine, and other negative images that were available to students from dominant groups. It is not their fault, Aziza argued, that these students do not know otherwise:

Samira: We were totally frustrated because **we were totally seen**, imagining [*the*] Africa that we know.

Aziza: You know, ah, the media always shows/represents [*montre*] the negative side of others [*le côté negatif des autres*]. I already mentioned the media because they, it is not their fault if they [White students] always see on television the negative side of Africa. OK, there are some people who think that Africa is a country. They don't even know that it is a continent. You see what I am tryina say? (group interview, English, emphasis added)

Still, one has to ask: Is it really "not their fault if they always see on television the negative side of Africa"? One answer might be that it is not their fault so long as they are not reproducing these negations. It *is* their fault, Hélène Cixous (1994) would argue, if they reproduce them. To illustrate, Cixous (1994) discusses the examples of slavery and the Holocaust. Not to know (about) slavery and its impact on the African peoples, Cixous contends, does not remove the historical responsibility from the child of the West; that is, that child cannot be exempted from the historical responsibility for the Holocaust or for slavery whether the child knows about them or not. One has to be responsible for their lack of knowledge:

> Ossi: There is one person who asked a girl who comes from Ethiopia, the girl was asked, "Did you have, do you have a house in Africa?" She asked that! [laughs] The girl, she is like, "Of course! Where do we sleep, outside?" (group interview, French)

Ossi is not alone in narrating such naiveté, even racism, and uncritical cultural information, and uncritical imaginary consumption. As bell hooks (1992) argues, consuming the Other uncritically may result in pain and wounds. The Other is not a puppet or a marionette; on the contrary, the Other has to be engaged as a full subjectivity, with history, memory, language, culture and agency. The Other has a name. The girls are worth quoting at length:

> Aziza: Like us, when we told them that we came from Somalia, in our early days in the school.
>
> Ossi: Nobody knew, nobody.
>
> Aziza: Nobody knew what Somalia is, or, except...[interrupted]
>
> Ossi: The war, the poverty, the famine.
>
> Aziza: The media.
>
> Ossi: They didn't know Somalia. They didn't know that there is a country called Somalia, till the war broke out.
>
> Amani: "Oh, you are different than the Somalis on television."
>
> Asma: That is what they told us.
>
> Asma: Really different than the Somalis we have seen on TV.
>
> Amani: What is not good, they don't have an open mind. OK, they don't try to question what they receive. So, if they don't find the exact information on something that they don't know, what they do is, they depend on the media.
>
> Aziza: I even have an example. One person came up to see me and asked me, "Do you really dress like that?" talking about the way I was dressing when I came here. "Do you really dress like that when you were in your country?"
>
> A female voice: It's true!

Asma:	No, we put on underwear [*petite culotte*] and then we walk naked [laughs].
Aziza:	And me, I said, with my eyes I said, "You making fun of me [*mon queue*], ah, who do you think I am?" I said. "Listen, trousers and jeans and all of that also exist back home. Do you think it is only here?" So, you see! (group interview, French)

Within the dominant representation, the girls continue, Africa is stereotypically cited in terms of war, genocide, awkwardness, backwardness, and poverty.

Ossi:	Africa for them…[interrupted]
Asma:	But we are more…[interrupted]
Ossi:	The forest, the jungle, the poverty, the war.
Samira:	Don't forget the animals: the lion, the animals, the giraffes.
Aziza:	There is one student who asked me, "Do you live, when you were over there [*là-bas*], do you live with lions?" (group interview, French)

As African students have, one has to take note of the fact that these negations of the African subjectivity and humanity are by no means unique to the visual mediatic representation. The arts, literary works, especially fairytales, children's books, and novels, and the daily newspapers are also sites in which Africa and Africans become *sauvage*.

Amani:	*You know why they are saying what they are saying*? Because of the fairytales they read in children books [*les petits livres*]. Ah, *Maxime dans le Jungle* [Maxime in the Jungle], ah. *You know* it is, it is…[interrupted]
Ossi:	*Le Roi dans le Jungle* [The King in the Jungle], *Le Lion* (The Lion).
Amani:	It is impression, and they think that we are a bunch of savages.

These impressions that are processed consciously and unconsciously through popular culture colonize people's imaginations, thus making them unable to imagine and see Africa and Africans otherwise. For example, it was hard for some White students at MV to imagine that their peers who came from Africa could be as rich materially and culturally as they were, if not more so, in some cases. Some African students fled their homelands only because of civil unrest, leaving behind or bringing with them substantial cultural and material wealth.

150   Chapter Four

> Asma: They don't know Africa the paradise on earth. They don't know that there we were living like the...[interrupted]
>
> A female voice: The kings.
>
> Asma: Really like princesses. But here it is not the same. They don't even know that, they have no idea of that.
>
> Aziza: Because over there, you know, *c'est la vie*, it is only because of the war did we have to move. (group interview, English)

Economy of Inhospitality: Forging a Separatist Culture

In this striated atmosphere of negativity and negation, claiming an African identity has become an unapologetic act of resistance, a political statement; and African students taking up Hip-Hop identity and learning Black English as a second language have become a second layer in this act of resistance, thus forging a different kind of being, a different cultural space, as we shall see. The virtue of being, however, Levinas (1998) has argued, has the social consequence of not being accepted. When they were inhospitably received by the dominant culture, African students looked for alternative identities, histories, cultures, and languages that were, on the one hand, subversive, and on the other hand, reflexive of who they were. They needed to centralize themselves to be able to speak; to strategically essentialize (Spivak, 1990) themselves, their identities, and their politics to make sense of a world that certainly did not want to make any sense of them; and eventually to "forge separatist culture" (Solomon, 1992). In this economy of inhospitality, where African students were blotted from the imaginary of the nation, and negatively imagined and poorly treated both inside and outside the school, it should not be a surprise that they stuck to their own cultural, religious, and linguistic groups in public and private spaces.

At Marie-Victorin, African students used their linguistic and cultural heritage as demarcation, as mechanisms to produce metaphoric as well as physical spaces. They gathered collectively in the cafeteria; played soccer and basketball almost exclusively; and in many instances, conducted their in-class activities together. As a significant symbolic capital, language became their solace. It was where they bonded, created a sense of community, and thus were able to combat the symbolic violence of this economy of inhospitality. This unfortunately created a too-different-to-mix-with attitude on the part of the students who came from the dominant culture. The girls put it thus:

> Amani: *Just live with your friends*, yah, you are going to be with those who understand you.

Aziza: This is why, this might explain why Somalis are always in their corner, because they tried the other corner, they are not accepted. They are not, *they're not welcome, you know. They say, "Oh no, he is too different. Oh, he is from, oh, he's from another place. He doesn't really, he doesn't know English."* You see things like that.

Asma: He is going to escape more quickly.

Aziza: This is why, this is why, you know, you go with your, your, your Somali friends, because you are going to understand each other. You could speak the same language, you have the same mother tongue, this is more than good, you see. Because they don't want to accept you because you are different, you don't speak English very well, you are an immigrant, you know, things like that. (group interview, French)

What is noteworthy here is the role language plays in demarcating social and group boundaries. Language has become an exclusionary practice, where the Somali language, for example, was deployed to exclude White Franco-Ontarians, and in the early days at MV, White Franco-Ontarians used English to exclude Somali-speaking students. However, as Jacques Derrida (2000) has argued, within an economy of hospitality, the ethics of reception lies entirely, or almost entirely, with the host. That is, as the host, White Franco-Ontarians bear the brunt of the ethical responsibility of having made African students feel that they were left out in the cold, with no personal or academic support. Yet, African students needed to function within this economy, and they used different strategies to do so. One strategy was to play the game with the same rules as the dominant groups. As Hassan put it, "*Je joue avec le système ou quoi!*" [I play with the system or what!]. This meant learning English, dressing in normative ways, "being nice," and performing well academically. In supporting Hassan, Samira (F, 16, Djibouti) set up the rules of the game this way:

In playing their game [*en jouant leur jeu*], you know, I play their game this way. They tell me "*tu es belle*" [you are beautiful], "*Oh, merci beaucoup*" [oh, thanks very much]. "You do that?" "Oh yes." "Are you going to be with me [as a fashion show partner]?" "No, thank you very much, but I already have someone else." That is the game. They want to play the game! (individual interview, French)

Some have argued that these rules are White, middle-class, and heterosexual male in nature (cf. Henry et al. 2000; hooks, 1992; Collins, 1990; Carby, 1986, 1992; Love, 2012). John Ogbu (1986) refers to it as "acting white," which I will discuss in the next chapter. For now, it is worth noting that the separatist culture is not a luxury nor is its execution fully conscious.

On the contrary, it was forged out of necessity. When African students' desire to fit in did not materialize, they used their language, culture, and religion as important paradigms of boundary setting, especially to demarcate *zones of comfort*. This demarcation took place in and through complex processes of encoding and decoding. For example, when a Somali-speaking student does not need to utter or semantically say much in order for other Somali-speaking students to understand him/her, this is because there is an already established unconscious decoding of each other's body, gender, race, language, and culture (see also Hall, 1997). This is not the case between Somali-speaking students and White Franco-Ontarians.

> Hassan: But the way I treat, say, other Somalis and students from another race [Whites for example] is a bit different. For when I'm with a Somali, I speak differently and we understand each other. But this difference is not out of malice, you see. The way I speak with a person from my culture is simply different than with a person from another culture. It is possible that we critique each other and speak in a tone that might be misunderstood. (individual interview, French)

To speak—in a tone or voice—is to assume a history, culture, memory, and language, which in turn assumes positionality, subjectivity, identity, and politics. After all, speech is always located in time and space.

Conclusion: Gimme the Low Down

Focusing again on Marie-Victorin, this chapter was divided into two sections. The first section dealt with the memories and histories of language learning in Africa as well as in Canada. In it, I addressed students' relationship to language and the sites of language learning. These sites include popular culture, Black popular culture in particular. By Black popular culture I mean music, TV programs, and movies. The second section introduced the ways in which Africa and Africans are culturally represented and imagined, and the impact of this on the politics of forging a separatist culture. Africa and Africans, I showed, are either utterly negated or negatively represented, which, in turn, impacts their processes of identity formation. This continues to create a striated rhizomatic process of becoming Blackness. Finally, African students identified Hip-Hop and Black English as sites of investment and desire, which I discuss further in the next chapter.

Notes

1   Here Asma is talking about her pleasure in learning to engage in conversation in English with students who used to look down on her and other African students because of

her/their very limited knowledge of the English language. This is the pleasure of knowing.

2 In my case, it was the Arabic language that dominated my mother tongue (Nubian), and became my first language. I therefore make the distinction between first language and mother tongue (see also chapter 1).

3 This is why during my university years in Sudan we used to mock those who "spoke like a book." These were individuals who spoke with lexics that nobody understood: The longer the words and more complicated the sentences, the more cultured and educated those persons were, or so we thought.

4 In my focus group interview, the boys narrated similar stories (mostly in English):

Sam:	L'anglais [English], uff, dad somethin', da'd, I had to, you know, learn [meaning: English is something I had to learn]. 'Cause, when I came, when you go somewhere, you know, around, you know, you go to a new country, you know, you have to, you have to get around.
A male voice:	You have to learn the language.
Sam:	Yah, you have to learn the language, yah.
A male voice:	Yourself to learn.
Sam:	Yah, and then to understand what people are saying in, what more people, you know, their moral or their views on things.
A male voice:	That something you need.
Sam:	That something that you have to know. I didn't have a choice, so I had to learn English, you know.
A male voice:	To communicate.
Sam:	To communicate with people, you know. If I didn't know then I will be deaf, you know. (group interview, English)

5 In another context, Asma argues that one of the reasons for feeling the urge to speak English was that "I didn't want people talking behind my back. I wanted so badly to learn English to show them that I could do it [laughs]. And to speak English like they do. And I am really, really, *I'm happy I did that. I'm very proud of myself*" (group interview, French).

6 Mr. T. was a host of a local Canadian Rap music program called *Rap City*, which is based on U.S. Rap music.

CHAPTER FIVE

"Peace and One Love!"[1]

A Rhizomatic Third Space:
Race, Language, Culture, and the Politics of Identity

Thus far, especially at Marie-Victorin, the modernist and unoblivious language of Black and White in the African student discourse is as irrefutable as the politics behind it. This pellucidity stems from students' own consciousness of their racial, gender, sex, and class social locations which, I have argued, in the case of all immigrants, is a product of socialization and displacement. In other words, what one becomes is an accumulative history and memory that is built in and through one's everyday interactions. In these communicative everyday interactions, at MV in particular, African students became aware of particularly their racial identity, which in turn was implicated in how they socialized their gendered, sexualized, and classed identities.

Juxtaposing my ethnographic gaze as the researcher against their narratives and bodily performances, and focusing once more exclusively on MV, I argue in this chapter that African youths are already in a rhizomatic third space. This is a space of in-betweenness where, by virtue of being displaced subjects, African students find themselves in-between cultures, languages, and belief systems. It is where gender, racial, and sexual identities are articulated through linguistic and cultural communicative performances. As we shall see, the cultural and linguistic memories and history that students brought with them from Africa were not all negated. On the contrary, they were performed concomitantly and in chorus with the new (Black) North American culture and linguistic practices. As a result of translation, the "old" no longer looked completely like the "old" nor did it look completely like the "new," but the two combined. To elucidate, I shall discuss two significant incidents, but before doing so, I show the impact of Blackness on students' identity formation and identification. It is through language, I conclude, that one can detect students' desires and investment in becoming Blacks. Culture, gender, and sexual identities are also performed in this rhizomatic third space.

Possessing Black Identity, Learning Black English

Identity as a process of identification and citation, I have argued, can only be accessed through performance (see Chapters 1 and 2). I have argued as well that African youth linguistic and cultural performances were, indeed, citations of the language of Black and White (chapter 4). That is, when African students came to North America as displaced subjects, they were positioned and asked through overt and covert mechanisms and structures to racially fit somewhere. These mechanisms included, among other things, teachers, curriculum, and university professorial representations (all White, and exclusively Eurocentric) and mediatic representations (negative and negating). Having to racially fit somewhere was directly implicated in student identity formation and language learning. In this section, I focus on the latter, especially BESL learning. Through linguistic analysis, I expand on the BE features I discussed in chapter 4: (1) the absence of the auxiliary *be*, (2) negative concord, and (3) the distributive *be*. The first two features were spotted in my interviews with younger females (fifteen years old or younger), which supports the argument that younger females were impacted by Hip-Hop as much as the boys and more than the older girls. Unfortunately, however, the data is limited to moments of code-switching and to interviews conducted in English, which are fewer than the interviews conducted in French. Nonetheless, I have collected enough data to support my arguments.

The Absence of the Auxiliary Be

In his now classic study, William Labov (1972) documented that omitting the auxiliary *be* is a common linguistic feature in Black English (BE). According to this feature, instead of saying, "they *are* jumping," one says "they jumping." I found nineteen occasions in which the auxiliary *be* was omitted. Here they are: "they, like, jumping," "no, it's true because we, like, so mad," "we, like, so bad," "and they, like, listening," "it's not, we not actually nurses, but we, like, keeping on insulting people," "and we, like, doing activities," "they selfish," "I just, like, laughing at languages," "they so cool," "everybody has opinion, these people, they mental," "Why? OK, I don't know, 'cause they stupid," "all my friends, we, like, laughing," "oh and we like, 'oh yah, we playing basketball, yah,'" "I just laughing," "and he is like, 'yah, you my second wife,'" "and we, like, all fighting," "that's why, and we, like, running away from you," "and we like, you know, you know, I was like, '*prennez la balle et jouez.*'"

Negative Concord

This is another Black English linguistic feature whereby the negation is doubled. Consider this sentence from Labov (1972, p. 194):

> Huey: And he said, "Nobody talks about my mother."

> Michael: Well I am not nobody; I am somebody. That's what he said. "I am not nobody; I'm somebody."

Michael's phrase "I am not nobody" would have been corrected to "I am nobody" in a "regular" classroom. Michael uttered what would be the norm in Black English, also known as African American Vernacular English (AAVE). I detected this linguistic phenomenon on four occasions in my interviews with the girls. In talking about her physical education teacher, who she found unpleasant, Najat said:

> It's like, everybody, you know, all he cares about is his daughter, you know. If somebody just dies or if I decide to shoot somebody, you know, he is *not* doing *nothing*. (individual interview, English, emphasis added)

In the same interview, Najat continued to complain about her physical education teacher: "It's like, 'Monsieur, you *don't* have *no* feeling,' you know." Third, while explaining how a group of African boys saw the relationship between basketball, Hip-Hop, and other Black cultural practices and the school, Aziza contended: "But they *don't* want, like, *nothing* to do with school. They hate the school, they do their own fun like playing basketball, and dat all they care about." The fourth and final occasion was during my female focus group interview. Talking over another student, one female student said:

> I go, "no, Monsieur. We ain't playing volleyball. I'm playing basketball." And he goes, "No." I go, "Wha, too bad!" And we *don't* do *nothing*.

Distributive Be

In her study of Puerto Rican youths in New York City, Lynn Goldstein (1987) defined the distributive *be* as "a form characteristic only of black [sic] English in which uninflected *be* is used to indicate qualities which are permittent rather than permanent" (p. 418). Goldstein gave this example of William, who chatted away that "When I watch a movie, a scary movie, right, I *be*, you know, I sometimes *be* thinking of it, you know, how you sometimes *be* scared." I spotted the distributive *be* on four occasions in my interviews with the girls and on one occasion with the boys: (1) "He **be** like, '*Oh, elle va être bien. Oh, elle va être bien.*'" (2) "I **be** saying this, tha, you know, just because I'm your daughter, man, you don't have to give me, tha, you know." (3) "So, I **be** like, staying three days. '*Bonjour,*' you know, 'madame.' 'Where were you?' I was like, 'Madame, I was celebrating. You have a problem? Let's go!'" (4) "I **be** back."

I also noted some lexical expressions that are specific to Black English. For example, expressions such as "he is wicked," "he is bad," or "he is nasty" are used in Black English to signify exactly the opposite; that is, "he is really, really good" (see Smitherman, 2000). In the following excerpt, Najat addresses the difference between the new student council, which is predominantly White, and the old one, which was multicultural and multiracial: "Last year was like, mostly *multicultural*. They didn't know each other and then they have **wicked**, you know, things. This year is like, yak." Talking about her White geography teacher, Najat continues: "I was like, 'Monsieur, I wish you can buy your wife a ring.' 'Where?' 'At Eaton's,' and then he goes 'OK, I'm gonna do that.' [laughs] He is so **cool**, he is so **wicked**."

Beside the BE lexico-semantic features, phonological features can also be detected, especially in the boys' speech. Taking on the role of the MC (master of ceremonies) or the DJ (disc jockey), Sam in chapter 4 was "checking the mic." In typical Rap style, Sam said: "One two, one two, mic check. A'ait, a'ait, a'ait." "A'ait" [a:ait] is in fact "all right," and phonetically pronounced à la BE. I noted this expression on many occasions in the boys' narratives.

The last feature of Black English is linked to what could be called "speaking through the female body." This is a concomitant act, a joinder, a juxtaposition between verbal and bodily expression, where one snaps one's fingers, moves one's head left and right, and utters a sentence such as "Excuse me!" By stressing the end of the word *excuse*, as "excuuuze" [ekskyooz], the speaker means to question the credibility of the interlocutor or simply to "give attitude." I asked Najat:

Awad: One thing I noticed is that you speak some kina [snaps finger], kina attitude.

Najat: That's like when somebody gives you attitude and that, I actually I wonna go and beat 'm up but, some of them do, but 'm not like that

Speaking through the female body is a symbolic illustration of how race and gender have turned into performative categories. In the case of African students at MV, however, it is more complex. Much like learning BESL, speaking through the female body becomes an act of desire and belonging. But desire and belonging are more complex categories in this context; they oscillate between striated and smooth spaces, between making and being made. Is Najat's desire for Blackness and BESL her own, or is it a reaction to how she is expected to behave as a "Black" person? I answer this question in the concluding chapter, but for now, one can say both processes (making and being made) are taking place in Najat's case and in the case of many African students at MV. The situation is different at Maxwell High and Sunnyside; I address that in the next chapter.

It is worth noting that when Najat snaps her fingers and gives attitude, she is using her agency and citing her own Blackness, but as we saw in chapter 2, this citation is not totally free from the eyes of power, the White gaze. Najat plays on this tension by going so far as claiming expertise on Black music and "Black stuff." As she put it, "Sometimes I hang out with friends, you know, and my friends are like, when White people wonna come and I will start talking to them, and here it goes: 'Hey, you guys wonna hang out with us?' And they hang out with us, and I will be like, teaching them how to do reggae, how to do Black stuff, you know."

"Black stuff" includes language as well. Here, clearly, the impact of Black English is prominent in the speech of both the boys and the young girls (such as Najat). They are influenced by the style as well as the linguistic content. Given the pleasure they take in listening and the desire expressed in their becoming Black, Hip-Hop/Rap becomes the medium through which African students access Black talk. The process of learning ESL now has a target other than "standard" English, and learning is implicating and implicated in identity formation, desires, and, above all, politics. One becomes Black because one is learning BESL, and one is learning BESL because one is becoming Black.

Besides being a medium of language learning, Hip-Hop/Rap for African students is also an expressive cultural space, a "language" where they access human and cultural experience of diasporic North American Black peoples. Their identification with it is generational on the one hand, and directly connected to their lived experience on the other. Reflecting on his investment in Hip-Hop/Rap, Jamal (M, 18, Djibouti) put it thus:

> Jamal: Rap is created as self-expression. Black Americans created Rap for this reason, to express themselves. How do I say it? Their ideas, their problems. If we are influenced by Rap, it is because we are young. It is for that we connect with Rap. If we could invest in Rap, it is because they [Rappers/African Americans?] speak about or they have the same problems we have. This is why we can integrate in Rap, *you know wha 'm mean*?
>
> Sam: *Wardap* [laughs]. (group interview, French)

"They have the same problems we have." We have seen that African students have experienced what it meant to be Black in Canada. Being considered as and treated as an *involuntary minority* is central to this experience. John Ogbu (1983, 1990) distinguishes between voluntary and involuntary minorities. The former are the professional, middle-class immigrants who voluntarily move from one place/country to another. They tend to have a comparative and dual system that allows them to compare and contrast languages, cultures, and belief systems. Their educational experiences in their new "home" tend to be influenced by their experiences in their homelands, which are usually good and pleasant. Significantly, when they encounter discrimination and other forms of social injustice, they tend to brush it off thanks to their pleasant experiences in their countries of origin. Involuntary minorities, by contrast, are the people who find themselves involuntarily in a minority situation. This is the case with, for example, African Americans who found themselves in the United States thanks to slavery and the Middle Passage. Involuntary minorities tend to have high expectations of their society, thinking like majoritarian groups, but because they have only one referential system that tends to be embroiled in and built around the history of discrimination and racism, they tend to be mistrustful of both the education system and the society at large. African students expressed the importance and the significance of historical continuity:

Juma: I think that we [continental Africans] are more lucky, we are more lucky than they [Canadian- and U.S.-born Blacks] are, or what? Because we were born somewhere, and we believe in something over there. We are more lucky than them.

Sam: We are from the motherland, you know wha 'm mean? (group interview, French)

The struggle over historical continuity is also a gendered struggle (hooks, 1992), and both are expressed in Hip-Hop and Rap.

Gender, Gangsta Rap, and African Youth: Who You Callin' a Ho?

Obviously, not all forms of language that are appropriated and cited, especially by the boys, should be uncritically engaged. Some of it is certainly horrifying and alarming. The boys not only used language violently but also abused it, and, in doing so, they exhibited a problematic form of masculinity. Often in Gangsta Rap, masculinity is equated with how "hard" or tough one can or should be, which is articulated in part in abusive language, including name-calling—"bitches" and "hoez" (whores). If the boys were influenced by Gangsta Rap, then Shapir's expression "all my niggers and my bitches" is not coincidentally performed and cited.

Joan Morgan (2004) and Ebron (1991) have argued that the use of "bitches" is a product of a public space that is predominated by men. It ap-

160   *Chapter Five*

pears that some African boys problematically take up, cite, and perform this language. However, it doesn't go unchallenged. Following the lead of Rappers such as Queen Latifah, Salt-N-Pepa, Lauryn Hill, Common, Mos Def, and Kanye West, a number of male and female students had reservations about this sexist language and cultural practice. Omer (M, 19, Ethiopia), for example, stated that:

> Rap is *cool*, right? You also watch, well, the songs, but I don't really like the people, the values of *Hip-Hop*; always insults of, although it is a small group you see, they always speak of violence, like *bitches* and things like that. I don't really like that. That is why I don't listen very often to Hip-Hop, but I only look around. (individual interview, French)

Omer's narrative points to an internal *agentic desire*; that is to say, he likes some parts of Hip-Hop and Rap and dislikes others. With agentic desire, agency and consciousness do not allow for a wholesale either/or. One is not a mimic, but an agent with contradictory desires. It is worth noting that although Omer is not a permanent dweller in the Hip-Hop scene, he is a permanent resident in the reggae scene. I noted this same agentic desire of Hip-Hop in female students. For example, even though she calls herself a Rapper and she does Rap, Najat contends that "you know, some Rappers are like, so rude. They all talk bitches and hoez. Who you callin' a ho?" (individual interview, English) Other females agreed with Najat:

Samira: OK, *Hip-Hop*, yes I know that everyone likes *Hip-Hop*. They dress in a certain way, no? The songs go well. But, they are really, they have expressions like *fuck*, *bitches*, etc. Sorry, but there is representation.

Amani: *No, no, that's the wrong side of Hip-Hop.*

Asma: *That's Rap.*

Amani: *Hip-Hop, listen, listen, Hip-Hop is poetry. Don't ever insult Rap 'cause it's poetry. It's something alive, it's, it's well done.* But you know, Awad, *there is all kind of styles.* There are many styles, out of which you have to choose one or two. (group interview, French)

At stake in Amani's comments is the notion of agency and style. Complexly understood, there is good and bad Hip-Hop/Rap, and what one chooses and takes up becomes a performative act of agency. For Amani, it seems, there is agency in what one wears, says, and performs. When intersected with hegemony, however, her idea of agency has to be complexified. There are historical and social structures that hegemonically influence and in some cases inculcate how one structures one's life and desire. According to Stuart Hall (1997), a central component of this hegemonic structure is capitalism. It impacts the distribution of symbolic capital and resources and determines the rules of the market. As individuals, Hall (1997) contends, we hardly ever ask this question: Why do we consume what we consume? Is it because of individual

> Everybody lying
> Talking about me
> But they can't see
> I'm a grown now
> They can't faze me
> ***
> We turned every base into crack
> We turned Hip-Hop into Gangsta Rap
> (Lemon, 2012)

pleasure and desire, or is it because we have to? That is to say, do we consume what we consume because we do not want to be left out or left behind?

Hip-Hop and Rap are no different in answering in the affirmative to these questions. Originally, they were created as counter-hegemonic discourses and practices, but interestingly, they themselves became hegemonic spaces (see Forman & Neal, 2004). They represent as much as they misrepresent. By centralizing violence and toughness, Hassan argues, Rap violates the sacredness of Black peoples' lived experience. Therefore, for Hassan, the responsibility of what to buy falls squarely on the consumer. As he put it,

> Hassan: Occasionally, Rap has an inappropriate language for the life we live, a world of violence and all that. Even if what they do is to sell music, there is no need for someone to give them moral courage [laughs]. Seriously! They want, they want to sell 4 million dollars. They want to do it, even if they use violence. But the person who buys has to decide between what he should buy and what he shouldn't buy. Yes, I think Hip-Hop is influential. A lot of people are influenced by Rap and Hip-Hop. There are a lot of people who are influenced by them. (individual interview, French)

The boys of all ages and the younger girls (twelve to fourteen years old) were clearly influenced by Rap lyrics, syntax, and morphology (in the broad semiological sense). For the most part, the older girls (sixteen to eighteen years old) tended to be more eclectic in how they related to Hip-Hop and Rap. This was evident in how they dressed, what language they learned, and their tastes in music. They oscillated between national traditional music, rhythm and blues (R&B), house, soft rock, and techno.[2] They kept an agentic desire:

> Amani: [...] Don't ever insult Rap 'cause it's poetry. It's something alive, it's, it's well done. But you know, Awad, there is all kind of styles. There are many styles, out of which you have to choose one or two.

Aziza: OK, I might listen to songs, some songs. Some songs I don't like, [others, I] really really like. There are some songs that I don't like, and some songs that I like, you know. (group interview, French)

For Omer, this agentic desire is an expression of maturity, which he sees as more prevalent in females:

Omer: Girls always think. If you watch a fifteen-year-old girl and a fifteen-year-old boy, if they are thinking about the same thing, the fifteen-year-old girl is more mature than the fifteen-year-old boy. Girls are always more mature than guys of the same age. (individual interview, French)

Male or female, old or young, eclectic or totalizing in taking up Rap, Hip-Hop, and other Black musical productions, African students have demonstrated a desire for and identification with Blackness. Their narratives also show that these youths were quite cognizant of this identification with Blackness, and the impact of race on their choices and desire. In the following conversation, Mukhi reflected on the impact of Rap (just one among many Black popular cultural forms) on his life and the lives of people around him:

Awad: But do you listen to Rap, for example? I noticed that there are a number of students who listen to Rap, ah? Is...

Sam: It is not just us who listen to Rap, everybody listens to Rap. It is new.

Awad: But do you think that that influences how you speak, how...

Mukhi: *How we dress, how we speak, how we behave* [italics added]. (group interview, English)

The situation was exactly the same at Sunnyside and Maxwell High, where "Hip-Hop is who we are," as Phil (M, 17, Nigeria) put it. In my interview with Sunnyside and Maxwell High students, all agreed that, "it is a nobrainer that we identify with Hip-Hop; where else would we go?" (Phil sums up the sentiment of the conversation).

Identity or Identification: A Question of Desire

Why do we desire and invest in certain representations? What is the role of desire in how we are interpellated, and what role does interpellation play in our identity formation processes? When it comes to African students at MV in particular, finally, why are they influenced by Hip-Hop/Rap in how they dress, walk, and talk? Thus far, we have seen the impact of Hip-Hop/Rap on students' linguistic practices, especially in learning BESL. Learning here was neither haphazard nor without its politics, investment, and desire. In this section, I seek to decipher the impact of desire on African students' identity formation processes. I contend that *one invests where one sees oneself mirrored.*

Hassan once asked rhetorically, why would a Black/African person invest in or play hockey? An African student, Hassan continued, would have a myriad of reasons to play and even appropriate basketball as a "Black" sport. Such reasons may include, among others, the affordability of basketball equipment (a net and a ball) and the representation of Blackness on the basketball court and among professional basketball players, including talented continental African players such as Manute Bol and Hakeem Olajuwon. In responding to my query on why African students play almost exclusively basketball and soccer, Hassan (M, 18, Somalia/Djibouti/Ethiopia) said,

> What is good for them [White Canadians] is not good for me. African students liked basketball because it is the only sport where you only need a ball and a net. You don't need things that would cost 4,000 dollars to go to a place that would cost 200 dollars every month [laughs]. Moreover, they are influenced everywhere because a lot of basketball players are Blacks; there aren't other people, how do I say it, African or Black people who play hockey. So, why that, why venture into this sport [hockey]? (individual interview, French)

Analogously, the desire on the part of African youths, particularly boys, to invest in basketball is no different from their desire to learn BESL. This desire, significantly, is anchored in an organic process of identity formation. That is, in a highly racialized context where African youth are asked to racially fit somewhere, they are interpellated by Blackness. By interpellation I am referring to the subconscious ways in which individuals, given their genealogical history and memory, identify with particular discursive spaces and representations, and the way this identification participates then in the social formation of the subject (identity). Put otherwise, as ethnographers, African students looked around and translated the Canadian/North American context. In doing so, especially in their early days in Canada, they identified with Blackness as a space of investment and desire. As the girls contended,

> Amani: We have to wonder why we try to really follow the model of the Americans who are Blacks. Because *when you search for yourself, search for identification, you search for someone who reflects you, with whom you have something in common.* [italics added]
>
> Aziza: And of course...

164   Chapter Five

> Amani: What is the big difference between the Blacks [in Canada] and those who are in America? We have the same past. We have the same history.
>
> A female voice: Plus the race.
>
> Amani: And we have the same race. (group interview, French)

Hassan supported the girls' view:

> Hassan: Yes, yes, African students are influenced by Rap and Hip-Hop because they want to, yes, they are influenced probably a bit more because it is the desire to belong, maybe.
>
> Awad: Belong to what?
>
> Hassan: To a group, belong to a society, to have a mode/fashion [*un modèle*]; you know, the desire to mark oneself, the desire to make, how do I say? To be part of a *Rap* society, you see. It is like getting into *rock and roll* or *heavy metal*. (individual interview, French)

One may conclude, then, that *identification is the inauguratory event or the starting point in the identity formation process*. Mukhi (M, 18, Djibouti) explored the issue of identification, arguing that

> Mukhi: We identify ourselves [*On s'identifie*] more with the Blacks of America. But, this is normal, this is genetic. We can't, since we live in Canada, we can't identify ourselves with Whites or *country music, you know* [laughs]. We are going to identify ourselves, on the contrary, with people of our color, who have our lifestyle, you know. We are not rich, for example, so we cannot identify ourselves with rich people. (group interview, French)

Mukhi evokes biology and genetic connection as a way of relating to Black America, and his identification with it is clearly stated. For all the students I spoke to, this identification was certainly connected to their inability to relate to dominant groups, the public spaces they occupied, and their cultural forms and norms. In my conversation with her about the genre of music she was listening to, Najat (F, 15, Djibouti) supported Mukhi's view:

> Awad: But do you listen to Rap music?
>
> Najat: Yah, I listen to Rap, reggae. all kina music, except for classic, heavy metal, and country [socially considered "White" music].
>
> Awad: No way?
>
> Najat: Not my type.

Awad:	Forget it [laughs].
Najat:	Not my type, not my type!
Awad:	Period. Ahm, do you actually, ahm you don't like them because you kina of heavy…?
Najat:	Heavy [metal], oh God! First of all you don't make any sense, and then they like, coming blablabla. I can just go in there and just go blablabla, and then my head, yak. (individual interview, English)

Summarizing my contention about the link between identity and identification, and lending support to Mukhi and Najat's views, Aziza (F, 18, Somalia) is worth quoting at length. She put it thus:

> OK, ahm, me, what made me feel good when I came here is that I saw, ahm, when I see the Blacks who come from America or Canada, I tell myself, or rather, I used to tell myself, they are Blacks like me, they have the liberty. They are they are chic. They are good and beautiful and all that. They dressed up really differently; you see things like that. It is like, that, that I used to see myself, wow! But I never saw, I never thought that they also were living in misery like racism and all that. They were pushed around every time. For example, they go to look for work, he is going to be pushed by, you know [Whites?], I never thought of that. I always think of the positive side. I told myself, "Oh, super, they are Blacks like me, my brothers and my sisters," you see. They have the liberty. Oh, wow, it is super, you see. I am going to their side and all that. But also I never understood that they were also living in misery. It was always something hidden that they were as well living with racism. And me, I used to tell myself, like, when I came here, I have never thought that I will be a victim of racism. But I was. (individual interview, French)

The moment of identification is patently pronounced here across gender and age. Aziza's narrative is of particular interest at this juncture for three reasons. First, it furthers my argument that moments of identification are quite significant in the process of identity formation. Rhizomatically, Aziza *named* Blackness as a site of desire and investment, thus translating the outside and making it part of her self. Second, to *name* is also to *be named*. The outcome of naming oneself and being named by others is where I situate the complex and rhizomatic process of becoming Black. Put simply, discursively, Blackness called upon, interpellated, and named Aziza as its subject. and in complex ways, Aziza in turn called upon and named Blackness as a site of desire and investment, as a subject location. This is a perfect illustration of the *rhizomatic process of becoming Black*.

Aziza's discovery of the Black plight in North America is indeed a cogent moment in this psychic process of becoming. That is to say, in her own discovery of how she is becoming Black, and the impact of becoming Black on who she identifies with, which markets she can or is allowed to enter and participate in, which doors are opened and which doors are closed, and what she can or does learn and how.[3] Thirdly and lastly, Aziza's sentence, "when I see the Blacks who come from America or Canada, I tell myself, or rather I used to tell myself, they are Blacks like me, they have the liberty" is particularly important. It points to a rhizomatic moment of realization and consciousness. Her phrase "or rather, I used to tell myself" points to something that has become a history, and names an accumulative memory and experience whereby what "I" used to tell myself has become part of my present reality. In other words, I became part of what I used to naïvely tell myself about: Blacks are my brothers and sisters.

Gendering and Sexualizing Performativity: A Politics of Embodiment

In the above quote, Aziza observed, "They [Black youths] are dressed up really differently." This observation articulates the gaze of an ethnographer who is interpellated by the camouflage and the collage of Hip-Hop. In this section, I decipher this gaze by looking at the impact of Hip-Hop on African students' lives, and the play of gender, sex, and age in how their choices came about—what I call the *politics of embodiment.*

To begin, Hip-Hop is an identity marker that is governed by desire, history, and Black fashion. However, as Weaver et al. (2001) have argued, Hip-Hop is also posited within a free-market, multinational capitalism and consumption that is "bent on making it big at any cost" (p. 9). As we have seen, Hip-Hop fashion is a camouflage of hairstyles and the latest fly gear: bicycle shorts, high-top sneakers, chunk jewelry, or "bling-bling," baggy pants, and polka-dotted tops. In the words of Paul Gilroy (1991), it is a "cut 'n' mix" of famous fashion trademarks and casual but expensive ones.[4] Because each piece is a fashion statement in itself, students put themselves through financial hardship to buy them. Omer (M, 19, Ethiopia) explains:

> [Hip-Hop fashion] is only *baggy*; no pants up to here [pointing to the lower side of his buttocks], just normal. It is *baggy* but normal, with basketball jackets like Polo and things like that, which have become à la mode, you see. So, on the one hand, it is a bit *gentleman*, and on the other, a bit Hip-Hop. It is mixed, you see. It is mixed. The vesto or garment on Hip-Hop side like Polo, you see, costs something like $100, $110, $130. It is expensive, but with quality. That is how you dress. My problem is to buy pants, clothes, you see. Now I want to buy a Polo jacket that costs 125 dollars at the Bay [a local chain of stores]. (individual interview, French)

Despite mammoth peer pressure, not every student succumbs to buying exorbitantly expensive clothes, nor to the motive, namely the consumerism, behind it. Pragmatically, Hassan argues that one does not need to buy an article of clothing for 80 dollars when it can be bought for 8 dollars:

> Hassan: You don't need to buy something for 80 dollars. You need to buy something for 8 dollars. Even if it is beautiful, it is convenient, you understand what I mean? Because there are a number of philosophers who say that appearance counts; it is our society. I don't dress for other people. I don't think of other people in order to accept myself when I dress. (individual interview, French)

Philosophically, Hassan is calling for a centered self where, first, one should care about one's look but it should not determine one's life, and second, race and gender are cornerstones. As we have seen, Hip-Hop is a racially gendered practice in that it is taken up primarily by African boys and younger girls. Found in their narrative, Hip-Hop is a "Black" fashion that is linked to being young and Black (in a transatlantic sense).

> Omer: It is called Hip-Hop because it is also a fashion; all Blacks dress like that whether you are Haitian or African, all Blacks dress like that. When we are young, we dress different, you see. When we are adult, we dress different. So, only, only to see, within the same group, to mark/recognize each other [*pour se reconnaître*]. (group interview, French)

For African students, moreover, Hip-Hop becomes an important signifier in their claim for a Black identity, especially when combined with Black English. In my discussion with Aziza about why Black/African students need both Hip-Hop and Black English, she said,

> More because they try to stick together, you know. To stay together, they need to preserve their own language, their own culture, their own fashion [*habit*]. When two Blacks say to each other, "*Yo whassup? Ya ya yo wadab ye ye*?," they are saying things like that to understand each other. They are like this because they are Blacks, you see. On the other hand, when he [Black person] speaks to a White person, he is not going to be comfortable like he will be with his Black brother. (individual interview, French)

Aziza is alluding to the impact of race on the process of identification and on how Hip-Hop is taken up. When deconstructed further, however, one can also see the centrality of gender in this process. Hip-Hop, then, becomes a gendered performance that involves the younger girls and the boys across ages. The older girls (sixteen to eighteen years old), in contrast, had a more complicated and nontotalized relationship with both Blackness and Hip-Hop/Rap. Even though they declared their full identification with Blackness, they understood Blackness as an inclusive category that can and does encompass a number of styles and fashions. As a result, much like their musical tastes, their dress sense tended to be eclectic: elegant middle class à la Parisienne, partially Hip-Hop, or traditional.

This eclecticism is expressed in and through liberal discourse whereby, when it comes to fashion, "dresses are for everyone," and what garments one chooses to wear is adamantly an individual choice. It is a question of taste, and as such, it should not concern anyone else. "It is just a choice," "Clothes are for everyone. Everyone can put on [clothes], Black, White, Asians, all, you see," "Clothes are for everyone. It is a choice that we made, you know, I don't wonna, I don't wonna dress like that. I wonna rather dress like this, you see! It is just a choice. It is it is nothing more, nothing less. It is a choice." These sentiments were heard all through my interviews with the older girls.

But we know in semiology that things do not mean; we put meaning onto them, especially what Roland Barthes (1983) calls "complex semiological languages": fashion and garments. Barthes (1983) explains that garments do not talk; therefore, they are already-always open for different reading and signification. As a corollary, the contention that garments are for everyone needs further examination. It is a contention that runs parallel to the *politics of embodiment*. This is a politics where our racialized, gendered, sexualized, and classed social identities are directly related to and influence the social positions we take up, the choices we make, and the different possibilities afforded to us. Therefore, the girls' contention does not account for the fact that, when it is taken up by a Black person, Hip-Hop takes on a different, extra meaning. Much like Rastafarianism, Rap, reggae, jazz, blues, dreadlocks, and braids, Hip-Hop is *socially defined* as a Black phenomenon or event (Kitwana, 2002).

Furthermore, given the influence of the French language and culture, Parisian fashion and style is exceptionally pronounced among the older girls. This is significant for two reasons. First, it displaces the tension and the dichotomy between "Black" and "White" fashion, however broadly they are defined, somewhere else: Europe/Paris. In doing so, these girls are calling for a nontotalized and more inclusive category of Blackness. Second, in the popular representation and imaginary, Europe is *seen as* a White space, even now (Stanley, 2011), and for this reason, these girls were accused of "acting White."

Aziza: When I put on clothes, there are some people, there are some Somalis who tell me, "Aziza, why do you dress like White people?" I say, "I don't. First of all," I say, "there is no such a thing which says that these pants are White, these sweaters are for Whites," you see. When people tell me that, I start to get mad, seriously. You see, I try to explain to them, "Listen, clothes are for everyone. There is no such a thing as White clothes, it doesn't matter to dress Black, OK. There are Whites in my neighborhood who dress like Blacks. They put on *large jeans, corkscrew, you know, big coats, you know*; sport things and all that, you see. Clothes are for everyone. *It is a choice that we made, you know, I don't wonna, I don't wonna dress like that. I wonna rather dress like this,* you see. It is just a choice. It is it is nothing more, nothing less. It is a choice." (individual interview, French)

Refulgently, Aziza demonstrates an inherent contradiction in the psyche of the older girls. On the one hand, she is ethnographically observing that Whites can and indeed do dress like Blacks, but on the other, she refuses to acknowledge that there is a separate category that may be called "Black fashion." It is significant to note, nonetheless, that these girls are quite cognizant of the fact that the very category they refuse to acknowledge—Black fashion—is the category upon which they are judged and positioned by the dominant groups. They refuse, in other words, to be easily positioned, and earnestly challenge the notion that one's clothing is one's self. The notion "show me your clothes and I'll tell you who you are" does not work with these girls. I had the following conversation with Amani (F, 17, Somalia), in which I asked her to reflect on the "acting White" accusation. She began by reiterating my question:

Amani: You [Awad] said, let us suppose that I don't know you [the girls], right?

Awad: Yes!

Amani: So, when you see us girls, with our hair, hands, you could tell that we were born in Canada. We are racially Black and you could completely identify us. This already influences you [to know] who we [the girls] are. So, this is really judgment. You think you know the being of this person.

Awad: No, it is not at all that. What I am trying to say is that there are some aspects of racism in it, Whites usually...[interrupted]

Amani: That explains why Whites react like that; [they] don't try to know who you are. They are going to judge [based on your clothes] instead of knowing you. This is the point. You see, that is the problem with [White] Canadians. Instead of knowing you, instead of asking you questions, instead of knowing the response to their questions, they judge. (group interview, French)

For me, the girls' music and fashion "choices" are products of the enigmatic position in which they find themselves. They have their own desires, but these desires are conditioned. Female agency itself, whether in Africa or in Canada, is governed by the socially constructed gendered identity. The female body is already prescribed in certain traditions, which include the notion that women are cultural, religion, and language keepers. Across ages, the boys, by contrast, appear to enjoy the leisure of different forms of North American and African patriarchal and heterosexual structures. These structures reinscribe the Father (in a Lacanian sense) as the central figure around which notions of family and respect are formed:

Musa: But we had, we also had the respect between women and men in Africa.

Sam: That's it.

Musa: But here [in Canada] there is no respect between women and men; we did, we did.

A male voice: That is the milieu, that is the milieu.

Musa: Yes, we had the religion which plays a very important role. We respect each other, the young respected the old, the old respected the young. The family respected the father. (group interview, French)

By invoking religion and the Father, Musa is obscuring three things. The first is his unproblematized idea that there is no respect between men and women in Canada; second, by citing the Father as the central figure within the family, the mother is put off the map (yet most of the MV students live with their single mothers); and, finally, the Islamic religious background of most of the students is firmly prescriptive when it comes to the female body, as we see next.

In the Name of *Elle*

According to Foucault (1980), when the body falls under strict surveillance, it tends to buy into prescriptive rules that work to disadvantage it. This was the case with girls. They bought into the idea that the female body should be the center of desire, fashion, cosmetics, and even virginity. For example, just before my focus group interview, the girls were looking at the French fashion magazine *Elle*. The conversation, mostly in English, followed in a "typically" female language and interest (see McRobbie, 1994):

Amani: Do you like it? I like it.

Aziza: This is nice; that is nice.

A female voice: And this, too.

A female voice: Oh not the skirt, you know. What kind of a woman? When you do.

A female voice: And of course, you have to have.

A female voice: Like me, of course, thank you.

A female voice: The shoes. That doesn't [Somali] lights and clothes for your head [Somali] and stuff like that…

This discussion about fashion comes as no surprise. A number of studies have examined the relationship between teenagers and fashion, cosmetics, and other "typically" female subcultures (Amati-Talai & Wulff, 1995; Conick, 2010; Jiwani, Steenbergen & Mitchell, 2006; Lea & Driscoll, 2012; McRobbie, 1994, among many others). This example is cited here to demonstrate that these girls are *caught in the middle*. On the one hand, they are typical teenagers "playing the game" (as Samira put it in a different context) and making use of what the Canadian context offers in terms of personal freedom—including control over their bodies and desires. On the other hand, however, they find that their bodies are already prescribed by religious discourse, where patriarchal, heterosexual, and generational questions are at the forefront. These questions are neither easily answerable nor resolvable. I had the following conversation with Najat:

Najat: No, I don't even go shopping with my mom. She is like, "Oh, you have to wear this." When, OK, we are going shopping one day, oh God, I don't know, I was in seventh grade, I don't know, eighth grade. My mom, I went wid her shopping, you know, and den she is like, being to this store, wid tide jeans and everything. I was like, "Mom, that's not my style, bye." I go to the next aisle [laughs], I put, like, on, ah [continue laughing]. She hates it when I wear, like, baggy clothes.

Awad: Yah? But you like baggy clothes, right?

Najat: I like baggy. They so comfortable, you know. But, she is like, "No, and I'm gonna put all your clothes in the garbage." I was like, "Oh, you can do that because you are buying some, so whassup." But…

Awad: Does she accept that you have a boyfriend?

Najat: Oh, 'm not supposed to date.

Awad: Why not?

172 *Chapter Five*

Najat: Till I get married. It's religion, but she doesn't know that I have a boyfriend.

Awad: She doesn't know?

Najat: No!

Awad: Wooo.

Najat: I be like, dead by now. I be like, you know. I don't know, people like, "Hi, oh my God, she is dead oh," you know!

Awad: What happened to her? Her mom killed her [laughs].

Najat: Because she has a boyfriend [laughs].

Awad: But do you actually have a boyfriend behind her back?

Najat: Yah, I'm not supposed to, like, come out and say, "Hi, I have a boyfriend."

Awad: But do you go out and meet them?

Najat: Oh yah, we go out to the movies, eh, you know.

Awad: Ahm, you don't have to respond to this if you don't want to.

Najat: OK.

Awad: Do you actually have sex with him?

Najat: No, that's like the last thing; I won't do that. Ah, ah, I respect my religion, you know. I'm proud of my religion, you know. But first of all, it's kina not fair not having a boyfriend, you know, not having sex, you know. (individual interview, English)

This is the tension and the complexity of the rhizomatic third space. Najat is struggling with her agency between, on the one hand, respecting religious codes and her mother, and on the other, fulfilling her desires in having sex, a boyfriend, and baggy clothes. Her struggle with the discourse of "honor," virginity, obedience, reproduction, heterosexuality, and "sin" is by no means an exception. I asked the girls during my focus group interview if they would have sex:

Samira: Having sex?

Asma: *Oh yah, I will have sex, OK. Yah, actually, actually.*

Samira: I can't say yes or no. Let us suppose for example…

Amani: *But I love our relation and…*

Absan:	Now, if I am going to marry this man, but I don't like him in an intimate relationship, sexual, I am trapped, I am trapped.
Asma:	*Ohm, let's say the S word, what's wrong with it?* [laughs]
Amani:	*You not Muslim any more.*
Asma:	*No, no, excuse me! Your man, your man,* it is not only you have sex; *how many have sex before they get married and they are still Muslims? If you do it, you are no longer Muslim? Is that what you saying to me?*
Amani:	*I'm talking about the way that the religion works. There is one way it works, not too many ways, OK! One way it works. And the way it works is that.*
Asma:	Get married.
Amani:	*Is that you not allowed to even [frequenter]* frequent/associate [with men] *ap ap, sorry, before you get married, OK, forget about sex.*
Asma:	It is not only how Islam is practiced.
Amani:	*Hold on, hold on, let me end, no, let me end. And then you, you, you are busy telling me, how am I supposed to ahm, ahm, marry the guy if I am not sexually attracted to him, right?*
Asma:	Yes, *that's what makes a good marriage, chérie. A grand passion!*
Amani:	*Hold on, we know that* [girls talking].
Samira:	I *didn't say I was religious. I say I'm Muslim, OK? Heart: from toe to toe* [girls are talking in Somali]. *I don't have nothing, I am still a virgin. So, don't you say* [laughs].
Amani:	*We are talking about the if, we are not talking the facts.* (group interview, French)

It is precisely the "ifs" that govern these girls' lives: if they have sex, this or the other might happen; if they lose their virginity, again this or the other might happen. For reasons beyond the scope of this project, these "ifs" do not seem to apply (at least not the same way) for the boys. Nonetheless, the internal dialogue in these girls is clear. There are, first, religious codes and interpretations of these codes, and second, situational gender desires. Evident as well is the disagreement among themselves, which leaves them with personal choices that might go against religious codes. As Asma put it:

> If I see a guy and I wonna get married to him, and if I get married to him and have sex after the marriage, how am I gonna feel if it's not good? Do I have to get divorce? Excuse me, but I am gonna have to check with him [laughs]. And I'm gonna

see if it feels good, and if I'm gonna commit my life to him. Listen, I need a partner to satisfy my needs to life. I am going to [have sex]. I am going to. 'Cause I need to be sure [that] the person I'm gonna commit my life [to/with] will be really there: to satisfy my need, every single day of his life. Thank you. I rest my case now. (group interview, English)

The Ideal (Hetero)Sexuality

Whether male or female, students' behavior and narratives are marked by a striking heterosexuality. In the interviews excerpted above, for example, even though men were not physically present, they permeated the females' discourses and imaginary. Like knights in shining armor, men come and save the girls from questions of "honor" and virginity, securing them financially and satisfying them physically. Women are thus turned into mothers, child bearers, and available sexual objects. In some cases, such as Amani and Aziza, African students come from families where men have more than one wife. These female students contended that polygamy is "disgusting," "denigrating," and "abusive" to women, and wondered why they didn't have the same rights as men. The ideal relationship for them is a partnership of marriage between a man and a woman:

> Asma: Me, I found that a marriage, a marriage is two partners. Two people who build a link, who have common feelings for the rest of their lives. (individual interview, French)

Yet, this ideal relationship may turn into a nightmare, a battle where men protect "their women" and women assault other women who are attempting to seduce "their men":

> Najat: She [her best friend Susan] is fine. Oh, gosh, she like, left [the school]. She is like, so sad because she gets the attention of the guys.
>
> Awad: Why? Guys like her?
>
> Najat: Check, she is nice and this, ahm, these girls, a bunch of girls, right? And then I was in the candy store and the whole thing, and then after that, what's called? Ahm, this girl comes to Susan, she is like, "you bitch" [because Susan befriended this girl's boyfriend]. And then Susan is like, "Hi," and then Mary [a West Indian friend of Najat] came, came, and they like, insulting us behind our backs. Mary came, Mary is like, giving them attitude, and then they all left [laughs]. It was so cool. I go, "Wait until I see them, I kill them." (individual interview, English)

When a woman calls another woman "a bitch," knowingly or unwittingly she is reinscribing the sexist language that sees women as seducers and sexual objects. As the seducer, she would most likely be blamed if she "fools around" with a married man, whereas he can brag about it with little censure or consequences. "Innocent" friendship between a man and a woman is inconceivable for African students at MV; all is understood in sexual terms. For their part, the teachers at MV reinforced these codes of behavior and did not escape being positioned themselves as sexual beings by students. Given the imaginary of beauty in the Western world, it is not surprising that for heterosexual women, the ideal is a White heterosexual man (with blond hair and blue eyes?).

> Najat: And sometimes she [the teacher whom Najat calls the "nun" because she is not married] is so desperate. Oh, she needs a man, I swear to God. She always goes like, "You have guest today," right? Now she is like, "Oh, don't forget, you know, to bring, you know, your boyfriend, a White man," blablabla. It's like, everything that you are telling, you know, we supposed to say no boyfriend at this age, no blablabla, but she is like, "Oh go get one," you know. (individual interview, English)

For girls as well as for boys, it is worth remembering that sexuality and sex are taboos. And unfortunately, how African students reacted to homosexuality and homosexuals was not a question I investigated thoroughly. Nonetheless, there were incidents where students exhibited some form of homophobia. For example, while I was filming Black History Month activities, a (gay?) African student was performing a sketch. Najat approached me and whispered in my ear, "You gonna put the fag on your camera?" Regretfully, I was unable to talk to Najat about her statement, or to the boy to whom she referred. However, the statement shows Najat's disapproval of homosexuals, which can also be read as disapproval of homosexuality.

Despite her disapproval, I knew at least two male African students at MV who were gay, but they were not part of this project. African students in general are confronted with the public discourse of sexuality in Canada, including homosexuality and lesbianism. In any case, African students in MV cannot escape sexuality. Building on my experiential knowledge as an African, two things are noteworthy. First (I fear generalization across the continent, but generally speaking), sexuality is neither an open discourse nor is it for public consumption in Africa. That is, unlike in the West, where sexuality is on display everywhere and people talk about it so openly, in Africa sexuality is still a private matter. In Muslim countries, sexuality is not only a private matter; it is restricted and a taboo. Islam has a significant role in this restriction. Discussion of the grounds for its prohibition of *el Liwat wa el Musahaga*—homosexuality and lesbianism—is beyond the scope of this project. In the present study, it suffices to say that students are caught between prescribed religious codes and personal choices. Second, homosexuality does exist in Africa; in Sudan, for example, the place I know best, there are houses designated as *beuoot el lawaita* (homosexual houses) that are usually known in the neighborhoods where they exist. Interestingly, lesbianism is never mentioned in African students' narratives. In sum, there are homosexual men at the school, but they are not willing to declare it or to talk about it in public (see also Heller et al., 1999).

The lengthy discussion in the sections above should be considered an introduction and overview of the rhizomatic third space, which I discuss next. To summarize, it is worth re-asking the following questions: After what we have seen thus far, will African students ever be the same? What is the role of the new Canadian context in translating and reproducing their Africanness? What role, in turn, does their Africanness play in translating the new context? What are the roles of gender, race, and racism in these processes? What are the capitals and rewards in this space? Finally, how are these capitals exchanged and performed? To answer these questions, I contend that African students choose, predominantly, to be a part of Africa *and* North America: at once continental *and* diasporic. To illustrate these arguments, I take what I consider to be two significant moments that might be seen by an outsider as moments of contradiction. The rhizomatic language of the third space is an attempt to understand these supposed "contradictions." It is set to argue that taking up and performing Hip-Hop culture, language, and identity does not necessarily mean a negation of being African. First I revisit this language and then offer my illustrations. Before doing so, I look at how students talk about their own fluid, complex, "contradictory," and rhizomatic identities.

A Rhizomatic Third Space—
Take I: Ethnography, Identity, and Cuttin' 'n' Mixin'

During my focus group interview with the boys, intentionally and provocatively, *j'accuse* Sam (M, 19, Djibouti) of "becoming Canadian." He said:

> Sam: I see myself as Djiboutian, man, I am Djiboutian 100 percent, man. *Don't judge a book by its cover, you know*. But no, *don't judge a book by its cover*. If, if someone puts on a certain style of clothes, you can't say that this person is like this or like that. Because *you don't know what he is inside. You have to know the person to judge him.* (group interview, French)

Following the logic of identity and performativity, this excerpt is vitally significant for many reasons, for five reasons to be exact. First, it points to the difficulty of *reading* identity ethnographically. This difficulty stems from the complexity and contradictory nature of identity (see also Hall, 2001; Meeks, 2007). Yet, second, students' identity performances are *read* semiologically. That is, how they dress, walk, and talk is judged and read by other people. This reading can either be positive or negative, and, interestingly, students are cognizant that others make judgments and read their bodies, clothes, and so on:

Hassan: Clothes for me are like, I say, people say that the eyes are the window to the soul. But they also say clothes are the representation of the personality. They say our society had developed, OK. They say one should never, never, like, judge on the appearance of a person, and you think they don't do it?

Awad: What you think?

Hassan: They do. My mother does it, my father, the principal, everyone does it. Teachers do it, but they don't say it, you see. This is why you have to respect your *outfit*: Show an image, because all what we are doing is projecting an image before people's eyes. And again, you have to play the system to your own advantage, you see. (individual interview, French)

Third, Sam's excerpt identifies the tension between the *verbal act of identity*—that is, the conscious signification that one gives to one's own identity—and *performance of identity*—that is, the spontaneous act of identity that is contextually specific and depends on the moment, audience, and topics. As Hall (2001) argues, there is an inherent discrepancy between the verbal act and the performing act of identity. When it comes to African youths in all three research sites but particularly at MV, part of this discrepancy is related to, first, the lack of meta-language that enables them to verbalize and signify their identities in totalized—or near totalized—ways and, second, the fact that there is no eloquent and "full" language that captures the essence of identity. This is precisely why it was important methodologically to make use of ethnography of performance, where I juxtaposed what was verbalized with what was performed.

Fourth, in the Euro-Canadian context, where Black identities are almost always cast in the negative, strategically, politically, and essentially, one may need to claim an identity to combat and resist this negativity. When Sam pronounces himself "100 percent Djiboutian," he is in fact claiming an identity that has become: a translated identity. Claiming a Djiboutian identity is a symbolic gesture in a market where being ethnic in the (formally) multicultural Canadian context might get you a job, but it is also where students are expected to be experts in their cultures. Fifth, and finally, Sam's statement "You have to know the person to judge him [or her]" addresses the issue of the imaginary: How can or should we go beyond what we see to imagine otherwise, to imagine subjects with full subjectivity and agency? To imagine otherwise, Blacks may be middle-class professionals, university professors, teachers, writers, poets, fashion designers, and so on, not only drug dealers, basketball players. and singers, as is commonly assumed in mediatic representations (Asante, 2012; Fisher & Model, 2012; Jackson & Moody-Freeman, 2011; Jaleh, 2012; Meeks, 2007; Razack, 2004).

These negative representations have a way of creeping into the subconscious and affecting people's perceptions, especially of Black people. Unfortunately, African students are no exception. Describing the difference between English-language and French-language schools, a male student at MV argued in English: "The difference [is that] when you go to English schools, they help you a lot, you know, the Black students, you know, 'cause they know always Black people have problems." Following a similar line of argument, during my focus group interview with the boys, Mukhi contended, "Now, now, it is part of their [African American] culture, *you know*, the drugs and all that." These conceptions did not go unchallenged by other students. Some students argued that drugs were/are a problem, but it is part of nobody's culture. Others reasoned that economic marginalization is a factor that pushes *some* members of the Black community to traffic and purchase drugs:

Sam: OK, me, I did not like what Mukhi said, because *everywhere you go there are bad apples. So, you can't judge people, you know*. But the drugs, *you know, it is not their culture, you know*, some of them use, it's like, everywhere. *It's not* [part of their] *culture, it is a problem.*

Juma: You can't call that style of living, *you know.*

A male voice: You can't say that. Some don't have a choice. (group interview, French)

These arguments indicate a dialogue among students about what it means to be an African in North America in general and Canada in particular. It is worth noting that Sam is not alone in claiming an African identity. Indeed, all African students have no doubts about their African identity. Here is a small sample:

Najat: 'M mean, am happy wid being Somali, you know, this is who I am, you know. I'm African and am proud of it, you know. I don't know everything in my culture, but you know, I love it. I won't say, "Oh, am not Somali." I won't say that. (individual interview, English)

Sam: I can't say that [that he has the same problems as involuntary minorities (Ogbu, 1983, 1990)—African Americans, for example] 'cause 'm from Africa, you know, straight from there man, hundred percent, you know. (group interview, English)

Asma: I see myself as African.

Aziza: Hundred percent African.

Amani: I am African, Somali.

Asma: Where you come from? Africa, I said. (group interview, French)

However, when I asked them to reflect on and verbalize the role African identities, languages, and cultures plays in their lives and in their engagement of the new Canadian context, their responses ranged from not knowing to describing either an essentialized, narcissistic, and Cartesian African identity that is stable and static across time and space, or a socially, historically, and culturally situated self and culture where African identities, languages, and cultures cannot escape translating and being translated by the sociohistorical specificity of the Canadian context. For African students, unfortunately, the Canadian context is an exclusive category where Blacks and other people of color will always be immigrants or imagined to be from somewhere else, unless they provide some capital which White society wishes to appropriate. When, for example, Ben Johnson was found guilty of using steroids in the Seoul Olympics in 1988, he immediately became Jamaican, whereas he was Canadian a few hours before his steroids scandal:

Asma: I say I am Canadian, I have the nationality, but I am not Canadian, 'cause in my blood I am Black.

Ossi: They're going to say that you are Canadian, do you understand what I mean? [laughs]

Amani: *Immigrant of, ah.* [laughs]

Ossi: Yes, voilà, immigrant or Black or, well, but I can't say he or she is Canadian.

Amani: *It is like Ben Johnson.* When he was discovered guilty of using drugs, they said, *"the Jamaican ah...."* [laughs]

Awad: Born!

Asma: When he won, they said, "the Canadian John, Ben Johnson and...[laughs]

Amani: *Glory, glory, honor.*

Asma: Hypocrisy, eh? (group interview, French)

By contrast, other students narrated a stable and never-changing African identity to which one can revert at will. Juma (M, 18, Senegal) put it thus: "But, I don't forget my culture. I don't know what will happen to it, but for me, my culture will always represent something [in my life or to me]" (group interview, French). Supporting Juma's view, Mukhi (M, 18, Djibouti) argued, "[My culture] will always be deep in my heart. I am not going to forget it. One day or the other, I am going to return to my culture or to my language, you know" (group interview, French). My own interest, however, lies with the third notion of identity: the complex, shifting, and historically specific. Here, identity is understood situationally; historical memories can fade away, and others can and do either replace them or translate them so they reappear in different forms and shapes; memories and subjectivities cannot escape historical and social forces; and, finally, the Old is not negated, but, students argue, the New is situationally appropriate and specific. In the following two excerpts, students express a deep understanding of culture, history, memory, and identity:

(1) Sam: However you live and however your lifestyle is and however you know and whatever you do, whatever surrounds you, that's your culture. That's what you will believe in. If you are Black in North America [for example], your culture is what surrounds you and what affects you in how you live right now, today, tonight, this second, you know what 'm mean? That's what it is, boy.

A male voice: Four hundred years, that's their [diasporic Africans'] culture.

Sam: That's something I know, but that's something that was destroyed. That's destroyed now, and you can't [just say they lost their culture].

A male voice: They lost, that's what we are saying, they lost it.

Mukhi: They lost it, but they gain another. (group interview, English)

(2) Musa: Here, we are in Canada, you see. We are going to keep our culture, but at the same time there is the new technologies, the new musics. There is also glamour and modernization of the cities and towns.

Mukhi:	The way we dress, the way we talk; we are in Canada. It is like we can't dress in, like, Raphar or our Galdoté, *you know*.
Sam:	*Tight jeans, you know.*
Mukhi:	The small *angoloté* [phonetic transcript] [it is actually called *macawiis*, *khameez*, or *koofiyad* for men and *direh*, *jalabeeb*, or *coantino* for women], you know, the small cloth we put around [the waist], it is like the way we dress back home. We need to mix in different genres of dress here. The way I am dressing now [à la Hip-Hop] is because I am influenced, you see, and that is why I dress the way I do. Back home, for example, we put on boubou and all that. But I don't find it embarrassing to go out like that. But I feel more comfortable with clothes like the ones I have on now, you see! (group interview, French)

Mukhi's last statement draws us closer to the complex language of the rhizomatic third space. In it, the New "mixes" with the Old in ways that do not look fully like the Old or the New, but the two combined. There is no longer simplistic, modernist opposition, but rhizomatic, complex, postmodern simultaneity of existence. Within the latter all is historically and socially situated. Therefore, given African students' identification with African American culture and language, the rhizomatic third space is performed through these symbolic capitals. Hip-Hop culture and language are performed side by side with African students' ("Old") languages and cultures, including French, Somali, and Arab/Muslim culture and lexicons. What is more, I also observed the phenomenon of what Rampton (1995) calls "crossing." This is a phenomenon where non-native speakers of a language recognize and use certain terms and expressions to create a bond and affinity with native speakers. As with the Black stylized English discussed previously, language is used here for purposes beyond simple linguistic expressions. This is the case with Juma. Juma is a Senegalese Wolof speaker who was living with Somali-speaking youths. During my group interview with them, someone knocked on the door:

A male voice:	Open the door, *boy*.
Sam:	*Who told you he will?*
Awad:	Who is it, what is it?
Juma:	*Diin Shimbir* [Somali: turtle bird]. [laughs] It's true, eh? (group interview, French)

Another example of crossing is the influence of the Jamaican patois. Given the fact that a sizeable percentage of African Canadians are of Caribbean descent (StatCan, 2011), and that they are accessible to African students in the city where this research was conducted, it is not surprising that some of their lexical features and musical genres can be detected in African students' musical and linguistic repertoires. Note these three examples:

(1) Sam: Me, I am African, the true African *man, you know*. I am Djiboutian *man, bumbo clatt, you know. I am telling you, man.*

(2) A male voice: Shit, you come closer *bumbo clatt* [*bumbo clatt* is an anatomy, a derogatory term in Jamaican patois (see Solomon, 1992)].

(3) Aziza: *Malcolm X, Martin Luther King*, they were all assassinated, why? Because...

Amani: *Revolution* [with Jamaican accent, pronounced: *ravalushan*], *all my people thinking.*

A third event of crossing is reggae, which had a musical influence on African students. Omer (M, 19, Ethiopia), for example, became the "expert" in patois and everything Jamaican/Caribbean, so much so that he was called "the Jamaican." He had dreadlocks and listened only to reggae. For me, Omer's case raises the question of desire in relation to learning. *We learn once we desire what we learn, and once we can gaze on the rewards and see them on the horizon*. Omer likes the drumbeat of the music and the cut 'n' mix in reggae, where more than one tune and lyric are played by a DJ. After he made me listen to a reggae song, Omer said:

> It's like that, it [the tune] continues for two minutes, three minutes, or something like that. It is for this reason I like reggae, in one lyric you find more than one song. The patois, I listen to reggae since 1991, you see. It is not a problem to understand, but I don't speak it. It is not a problem to understand what the song is about, but there are like some words that I don't understand. When I am in the shelter, I call sometimes my Jamaican friends and we listen together. I ask them then what this or that means. I have a desire to learn. With them, I can talk and this was how I learned patois. (individual interview, French).

A Rhizomatic Third Space—
Take II: Multiple Selves and the Language Question

Thus far, in the discussion always focusing on MV, African youths have expressed complex, shifting, contingent, and multiple selves. My aim in this section is to show, ad interim, that each of these contiguous identities is expressed in and through language. In the excerpts below, for example, different linguistic and cultural capitals are performed by African youths, with, of course, various degrees of availability, mastery, and production. These capitals include: French (lines 1, 3, 4, 8, 10, 11, 12), Arab/Muslim culture and language (lines 2, 5, 8, 12), Somali (line 12), Hip-Hop identity, dress, and culture. and Black English (lines 4, 6, 9, 13, 14, 15, 16, 17, 18, 20, 22, 35, 36, 37, 38, 42, 45, 47, 49), and patois (lines 19, 25). To reiterate, my contention is that each of these symbolic capitals represents a subjectivity, an identity within the speaking "I"; and to illustrate, I will revisit what Aziza said in Chapter 2. Reflecting on moments of code-switching between English and French, Aziza observed, "It is like you're detached from your French side when speaking in English." Her "French side" is part of who she is, part of herself, identity, and subjectivity. It is a "she" within her. Thus, there is not one "I" but multiple "Is" within the speaking-subject (see Cixous, 1994). Each "I," according to Cixous, is brought out and brought up depending on whom one is speaking to, what one is speaking about, and when, where, and how. Ad interim then, one may argue that each linguistic code-switching from English to French to Somali etc. is indeed or can be taken as a performative act of each "I" within the self. That is to say, when a student code-switches from French into Somali, she is slipping from one subjectivity, one "I," into another "I." In the following excerpt, for instance, which is taken from a video recorded at the end of my focus group interview with the boys, African students demonstrated the subjectivities, the "I"s available to and within them. These subjectivities are performed through linguistic and cultural capitals. (In the transcriptions I italicized Arabic terms and also italicized English-language sentences in mostly French-language sentences and French-language sentences in mostly English-language sentences. I transcribed the Somali, Hip-Hop, and AAVE expressions and provided their rough translations, which are at the end of each sentence):

A male voice: Alors ferme la voilà ah ferme [So, close it!].

Sam: *Wallahi* [in the name of Allah], I don't believe that, man, you know, *wallahi bellahi* [I swear in the name of Allah].

One male voice: Ça doit être 50 pièce *man. Wardap!* [It must be 50 bucks, man. I swear!].

Juma: Yo, toi. [You, you]. [noise, laughs]

Sam: [laughs] Juma, man, *wallahi bellahi.*

Juma: *Yo, yo, bouggie,* c'est moi. *Watch the music!* C'est le même mot qu'on-avait. Tu sais qu'est-ce que j'ai dit à Madame Davy? Je l'ai ménacé verbalement. [Hey you, bouggie, it is me....It is the same word we learned. You know what I told Mme Davy? I threatened her verbally.]

A male voice: Ehha!

Sam: *Wallahi,* fuck, *c'est pas vrai,* man. I be back. [In the name of Allah...it is not true, man.] [TV background]

Awad: Viens, viens, viens ici! [Come, come here!]

Juma: Oh, where you going, man, sit down, have a seat, man. From your...*c'est quoi?* [...what is it?] [laughs]

Sam: *Je reviens,* man [...], you know. It's from Mecca, you, represen'in [pronounced: *repreze'in*] you know, Mecca a'ait [pronounced: *a:ait*]. You ask. [laughs] Waxaan faley waan faleyba. [Somali: You did worse than me.] *Wallahi bellahi,* hooyadey [Somali: my mother]. A'ait a'ait. You know wha a mean? Represen'in Q7, you know, you know wha a mean? [I'll be back...you know. It's from Mecca, you, representing you know, Mecca, all right...You did worse than me. I swear in the name of Allah, my mother. All right, all right. You know what I mean? Representing Q7, you know, you know what I mean?]

A male voice: Q7 in the house.

Sam: Yo, a'ait. This my man Jamal, you know wha a mean? [You all right. This is my friend Jamal, you know what I mean?]

Jamal: Q7. [Crew or gang name]

Sam: Represe'in AQA, you know, dig it, you know wha a mean? [Representing AQA, you know, you understand what I mean?]

Jamal: Yo, ward'ap. [You, I swear!]

Sam: It mean you know me. Sam AQA, you know wha a mean?

Jamal: Ras-ta, wardap, 'n the house. [The rasta is in the house, or present.]

Sam: A'ait! [All right!]

Jamal: Wheda book, yo, wordap, kick it like this man. [Where's the book, you swear, kick it like this man.]

Sam: Kick some freestyle, yo, wha that? Shapir, you know. Represe'in. Check dem, check the last style 'f me man. Tura, tura, tur around. Yo da de last style. Show dad shit, man. Yeeh, wardap. [Kick some freestyle, you, what is that? Shapir, you know. Representing. Check them, check the last style of my man. Turn, turn around. You, that is the last style. Show that shit, man. You, I swear!]

A male voice: African style and shit, you know wha 'm sayin [you know what I am saying]? Just trying to keep.

Sam: Da [that] mean you don't have to rap up, you know.

Jamal: Ya mon! [with Jamaican accent: You man!]

Awad: Go, go, kick it, kick it!

Jamal: Musa in the house.

A male voice: It's just like we've the [...] you know, M U S A.

Jamal: Musa!

Sam: You know wha a mean? [You know what I mean?]

One male voice: Ya mon!

Jamal: Italian boy from Sicily. [laughs]

Sam: For real, for real!

One male voice: For real man, for real.

Jamal: Niggas [Not audible: don't ask to come back?].

A male voice: Niggas.

Sam: Represe'in. [Representing]

A male voice: [...] in the Black who the nigga is. All the niggas wid dat watch, that shit, you know wha 'm saying? [...in the Black who the nigga is. All the niggas with that watch, that shit, you know what I am saying?]

Sam: So that's a rapper!

Shapir: No no no Bob, no nasty, no Bob nasty see this shit.

A male voice: I told you in those things where they…

Sam: Hold on, check 'at a'ait; check, one two one two my name is SA. Sa'am….[Hold on, check all right: check, one two one two my name is SA. Sa'am]

Juma: Ohh!!

Sam: Represe'in Q7. [Representing Q7]

Juma: Ohh.

Sam: I represen to the fullest don fool around. 'Cause amo, you know, 'm mighta hit you, so yo, ama, eh? You know 'm sayin? I won, won, I don't wonna give all my secrets, you know wha 'm mean? So, dat how it is. [I represent to the fullest [so] don't fool around. Because I am, you know, I might hit you, so you, I am, eh? You know what I am saying? I don't want to give all my secrets, you what I mean? So that is how it is.]

Juma: I don't wonna give all my secrets. [laughs]

Sam: Yo, that's enough rap. So, peace. Yo, time out! (freestyle group interview, primarily French and English)

There are many interesting aspects of these excerpts. First, it may be incomprehensible at a semantic level, but there is a reason for this. These excerpts are an outcome of freestyle conversation and were captured after a long group interview with the boys. As such, I am not interested in semantics but in the complexity of code-switching. Second, the influence of Hip-Hop/Rap language is exceptionally pronounced: "respect to my main man," "reprez'in Q7," "peace out, wardap," "'am outa here," "I am trying to say peace to all my niggas," "Wheda book, yo wordap," and so on. The contention that Hip-Hop influences African students' speech needs no second look or discussion. Finally, the lucidity of code-switching is remarkable. Given my previous arguments about the relationship between language and identity, one may conclude that these boys have entered a rhizomatic third space. But entering this rhizome space is neither gender neutral nor without hardship.

The rhizomatic nature of this third space is certainly conditioned by gender. Because of religious and social scripts and traditions, the female and male bodies of African students at MV are prescribed and interpellated differently. As we have seen, the female body seems to fall under a stricter religious and social code of conduct; it is not as free to float. One may thus conclude that, as part of the process of becoming Black, the rhizomatic third space is experienced either as smooth or striated space. The female body, I suggest again, did enter and experience the rhizomatic third space as a striated space. With a lot of difficulties, restrictions, and reservations, this was done either as an act of resistance or as a conscious utilization of one's agency. Indeed, the two examples below of the performance of the rhizomatic third space include the female body as a central figure. But first, it is important to look into how students understand and hence verbalize the rhizomatic third space.

I asked all research participants at MV: "How are African students engaging the new Canadian context, with its multicultural population and policy?"[5] The following two responses are as close as students came to the *verbal performance* of the rhizomatic third space. In their responses, neither Mukhi nor Amani see the New in opposition to the Old, and taking up the former is not a rejection of the latter:

(1) Mukhi: My culture is something I am proud of. I would like to keep my culture, but at the same time, you know, I am going to be very close to Canadian and particularly Black peoples. I am going to even be friends with them, you know, but also hold onto my culture. (group interview, French)

(2) Amani: You know, in any culture, there are advantages and disadvantages, strong points and weak points. I will keep the strong points and leave the rest. There are points we love about our culture and others we don't like. So, it's about making choices; do you accept the weak points [of your cultural heritage] or don't you? But that doesn't mean I am rejecting my culture when I choose a new one, I keep what's valuable in my culture. (individual interview, French)

What Mukhi describes as an ongoing negotiation between his and the North American Black/Canadian culture is something with which African youths are quite familiar. As he said in the previous section, "We need to mix in different genres of dress here." But this need for cuttin' 'n' mixin' of different genres of dress, language, and cultural norms, which I term negotiation, does not come to be by a conscious act. Indeed, a considerable portion of our negotiation with what surrounds us takes place unconsciously. In the case of African students, the New is not a path we open and slip into, nor is the Old a dormant and secure place resting in peace. Au contraire, negotiation requires arduous tasks and difficult choices.

This tension of negotiation is eloquently expressed in Amani's excerpt. The result of translating and negotiating the Old and the New is a language, a space of in-betweenness where the "strong points" are reproduced and the "weak points" are seriously questioned. This space of in-betweenness does not allow for simple claims. As much as African students have claimed Africa, they also have claimed Canada as a homeland: "It is our society" (Hassan); "We have the same past [as African Canadians]. We have the same history....And we have the same race" (Amani); "it is good to know your country [Canada]" (Ossi). Canada is now part of them, part of who they are and what they have become. They belong to *a* Canada, which is most likely Black. Nonetheless, they belong to an inclusive "we." For its part, Africa is now a rich history, memory, cultural, linguistic resource and symbolic capital. It gives them a sense of identity, helps them to articulate their desires, and aids them in the process of integration. When Africa meets Canada in downtown Montreal, Toronto, Calgary, or Vancouver, it is metamorphosed into new and not so easily recognizable forms. The product of this metamorphosis is double-edged, at once Canadian and African: a rhizomatic third space.

A Rhizomatic Third Space—
Take III: Are These Really Moments of Contradiction?

To further illustrate the rhizomatic texture, nuances, and complexity of the third space, in this last section I introduce two extracts from my weekly journal entries. The significance of the two moments these excerpts describe stems from the contention that they can be (read as) moments of contradictions. The language of the rhizomatic third space is developed precisely in order to argue otherwise, to make complex the identity reading and the reading of identity. They may be moments of tension, but not of contradiction. As displaced subjects who encountered new social, cultural, and linguistic spaces and practices, African youths have *become*. They have become a product of translation and negotiation. To negate the Old or the New is to obliterate part of what has *become*. Because the rhizomatic third space is an extremely complicated language of in-betweenness, it does not have a fixed shape or form. Its rhizomatic shapes and forms are complexly performed in these extracts:

> 1. February 12, 1996. It was during lunchtime that I was sitting in the foyer of the school, just under the best students recognised by the school. Najat [F, 14, Djiboutian] and a group of Black girls were holding a tape recorder which they brought with them. They stopped in the middle of the foyer on their way from the gym to the library; two girls wore *hijab*—Islamic headscarf. "School sucks," Najat said to me in English. At the beginning of her second sentence, one of the girls with her plugged in the tape recorder: It was LL Cool J [an African American rapper] rapping. Najat turned around and spoke to one girl in Somali, and hereafter everyone joined in the dance. Hands were moving, bodies were swinging and the girls were talking in Somali, French, and English. Two girls were putting on Islamic *hijab*, others were in the Somali national dress of boubou—a piece of cloth put around the waist, others were dressed in baggy Hip-Hop dress.
>
> Later that day, around 5:30 pm to be exact, I saw the same group of girls. They were part of Black History Month (BHM) activities. They changed their clothes, along with other girls, either to Hip-Hop or traditional African dress from South Africa, Somalia, Gabon, and Zaire [now known as Democratic Republic of Congo], among others. All participants in BHM activities continued to practice intensely for 45 minutes. They then took a break, during which Yusuf [the acting African elder and the sole organizer of Black History Month events (he received no help from the school or from any teacher)] was acting as the DJ. Yusuf played LL Cool J followed by Queen Latifah followed by Toni Braxton followed by African music from Zaire, Egypt, and Somalia. Almost every single person in that space was dancing, and those who knew the songs, including most of them, seemed to mimic and recite them. The hairstyles seemed to vary from dyed to dreadlocks to African braids; and

during and after the practice, everyone was code-switching between English, French, and mostly Somali language.

2. April 4, 1996. Picture this: it was lunchtime. Amani, Aziza, Ossi, Asma, Samira, and five African boys were sitting on the ground of the second floor reviewing for a test. The girls were dressed very elegantly and à la mode: tight jeans with wide bottoms, white and coloured blouses with long or short sleeves, black and white sweaters, and two had Victorian hats. The hair was a fashion show: braids, ponytails, dyed short hair with a long braid descending by the side, and corkscrew style. Their faces were beautifully done with soft makeup. The boys, on the other hand, dressed either in a Hip-Hop style with baggy clothes, topped with sports sweaters or baggy basketball T-shirts, or in traditional African dress. Interestingly, the two boys who wore traditional African dress also dyed their hair blond and brown like the girls. Boys as well as girls were code-switching primarily in English and Somali, but also in French whenever they were talking academically. They were discussing nineteenth-century European literary trends, among them humanism. Michael Jackson was playing on Aziza's tape recorder, and some were dancing to his music.

Conclusion: Gimme the Low Down

Clearly, the code-switching in these excerpts is no longer just linguistic, from English to French or Somali, for example; it is also cultural. Africa, Islam, Black popular culture/Hip-Hop, including LL Cool J, are all to be found in the same space. In this rhizomatic space, the New mixes with the Old in ways that do not polarize or oppose each other. These nonoppositional performances and mixings can only be a product of "in-betweenness." A third rhizomatic space is thus created and given birth to. It is clear both boys and girls entered this complex space of in-betweenness, though girls entered it with considerable difficulties, reservation, and restriction. This is because male and female bodies are prescribed differently in religious and social texts and traditions. Yet, importantly, the translation and negotiation of the Canadian and North American context in general was highly influenced by racial apparatus. Language, culture, gender, and sexuality are all part and parcel of this apparatus. In a climate of negation, I have shown, African youths felt the need to claim an African identity, a New ethnicity (Hall, 1990) that needed language, history, politics, and a location where one could be able to speak and desire. The end product is a rhizomatic third space of in-betweenness where the Old intermingles with the New. To be in this space, for African youths, is to become, and yet to become a double-edged product, an ambivalent one.

Notes

1   As I indicated in chapter 4, this is typical Rap language that is usually said at the end of a lyrical performance to show love for the audience. The phrase was cited by a Somali-speaking boy at the end of a focus group interview.

2   Listening to house and techno music, however, because they are socially read as "White" music, provoked the accusation of acting White (Ogbu, 1986). Using his ethnographic gaze, Omer observed, "But first of all, Amani, she is different from the others like Ossi, Asma, and Aziza. They are Somali of the, how is it called, *house*, you see, *techno*....Techno is the music tchtchtchtch, like that, you see. They listen to these kinds of music, whereas Amani listens to R&B, slow music like Whitney Houston, Toni Braxton....Amani, she always liked R&B music, Whitney Houston. So, she prepared, she really chanted, you see." Listening to R&B or house is not exclusive, as Mercer would have argued (1994). On the contrary, one can listen to R&B, soft rock, reggae, and Rap all at the same time. Of interest are the notes I made on several occasions in the school when Amani was invited to sing, particularly R&B music. One of these occasions was the Black History Month, when Amani sang Toni Braxton's "Unbreak My Heart." I wrote in my diary that "this performance by Amani was an illustration of race performance where she did not only recite Braxton's song but, more significantly, she took on the role of a 'Black' singer."

3   Omer argues that the plight of Black people in North America, across genders, is worse than that of Whites, including White women. Even though Blacks and White women are both in socially disadvantaged positions, White women, he argues, can be found in principal, vice principal, and managerial and top positions, but Black women and men, save for rare exceptions, are nonexistent in these positions. Despite enormous progress made since this study in mid-1990s, Angela Davis (2011) argues that we still have "a lot of work to do." For Omer, "Even, even women, White women, you see they are vice president, president, you see. Do you see any Black in these positions? This is not equality. You see even Blacks are worse than women, than White women. Look, this is what I am talking about, you don't see a Black person as a vice principal while you see two, three hundred in this school, wherever you go in high schools, you will see plenty of White women who are principals, or vice principals. Or, you can also see two women, principal and vice principal. Do you see Blacks as principals?" Brian (vice principal at Maxwell High) agrees with Omer and Davis that "we are only starting to scratch the surface."

4   It is worth noting that Black America is famous for cuttin 'n mixin, and it does so consciously (Love, 2012). It is a phenomenon that might be called *ad interim mob branding*. To explain, as we know, there are certain fashion companies that market their products to Black America (FUBU, for example), but most companies do not. In a very shrewd way, Black America targets companies that do not market to them (e.g., Tommy Hilfiger) and mobs it. For a period of time, they take it over and, mostly through Hip-Hop, they popularize it for the rest of the U.S. population and the world. Interestingly, once others start to take up the fashion, Black America moves on to the next brand, label,

or company. This mobbing is not wholesale. That is, you do not dress Tommy Hilfiger from head to toe; you highlight Tommy Hilfiger (with a T-shirt, for example) and mix it with something else. This way, you give yourself the freedom to move in and out of certain labels and fashion.

5   African students, it seems, have bought into and were ready to defend the praxis of the Canadian "mosaic," as opposed to the U.S. "melting pot":

Musa: Juma, look, in Canada, there is respect for the cultures of others.

A male voice: OK, in the U.S., there is no respect for culture, everybody has to be Americanized. Everyone has to be American. Here, in Canada, it is different. Once you have a culture, people respect it. You dress however you want to. You have your Muslim religion.

Juma: This is also the case in the States.

Musa: It is rare in America, it is rare, but everyone has to be Americanized. In Canada, it is called the Canadian mosaic, this is what exists in Canada. This is why in Canada people say Canada is the best country in the world, you see! (group interview, French)

CONCLUSION

What's the Dillio?[1]

Towards a New "Ticklish Subject": Pedagogy of the Imaginary as Integrative Antiracism

> In South Carolina, I had been an African. In Nova Scotia, I had become known as a Loyalist, or a Negro, or both. And now, finally back in Africa, I was seen as a Nova Scotian, and in some respects thought of myself that way too...But even as I learned new words and phrases each day, I wondered just who exactly I was and what I had become...Without...any people with whom I could speak the languages of my childhood, what part of me was still African?
> Aminata Diallo, cited in Hill, *The Book of Negroes* (2007, pp. 385–386)

Within an economy of power where Blackness finds itself sealed into objecthood, and where its meaning is closed and its multiethnic, multinational, multicultural, and multilingual nature is repudiated, the ultimate question I have asked in this book is: How do those most affected by this economy react to it? I purposefully did not take for granted the category of Blackness and simply investigate how "Black" people react to this economy. I entered the very category, so to speak, and tried to read it from within. In doing so, Blackness becomes a free-floating signifier, a multiple and contested site of meaning, a thing-in-itself; no longer an Other, a phantasm, a lack or a negative capital. Nonetheless, as we saw in Chapter 2, this economy is neither blameless nor without harmful effects. Even though it is not an imposed act, paralyzing those who are most affected by it (continental African youths, in this study), this economy becomes a schema that creates "a third-person consciousness" (Fanon, 1967, p. 110). It is this complicated, multilayered, and rhizomatic third-person consciousness that I have attempted to delineate, work through (Derrida, 2000), and trace. Here, I have shown that the Black body is displaced by an atmosphere of certain uncertainty; it becomes hyperconscious of itself, and no longer represents only itself, but becomes responsible for ancestors and indeed a whole race.

To trace how this economy works on the Black body, I deployed Deleuze and Guattari's (1987) notion of the rhizome. For Deleuze and Guattari, the rhizome is a tree that welcomes the sun, the snow, and the rain, but its shape, form, thickness, and greenness, as I explained in Chapter 1, is never sure or predictable. Therefore, one constantly has to ethnographically observe both how it receives the rain and the final product it produces. Horizontally positioned, the rhizome is not a point we reach; it is a way of becoming that is always in "a middle (*milieu*) from which it grows and which it overspills" (p. 21), and which we are forever struggling to attain. I deploy the rhizome because it is a notion that resists verticality and chronological lines of flight, where its growth is conceived in a nonlinear, nonarborescent, and unsystematic line. Radically conceived, almost anarchist in nature, the goal of the rhizome is "[t]o reach, not the point where one no longer says I, but the point where it is no longer of any importance whether one says I" (p. 3). The rhizome, then, is a metaphor for identity that is invoked here, among other reasons (see Chapter 1), to indicate the multiple, multiplying, complex, complicated, fluid, and infinite lines of flight and possibilities of identities and becomings.

Thus, I introduced *rhizomatic identity* as an assemblage, an interbeing, an intermezzo: an existential place of consciousness where we-subjects, owning our own subjectivity, practice constant experimentation and nomadism. Rhizomatic identity is a line of flight that welcomes sociality with everything that it brings (the good and the ugly), but there are no guarantees about what its final product might look like, or what maze it has to go through to get there. As such, rhizomatic identity finds itself in a constant state of flow, de/reterritorialization, and multiplicity.

As a rhizomatic identity, this assemblage finds itself assiduously oscillating between two extremes, two identities, two spaces: *striated* and *smooth*. The former refers to the power that controls, sedates, imposes, and limits, whereas the latter is a welcoming space where people are free to become themselves and to assemble themselves, and with others as they desire. In the smooth space, Deleuze and Guattari explain, we become nomads; we do not walk around aimlessly, but really we do not know or cannot fully predict the storm that is coming our way. So, we find ourselves in a constant, vigilant move between smooth and striated spaces. It is in this intermezzo between the smooth and the striated that I situated the *rhizomatic process of becoming Black*: this complex, complicated, and forever becoming process. The rhizomatic process of becoming Black, in toto, is an identity formation process that is infinitely deterritorialized (passive process of being assembled) and reterritorialzed (active process of assembling) sense of self and subjectivity.

We saw these two extremes in the three sites of this research: Marie-Victorin, Maxwell High, and Sunnyside. Marie-Victorin exemplified what it meant to find oneself in a striated space, both in terms of the arduous process of becoming Black and its painful final product. For this book, I focused almost exclusively on this school precisely because it offers such a stark landscape of the outcome of the arborescent, linear, and striated paradigm and space. By contrast, Maxwell High and Sunnyside were examples of smooth spaces. Despite the lack of diversity among the staff, the quality, dedication, and genuineness of the staff, especially at Sunnyside, and the committed antiracism policy at both schools made students feel welcome. Students appreciated this economy of hospitality (Ibrahim, 2005), as we saw in Chapter 3. In my conversation with Jean-Yves (M, 16, Congo), he captured both the essence of striated and smooth spaces and the ethnographic differences between Marie-Victorin (representing the striated) and Maxwell High and Sunnyside (representing the smooth). Cited in Chapter 2, here's my conversation with him in Maxwell High:

JY: Man, I am glad to make the switch [from a French-language school to Maxwell High].

Awad: Why?

JY: In the French school, you feel like you don't belong. It is "their school" [making a quotation mark gesture]. Here [at Maxwell High] you feel you belong even if you don't speak English. Everybody is so welcoming, and whassup with their French, man [referring to the linguistic variety of French spoken by Franco-Ontarians]? I don't understand most of it, yo yo yo y'knanhmsayin' prof?

Awad: I guess I do. [laughter] (individual interview, English)

When I relayed Jean-Yves's comments to the principal of Maxwell High, he said,

That warms my heart. You know, Awad, we work really hard here in the school. There are four basic principles that guide our philosophy and actions. We call these principles "Welcoming the World." We try to remind our teachers and instill these in our students. They are (1) creating a safe school, (2) increasing student achievement, (3) building a sustainable community partnership, and (4) supporting student leadership and engagement.

In my discussion with the students at Maxwell High, they all said that they knew about these principles and have attempted to implement them in their lives. It is worth noting that the principal of Maxwell High is a White man who is deeply committed to social justice. One time he told a group of Teacher Education Program students who were doing their practice teaching at the school to "go find another job if you are not committed to social justice. Especially in our school [Maxwell High], you can't afford not

> How many schools will you find where 6 months ago kids were in a refugee camp and now they're up singing and dancing onstage?
> —Sherifa (Maxwell High, F, 15, Somalia)

to Welcome the World because the world is already here in our school; and the need is so great that this is not a 9 to 5 kind of job." With help from his vice principal, Brian, once a month this principal leads a short workshop with teachers on how to best implement social justice. One workshop I attended was on how to sensibly acknowledge diversity, using Peggy McIntosh's (1998) features of "White privilege." McIntosh's exercise requires participants to take a step forward or backward if statements that are read aloud apply to them personally. It was an uncomfortable feeling when all the staff of color (including Brian, David, myself, and three other teachers) found ourselves in the back of the room while the rest of the staff (all White, including the principal) found themselves in front of the room. The principal then talked about privilege, the need to be mindful of it, and how best to channel it "for the benefit of our students, not for our own personal benefit."

Sherifa (F, 15, Somalia) thinks the principal and vice principal are "inspirational": "They know almost every student by name. I have no idea how they do it. I can't even remember my sister's name [laughter]. When you go down to the daycare [in the basement of the school] and you see high school students dropping their kids, and then parents from the neighborhood dropping their kids, it gives you a chill. This is not just a school, it is a big family" (group interview, English).

The story is no different in Sunnyside. Even though Jenny (F, 16, South Sudan) did not have the best experience during her co-op program (see Chapter 2), I had the following conversation with her, which sums up my reading of the situation in Sunnyside:

Awad: So you hated your co-op?

Jenny: Prof, that was a killer [laughter]. But you know what, I love the school. I love my teachers and I love, love, love [her trades teacher]. He is soooooo nice, and oh my God. he's sooo cute! [laughter]

Awad: Yep, he is. [laughter]

Jenny: Isn't he? OH MY GOD! OK, I better stop. [laughter]

Awad: Sorry to shift gear. Is that OK with you?

Jenny: NP [no problem].

Awad: Let me ask you a delicate question. You were born here in Canada, right?

Jenny: Yes.

Awad: Do you sometimes forget you are Black, and what happened during your co-op kina wake you up?

Jenny: That's a hard one. I don't forget I am Black, but I am not thinking about it all day. I don't sit with my friends and say, "You know, I think I am Black" [long laughter]. What happened during co-op was just stupid [she was treated differently than a White student]. I have to admit this is a damn good school, and I love it. Everybody gets along.

Jenny's last comment speaks to several ethnographic journal entries I made on Sunnyside. One of them reads:

June 6, 2007: When you walk in the door and see a whole bunch of different people sitting and playing in the foyer, parking lot, or the gym, there's so much more harmony than the normal big schools and so much more sense of community. The diversity at Sunnyside is a point of pride it seems. In fact, rather than causing misunderstanding, students expressed their feelings that being in the school with such diversity is educational: "You learn new things about people everyday," one student told me today. Another student noted: "The same way the cultures are for us on the sports field, we're like that in the school." I saw the school psychologist [a White woman who has great rapport with African youth] during lunch time. She believes the diversity at Sunnyside plays a huge role in creating this environment, this *economy of hospitality*. She suggests that one needs only to look in the hallways to see "how happy the kids are to be here, and the mix of kids jiving—everybody can find a good place here." It is significant that her observations and experiences in Sunnyside contrast with her experiences and observations in other schools. "Sunnyside is very strong. It is strikingly noticeable...unique." Having worked at many high schools in [the city], she notes "it is a different culture here." It is not surprising that, during my interview with them, African/Black students overwhelmingly describe Sunnyside as a "home" and their fellow members as "family": "We know each other here." Despite being a big school, the general sentiment of students is that "everyone's mixed together, we're like a big salad," Jenny said. The terms used in Sunnyside are strikingly similar to Maxwell High.

If Marie-Victorin is an exemplary illustration of what a striated space looks like, one may conclude that Sunnyside and Maxwell High represent the opposite—what a smooth space looks like. Thus, as far as African students are concerned, the ultimate conclusion of the book is:

There is no one process of becoming Black. There are multiple, complex, contingent, shifting, multilayered, and *rhizomatic processes of becoming Black*. These processes oscillate between smooth and striated spaces. As such, we can never assume their shape or form: We need to phenomenologically and ethnographically observe them to realize not only what they are (their actualized shape and form), but also what and how they have become. If we do so, then as this book shows, we realize the complexity, the contingency, and the temporality of Blackness, thus creating a *rhizomatic Blackness* or a *rhizome of Blackness*: that weblike figuration of identity with infinite possibilities and lines of flight.

Put otherwise, unlike the students at Marie-Victorin, who experience the rhizomatic processes of becoming Black, the students in Sunnyside and Maxwell High, most of whom were born in Canada, experience the multiplicity, complexity, and rhizomatic nature of Blackness, which is experienced differently by different people. My goal in this book was to trace ethnographically how people experience both: the *rhizomatic processes of becoming Black* (MV) and the *rhizome of Blackness* (Sunnyside and Maxwell High). In both cases, the outcome was a strong desire for and identification with North American Blackness, especially its popular culture, specifically Hip-Hop. Hip-Hop emerged as a site of identity formation and language learning, as well as a site of empowerment and resistance.

What I have argued in this book, and, I hope, have demonstrated, is that:

- Blackness is an already-always rhizomatic category: a free-floating signifier whose meaning is both contextual and contested. Continental Africans at MV, for example, had neither the conceptualization of nor the lived experience of what it means to be Black in North America before they immigrated. By contrast, African students in Sunnyside and Maxwell High both embodied and knew full well the rhizome and the rhizomatic nature of Blackness.

- There are no linear, systematic, or facile ways of becoming Black. The rhizomatic processes of becoming Black are meant to invoke both the rhizome of Blackness (its multiple meaning) and the complex, unorthodox, and multilayered ways in which the category is taken up. They are rhizomatic processes precisely because they oscillate between two extremes, two contexts, and two spaces: striated and smooth.

- Focusing primarily on Marie-Victorin, I have shown what a striated space might look like, and explored its psychic and identity outcome. Sunnyside and Maxwell High represented the other side, the smooth rhizome of Blackness, where complicated and hopeful lines of flight were brought into existence.

Be it recognition (in Maxwell High and Sunnyside) or misrecognition or even negation (in Marie-Victorin), I have seen what Slavoj Žižek (2000) calls the *ticklish subject* in all three schools. For Žižek, a ticklish subject is a subject full of desire, hope, and in many cases, success. It is a subject that is grounded not in the negation of the negation, that is to say, imagining "a world simply deprived of the Other that exerts oppression on them," but, to the contrary, in a radical pedagogy that "is mediated by the Other" (p. 72). Here, if one "is to get rid of the oppressive Other," Žižek (2000) explains, "one has substantially to transform the content of one's own position" (p. 72). It is this point that shapes this concluding chapter. I show, first, how African students, despite this bleakly painted tableau of hegemonic, repressive, and highly racialized structures, especially at MV, were able to be academically and socially successful and politically active. Focusing one last time on MV alone, I will offer their narrative and social experience as an alternative, radical antiracism pedagogy. This pedagogy has its own prescriptive dimensions. Second, I will offer an overall conclusion about the need to nourish and develop human subjectivity as always-already rhizomatic, contingent, temporal, contradictory, multilayered, complex, and agentic. As such, it is impacting and is impacted by social class, gender, sexuality, and, above all, race. I call this *pedagogy of the imaginary*.

Can You See Me Otherwise?— Take I: School(ing) and Social Consciousness

When it comes to deciphering and making sense of African students' academic performance at MV, there is a shortcoming in this research. I have extensive anecdotal narratives and ethnographic observations, but I do not have a systematized statistical analysis. The reason? The school did not (and still does not) keep statistics broken down by ethnic, racial, or national origin. (This is true for all three research sites.) Nonetheless, the anecdotal narratives and ethnographic observations I was able collect at MV were illuminating. Based on these and the emphasis on education in the African tradition (see especially Asante, 2002; Dei, 2009; H. Wright, 2004), one can conclude that African youths were by and large academically successful. In the graduation ceremonies in 1996 (and I also attended, informally, the graduation ceremonies in 2003), a considerable number of African male and female students received a sizeable number of academic *médailles* or prizes. This was also true during the two years when I was working at MV on another research project. In particular, one boy of Somali origin, Dema, drew laughter during the 1996 graduation ceremony because he received almost all of the *médailles d'or* of the academic subjects of grade 12; people were tired of clapping for him! When I went to congratulate him for his achievements, he jokingly said, "I will be back next year to collect the rest."

Some African students, including Ibri, Dema, Yusuf, Hassan, Asma, and Amani, were at the top of their classes. Ibri, for example, received three *médailles d'or*, for physics, mathematics, and French. It is noteworthy that some of these students were used by teachers as resources to explain mathematics and other academic subjects, particularly French, to students of all backgrounds. Speaking of Dema's competency in the French language, Hassan said, "Il est un maître du français" [He is a master of French]. Hassan continued:

> In French, he had the best grades. This is an OAC [advanced, almost college prep] class, right? There are words, when the female teacher [*Madame*] doesn't understand, she says to Dema, "Do you understand?" "Yes!" He then explains it to her. Seriously! (individual interview, French)

Hassan was being modest in referring to another student as *un maître*. Hassan himself was not only academically successful, but also one of the most politically and socially conscious and active students. In fact, when I talked to the principal about some of the issues concerning African youth, she referred to him as *the* person to talk to about whatever concerned African students, whether the issue was academic, social, or other. "I want to make history," he once told me. Hassan is a Somali speaker who was born in Ethiopia, lived in Djibouti, and spoke more than seven languages. At the school, he was the most stylish, exceptionally well spoken and well mannered, and one of the most "popular" students. Thanks to that, he was elected the first Black president of the student council, the first Black member of a federation of Franco-Ontarian high school students in the metropolitan city where this research was conducted, and then the vice president of this federation for two years. So he did make history. In his second year at the school, he was recognized as the most active student, and according to all students (African or otherwise), his student council was one of the most loved in the school history.

What made his council unique, students argued, was Hassan's ability to maneuver, put together, and bring out the school's true multicultural representation. It was a rare moment when the school motto—*Unité dans la diversité* (Unity in diversity)—actually worked. To illustrate Hassan's social and political talent, how his council came into existence is a story worth telling. Early in the school year Hassan expressed his desire to run for the student council presidency, but when an all-White, very popular group of students announced themselves as a team, he realized that he had almost no chance of winning. He looked around, he told me, and wondered about a counter-team. So, after a thorough consultation, he announced his team and his motto. His team was composed of an East Indian female, a Métis (First Nation) male, a Middle Eastern male, a White male, and himself; his motto was "Not Popularity but Diversity." His team won, and during the year they organized an impressive number of activities: social dances, general assembly every two weeks, a fashion show, Remembrance Day, two winter carnivals, and fundraising activities (with teachers' help and participation). The council also created *Le comité d'aide*—the help committee—to offer academic help to all students, and particularly African students who were new to the system and, as Hassan put it, would "like to advance their competency and take advantage" of the available help and expertise. The committee was made up of twelve students who were considered the top of their classes in particular subjects, and made themselves available once or twice a week at the school library. The council's most impressive achievement, however, was convincing the French-Language Board of Education to appropriate 15,000 dollars for the school library. By that time, Hassan was being consulted regularly by the Board on matters concerning Black/African students, and at the end of that year, along with Patrick, the Métis vice president, Hassan received the prize for the year's most active student, a letter of recommendation, and the *prix d'honneur*—the school's prize of honor.

By and large, African students were successful in establishing themselves and creating their own space and safe zones at the school. They created *l'Association des élèves africains*, a broad alliance of continental and diasporic African students that was established with the help of the Africanist principal who was later discharged by the French-Language Board of Education. *L'Association* was very vocal in addressing African/Black students' concerns, and it organized a number of academic and social activities, including Black History Month. In an informal way, *l'Association* became, by default, the African/Black student council.

Can You See Me Otherwise?—
Take II: A New Economy of Exchange

Clearly, African students were able to make history at MV, to be politically active and academically successful. In this section, I continue with Hassan's story for two reasons: First, because it does not stand by itself, as we shall see at the end of this section, and second, because Hassan, à la Obama, was one of the most socially and politically sophisticated students, and certainly the most articulate. Commenting on the success of African students at the school (including himself), Hassan argued on many occasions that *to be able to participate in exchange in any market, one has to understand the rules of the market.* That is to say, one has to possess the capitals of the market, to know the rules of the market, and, ultimately, to be authorized (and in his case, to have earned authority) to exchange with others in and within the particular market.

Hassan: So, there are all these structures and differences that you have to play with [*jouer avec*]. These include the fact that you have to have the competency to play with others, you have to know how to play with others. (individual interview, French)

To illustrate, Hassan gives the example of a Black man, a Ph.D. holder who is looking for work. For Hassan, the Ph.D. does not exempt this man from being discriminated against or even denied a job. However, his chance for employment increases if he knows the rule of the "game." Conservatively, the rules of the game in this case begin with being "elegantly dressed, with a suit and a tie." Because Blackness is imagined without a suit and a tie, Hassan contends, this becomes a moment to disrupt that imaginary. One way to combat discrimination, he continues, is not by taking up and confronting moments of discrimination, although this is necessary, but by strategically picking our fights, choosing the ones that make sense and will turn out to be socially, politically, and prodigiously productive. Taking up one fight at a time, it begins with the imaginary, the deep-seated stereotypes:

Hassan: To begin with, there are all these stereotypes about Black people. There is discrimination and all that, OK! The only way to combat discrimination is not by outing [publicizing] discrimination. Why do we have all this [discrimination]? We have to play their games to our own benefit. We don't have to do the impossible, you know. We don't have to do whatever, like killing someone because he did something to me. Do you show people the contrary image of what they think, even if you have a Ph.D.? Take a Black man [*un noir*] as an example. When you enter a place and you are not dressed like you should be, even with your Ph.D., people are going to reject you. But if you come in with a tie, or with a suit, with your Ph.D., they are probably going to accept you more than before. (individual interview, French)

To suggest that one needs to play the game to one's own benefit and use the same capital as the interlocutor is a vision that seeks success by working subversively from the inside, from within. Here, one does not look for alternative markets and identities—as the boys did when they chose basketball as opposed to volleyball and Hip-Hop as opposed to dominant identities. Instead, one chooses to affirm one's identity from within the particular *authorized*, *legitimized*, and *dominant* market and identity. Yet, Hassan is mindful of the fact that, in the case of Blackness, there are no guarantees even when one possesses the market's required credentials and capitals; that is why "If you come in with a tie, or with a suit, with your Ph.D., *they* are *probably* going to accept you more than before." By "they," Hassan is referring to the power bloc, those who have a larger control of the market, and who set themselves as the norm, the yardstick against which all is measured. Given the benefit they derive from the dominant structure, "they" have little incentive to imagine others differently, especially Black people, and thus decenter themselves. To do so would be to question their own power, and in some cases, to give up all or some of it.

As educators and antiracism workers, therefore, we need to deconstruct the social structure of domination, discrimination, and negation. Otherwise, some are damned to struggle all their lives and remain on the periphery of power with little or no resources and capital. Thanks to these hegemonic structures, Black/African youths, by and large, find themselves putting in twice the effort to reach an average position. They carry the burden of proving themselves, which means that in some cases they have to dichotomize, on the one hand, the school and the schooling process and, on the other, their personal desires, history, language, and culture:

> Hassan: But, I can prove it, I can do whatever I want to, dress however I want to,[2] have whatever I want to, and be myself. You do what you have to do, you have 100% in your classes, and you are well liked by everyone. It is really deceiving, it is really deceiving that despite all of these, we have to prove what we have to everyone, or who we are, and the others don't. The Africans or the Blacks have to prove themselves to everyone because it is the grandparents of others who have proved it....But our grandparents didn't prove it for us because they themselves were not free to do so. But we have to prove it ourselves. (individual interview, French)

One way to do so, Hassan contends, is to "flip the script," as Hip-Hoppers love to say. That is, in place of failure, one emphasizes pedagogy of hope, possibility, and success, and talks about the unsaid, the absent, and the silenced:

> Hassan: And the only way to do it [prove ourselves to others] is not to conform or buy into stereotypical data like: "Oh 50% of African youths had failed, they can't do it." What has to happen is to show them that 50% had passed, not only to show them the 50% that failed. But they only see the part that failed, they don't look for the part that passed. We have to show them the part that passed, that's what we have to do; and this is one of my objectives: to do more in this regard, to leave a dream...(individual interview, French)

To materialize this dream, Hassan is placing the onus squarely on himself. He is not waiting for someone else to do something about the social situation he sees around him. He is willing to "sacrifice" and take up that burden, and he knows the price he has to pay. As the old African saying goes, if the spirit is high, the body can only feel its height and weight. That is to say, the body does not have too many choices when there is a will, because we are guided by our will, not our bodies.

> Hassan: I am sacrificing an enormous amount of time. I have been in a chain of committees, for example, so there is always a price to pay. He who wants something, he is going to pay a price. You want something, you have to pay for it. You may have to prove something, your strength or whatever. Personally, I know I sacrificed: I missed evenings and there is my mother, anxious [*debordée*]. "You come really late at night. Why do you stay after school, occupied with so much extra work?" she says, you see! (individual interview, French)

Supporting Hassan's arguments, the girls showed an understanding of Black history in North America, especially the struggle for social change and equal rights. Whenever a Black person attempted to alter the plight of Black people, they argued in my focus group interview, he or she had to endure sacrifice, suffering, suppression, and sometimes even assassination:

> Amani: If you are a Black person who is busy trying to lift up your people and their spirit, you will be killed.
>
> Ossi: A number of Black people tried to change the world, to change reality.
>
> Aziza: *Malcom X, Martin Luther King*, they were all assassinated, why? Because...
>
> Asma: *Revolution* [with a Jamaican accent], *all my people thinking*. (group interview, French)

These are precious prices that Black people had to (and still do) pay to envision a more just and humane world. Yet these prices should not discourage us from taking initiatives or talking about what we know, because if we do not, no one else will. In a different context, Hassan argued that because there are no miracles when it comes to social change, *to be is to be an initiative taker*. This is his definition of leadership. I asked him about why he felt the ethical calling of leadership to do what he did. This ethical calling, what Shoshana Felman (1992) calls "ethics of the appointment," is directly related to his memory and the history of his upbringing: being between nations (Somalia, Djibouti, Canada), languages (more than seven languages), cultures, and borders. In sum, he had experienced enough in life to decide his own mind.

Hassan: The ideology I have found, how do I say it? It came out of me, out of, how do I say it? Out of my origin: I am a mixture of many things. For me, there are no borders [*frontières*]. For me, there are no obstacles. I don't wait for, I don't wait for miracles to come from the sky [laughs].

Awad: Which is going to open the door, eh?

Hassan: You see what I mean? I don't wait for that day when miracles arrive to my house and I put my spoon in them. I don't wait for the day when miracles come and spoon-feed me. If this happens, I would have to agree with the idea that all comes from outer space [laughs]. I am not this kind of person. I am the kind of person who is ready to experience everything; not everything, like, I am not thinking about drugs, or ah…I am talking about possibilities. I like to take initiatives. This helped me to expand my leadership ability. (individual interview, French)

The ethics of the appointment, Felman (1992) argues, leaves few options. It is a calling and an interpellation where one feels an obligation to speak up and to act. "If someone else could have written my stories," Elie Wiesel said, "I would not have written them. I have written them in order to testify" (cited in Felman, 1992, p. 3). As a Holocaust survivor, for Wiesel, to testify is *to vow* to tell, remember, and speak up. This ethics of the appointment becomes a central psychic strategy against discrimination and negation. It is a strategy commonly known as *confiance en soi*—self-esteem. Although it does not account for structural paradigms, and in most cases puts the responsibility on the individual actor, Hassan sees self-esteem as a means to find reasons, aims, and energy to imagine differently and to work with a pedagogy of love, hope, and possibility. Hassan wakes up in the morning and tells himself that he is capable of doing his everyday activities well; can make friends; and is capable of being the top of his class, if not the school:

> Hassan: *Tu sais quoi? Des fois je me demande si je pense pas mieux que des adultes.* [You know what? I sometimes wonder if I don't think better than adults.]

Hassan: First, I am talking about being comfortable in one's own skin, being comfortable with one's own identity. Self-esteem is when you have the will, when you have an aim, when you have a reason. Every morning, I wake up and I tell myself that I am capable of doing what I have to do much better. I am capable of reaching my objectives that I set for myself. And I study. I am capable of making plenty of friends, and don't care about race, color, language. So, I come to school, and I am here [in Canada] only five years. I know almost every student at the school, I made friends here and elsewhere. (individual interview, French)

Moments of contradiction are always illuminating. Hassan did care that he was the first Black president of the student council. The members of the council were purposefully chosen and described by Hassan as "multicultural," as I noted above. Yet, he knows there is a land beyond race, color, and language. To get to this promised land, Hassan advised the following: be open-minded, make yourself available, be fully present, find your interlocutor's interest, don't be shy, open channels of communication, and speak to people. This will not happen without loving and accepting oneself.

> Hassan: You should not sit on your behind, excuse my language, and wait for people, because that's just stupid. You have to converse, you have to be social. But before other people can accept you, you have to accept yourself. If you see me during lunch time, I sit with everyone and in every chair. There is not even one person who tells me, "*Yo, I don't like you, get out of here.*" I found this, a character that I found: speak to everyone, become friends, and they are going to accept you. There are no people who hate you for who you are; even if they exist, it's small minority that we don't have at the school. It may be in the city, but in the school we don't have idiots who hate you for your color or your sex or something like that. (individual interview, French)

This is another illuminating moment of contradiction: The personal can never be generalized, nor should it be. It is only that, personal. It leaves us with a rosy yet unsystematic picture. As we have seen, there are various and serious issues at the school, including the absence of Black teachers, the Eurocentric curriculum, the zero-sum participation of parents (where parents are always blamed for not showing up to parent-teacher meetings, thus giving a sense of superiority to teachers), the African students refugee situation (living on their own and surviving by themselves), the use of *le contrat*, and the insensitive treatment of African students (e.g., how they are streamed, talked to, and graded) by the principal, school administration, and teachers.

In this context of hostility and negation, where would African students go to vent and voice their concerns? As George Dei (1996) shows, "students do not go to school as 'disembodied' generic youths" (p. 31). Their moments of identification and their sense of belonging and ownership (both of the school and of what is taught) are vitally important to their sense of safety. Time and again, African students called for *safe zones* (individuals and places where they could go to complain without fear of reprimand) and for human connection and caring (being understood, loved, and cared for). They felt this sense of safety with the White Africanist principal, Monsieur Armond, who was discharged by the Board. He had a French background, had lived in Africa for a long time, understood African students and their peculiar situation, and voiced a very strong antiracism framework (see Dei, 1996, for full discussion and definition of antiracism theory and practice). Ironically, he was discharged because of his strong antiracism discourse and his unconditional support for African students. As the president of the student council, Hassan mounted a strike calling for Monsieur Armond's return, and testified in court to his good deeds and character. Yes, Monsieur Armond's case went to court, and the Board was found guilty, but again, when I finally asked, I was told because of confidentiality, the specificities of his case could not be discussed. It is significant to note, nonetheless, that Monsieur Armond was loved by African students because he showed empathy, mindfulness, caring, human connection, and unconditional support. In my interview with Aziza, we had the following exchange:

Awad: And they [the teachers] said that the problem with Monsieur Armond was that he was allying himself too much with African students.

Aziza: Yes, because he understood us very well. Because he was in Africa, he already understood Africans. In other words, he loved Africans. He was on good terms with Africans. That's it! You see? All these teachers here, there is not even one who has been to Africa, you see. They say, "Where is Africa?" [laughs]. It is incredible. They think that Africa is a country. *They don't even know that* Africa is a continent. (individual interview, French)

Given his encounter with Africa and Africans, Monsieur Armond was able to forge a new discourse and praxis that spoke to African students. His praxis[3]—that is to say, his connection between the word and the world, theory and practice, thought and action—showed African students that, contrary to most teachers, he cared. However, one does not need to go to Africa to care. Caring is a genuine human sentiment that knows no borders. In the same individual interview, Aziza talked about caring and having a diverse teaching body/staff and role models; different bodies bring different forms of knowledge. These, she argues, are directly related to students' identification and sense of safety:

We need a role model, you know. The African student is in need of a role model. When you see a teacher of color, the student will say, "Oh, yes, there is a teacher of color." It gives him a sense of safety. But if the student doesn't see any teacher of color, all teachers are Whites, the majority are Whites, he is going to feel marginalized [*égaré*]. (individual interview, French)

For African students, the will to care, to combat marginalization and racism, and to build human bridges is not a budgetary question. It is a will to question one's own location, power, and privilege; a will to help, to share, and to love. This has yet to materialize in Franco-Ontarian schools. In my focus group interview with the girls, they put it thus:

Amani: What is really stupid is that they organize weeks, a day as international day to combat racism. *Bullshit,, you know.* They only know how to create organizations and, *you know, how to spend big bucks, you know.* Francophone schools aren't doing as much as the English-language schools. Really, there are programs [in English-language schools] that are really geared towards immigrant students who want to integrate, but here...

Samira: Every time we ask the question...

Amani: I have to really blame the French-Language Board [of Education] because they are not making the effort to, to...

Samira: There is no budget, we don't have enough money.

Amani: Yes, to integrate you can only give hand and help, it doesn't take much. It is not budget that they need, their teachers could form their own organization to combat racism. (group interview, French)

In sum, African students are calling for a dialogic process of liberation and humanization, for a restructuring of power relations that allows them to be and to succeed. It is dialogic because as one is liberating oneself, one is also liberating the Other. "Liberation," Paulo Freire (1993) argues, "is thus a childbirth, and a painful one. The man or woman who emerges is a new person, viable only as the oppressor-oppressed contradiction is superseded by the humanization of all people. Or to put it another way," he continues "the solution of this contradiction is born in the labor which brings into the world this new being: no longer oppressor nor longer oppressed, but human in the process of achieving freedom" (p. 31). Yet, for Aziza, this liberation will not materialize without what may be called *critical literacy*, where one takes one's ignorance of and about the Other very seriously. The Other is not a tableau on which one may draw whatever one wishes; and if one is to eat the Other, as bell hooks (2003, 1994) has argued, one is better off knowing what one is eating. A crucial part of this critical literacy is learning how to receive, translate, and process information about the Other. This information should be critically processed, analyzed, and compared, and not naïvely devoured or consumed. In the end, it is critical literacy because it deals as much with what is said as it does with the unsaid, the unmarked, and the silenced. Juxtaposing critical literacy and media representation of Africa, Aziza contends:

> And I sometimes don't blame them [White students] because there is the media which plays a role in that [negative representation of North American Blacks, Africans, and Africa]. But they should not trust the media. They have to educate themselves and say: "I don't really believe it is like that. I am going to do research. I am going to study Africa. What is Africa?" And when you study Africa, don't focus only on the negative sides, study the positive sides as well; the two sides, you see. That is that. (individual interview, French)

"But they should not trust the media" is a call for a radical media literacy to decolonize the mind (wa Thiong'o, 1986); to talk about the left over, the silenced; to question one's own knowledge, location, and privilege; and to critically deconstruct historical and media representations and power relations. It is a call for a critical pedagogy that I call *pedagogy of the imaginary*.

Concluding the Conclusion: Towards a Pedagogy of the Imaginary

> Silence from and about the subjects was the order of the day. Some of the silences were broken, and some were maintained by authors who lived with and within the policing strategies. What I am interested in are the strategies for breaking it.
> (Morrison, 1992, p. 7)

> They were me; they defined me....For all they were concerned, we were so many names scribbled on fake ballots, to be used at their convenience and when not needed to be filed away. It was a joke, an absurd joke....[And now that] I had switched from the arrogant absurdity of Norton and Emerson to that of Jack...it all came out the same—except I now recognized my invisibility.
> (a rearranged text by Ellison, 1952, p. 508)

He is an invisible man because he is already defined, he is spoken to when it is convenient; otherwise, he is filed away, he is a text to be arranged to suit one's own imaginary. This is a joke, an absurd joke, and as we have seen, it is deeply violent. In her psychoanalytic discussion of the Lacanian "imaginary phase," Kathryn Woodward (1997) defines imaginary as "a mixture of fantasies of love and hate" (p. 44). Within this phase, one "reaches a sense of 'I' only through finding the 'I' reflected back by something outside itself, by the other; from the place of 'the other.' But it experiences itself as if the 'I'—the sense of self—was produced from within itself, by a unified identity" (p. 44). That is to say, at some point, the Other becomes a projection of the self, almost a fantasy created by the self. It is this fantasy, especially when it is the dominant imaginary, that we need to deconstruct and reckon with. In this study—particularly with regard to MV, which I highlighted for reasons of clarity and focus——the dominant imaginary marginalized certain identities and deauthorized the spaces where they were formed and performed.

I am offering *pedagogy of the imaginary* as an integrative antiracism strategy to bring these marginalized identities and the sites of their formation into the classroom so that they can be critically engaged and deconstructed, not passively consumed. To engage these identities critically is to assume their full subjectivity, multiple subject positions, agency, and shifting and contradictory nature. This does not allow for simple classification or categorization (based on visible racial, ethnic, or gender criteria), but works through intersectionality. Categorization sees the social constructs of race, class, gender, and sexuality as exclusive and independent categories, whereas an integrative antiracism framework of intersectionality examines these categories as dynamic, mediated in people's daily experiences, multiple, shifting, contradictory, and consciously linked to the struggles against oppression (see Dei, 1996, ch. 4 for full discussion). Put otherwise, categorization is a mode of thought that employs *either/or*, whereas intersectionality employs *both/and* perspectives when theorizing the simultaneity, embeddedness, and connectedness of myriad forms of oppression: "An integrative antiracism approach [of intersectionality] is based on the principle that myriad forms of oppressions are interlocked and that a study of one such system, racism [for example], necessarily entails a study of class, gender, sexual inequalities, homophobia and ableism" (Dei, 1996, p. 56).

Accordingly, one has to ask the following questions: Should African students be gazed upon whenever minority issues are discussed in the classroom? When a privileged, White person sees a Black woman, can he or she imagine this woman as a university professor, as middle class, or as a lesbian? Is this White person's imaginary uninhibited, unprejudiced, decolonized, receptive, and amenable enough to see that a Black man with dreadlocks and Hip-Hop clothes may be from a middle-class background, may be a manager or a businessman? In short, how do we as a nation, as groups, and as individuals imagine ourselves as well others? What impact does this imaginary have on others, and how can we as pedagogues work with this imaginary to make people imagine themselves and others differently?

The African students at MV, it seems to me, were casualties of fixity, of striated space. Like Ellison's *Invisible Man*, they were already fixed in an identity, already slotted in an imaginary, which in complex ways limited how and where they circulated their identities. Although rhizomatic in nature, their identities had a limited number of lines of flight. Here, a (fixed) identity is not based on who one *is*; that is, one's own social-cultural, national, and linguistic identity. On the contrary, it is based primarily on how one appears, one's racial identity: "Oh, they all look like Blacks to me!" This state of mind is thus largely dependent on already circulating hegemonic and historical discourses and representations of Blackness. Hence, such fixed identities do not hear how one sounds when speaking to a subject; all they require is a look, a set of clothes, an attitude, and so on.

The pedagogy of the imaginary addresses those who possess this state of mind and who can maneuver the sociohistorical structures that allow them to exert such symbolic violence.[4] Paulo Freire has called them the oppressors (1993): those who possess the power to represent, structure, and restructure nations and narrations, and thus write and rewrite them. Intentionally or not, this symbolic violence has been exerted on African students by denying them their full identities, which encompass more than their racial identity. Put differently, African students appear to have fallen prey to fixity, which imposed on them the already established North American order, discourse, and historical representations of Blackness. What we visibly "see" can be deceiving; and although we may all project preconceived identities on others in one way or another in our everyday interactions, when this imposition is coupled with power, its consequences can be traumatic, as evidenced by my encounter with the police officer in Toronto, and by student narratives contained in this book.

In formulating a pedagogy, we need to imagine race as well as gender as categories of visible subjects that occupy sites that are recognizable only through an actual, ethnographic, and *material encounter*, not an imagined one. In such sites, Blackness is already-always rhizomatic, and may refer to a gay, middle-class, writer, university professor subject; gender may refer to a lesbian, upper-middle-class, company executive subject, and so on. In other words, we need to imagine rhizomatically, where subject categories are always occupying different and multiple sites, though perhaps not in abundant numbers in some sites. Because the public imaginary has historically been colonized by a self-serving power bloc representing their own kind, these categories have rarely been represented or discussed as ever-changing. The presidency of Barack Obama is making us (or at least a good portion of the world's population) imagine Blackness differently. Unfortunately, the election in November 2012 showed that that is not the case in the United States, where the racial divide is very much alive, and given the Republican discourse during the election, a sizeable proportion of White America still holds exceptionally negative views of both President Obama and Black people generally and seems to be locked, despite the undeniable progress, in a nineteenth-century racial cartography of Blackness (Alim & Smitherman, 2012; Bonilla-Silva, 2014; Kantor, 2012).

The pedagogy of the imaginary in this context, then, is a hopeful yet critical pedagogy that "allows us to affirm multiple black identities, varied black experience. It also challenges colonial imperialist paradigms of black identity which represent blackness one-dimensionally in ways that reinforce and sustain white supremacy" (hooks, 1990, p. 28). It is a critical pedagogy that eventually will help us imagine, in the case of African students, for example, that Blackness has cultural, national, religious, and linguistic repertoires that differ from those evident in North American Blackness. Blackness is de facto multicultural, multilingual, and multiethnic. This is the *rhizome of Blackness*.

Within this pedagogy, the encounter is of particular significance in rupturing the normalizing gaze. Using a Foucauldian (1980) language, I understand normalization as a striated and coercive instrument and technology of power that imposes homogeneity, hierarchy, standardization, ranking, and classification. Here, given the nature of the gaze, the encounter is symbolic, where texts and representations become vitally important. Specifically, I am proposing Rap/Hip-Hop, and Black popular culture in general, as pedagogical moments—sites of encounter, if you like—with Blackness in the classroom. In doing so, I am pointing to lines of flight, the horizon of possibilities of using Black cultural productions, particularly musical, literary, and cinematic representations, as moments of rupture of what hooks has called colonial imperialist paradigms, where Black identities are represented one-dimensionally. As we have seen, Black popular culture (particularly Rap and Hip-Hop) are curriculum sites where learning takes place and identities are invested (see Ibrahim, 2004).

In the language of integrative antiracism education (Dei, 1996), proposing Black popular culture as a curriculum site is a call to centralize and engage marginalized subjects, their voices, and their ways of being, becoming, and learning. In addition, it revisits this question: In the case of African students, whose language and identity are we as pedagogues teaching and assuming if we do not engage Rap or Hip-Hop? This proposition entails a legitimization of a form of knowledge otherwise perceived as illegitimate (Ibrahim, 1999, 2004). As Giroux and Simon (1989) put it,

> By ignoring the cultural and social forms that are authorized by youth and simultaneously empowering or disempowering them, educators risk complicity silencing their students....This is unwittingly accomplished by refusing to recognize the importance of those sites and social practices outside of school that actively shape student experiences and through which students often define and construct their sense of identity, politics, and culture. (p. 3)

The encounter with Black cultural forms, therefore, is and must be seen as a moment of critical examination, instead of passive, exoticized, and essentialized consumption. Because Black popular cultural forms are also social and historical productions, they are as much sites of hope as they are sites of critique. Hip-Hop and Rap, as noted, are not exceptions to the dominant discourse of sexism and homophobia (Forman & Neal, 2004; Love, 2012; Rose, 1991). Therefore they should not be readily consumed but critically framed, studied, and engaged (Ibrahim, 1999). Yet, Hip-Hop and Rap are also sites of hope, a hope that will eventually broaden the horizon of possibility (Simon, 1992) that Blackness is seen and imagined for what it is: multiple, complex, multilayered, and always-already rhizomatic. A hope that would allow all students, but particularly those from dominant groups, to be able to see multiple ways of speaking, being, and learning. In Paulo Freire's language, introducing Hip-Hop and Rap in class, especially in the case of African students, is to hope to link their world, identities, desires, and investments with their words (1993).

To broaden the horizon of possibility, the late Roger I. Simon (1992) argued, is to create a critical pedagogical project that supports "the endeavor of creating specific social forms that encourage and help make possible the realization of an expanded set of differentiated human capacities rather than denying, diluting, or distorting those capacities" (p. 22). It is at the school that this possibility is brought into existence and students are armed to be their own subjects and understand their own possibilities. As far as African students are concerned, the encounter with rhizomatic processes of Blackness is a symbolic encounter with the silenced, the marginalized, and the unmarked. Here, Blackness becomes "a metaphor for freedom, an end to boundaries. Blackness is vital not because it represents the 'primitive' but because it invites engagement in a revolutionary ethos that dares to challenge and disrupt the status quo" (hooks, 1992, p. 37).

If this is so, then the pedagogy of the imaginary is an integrative antiracism pedagogy of struggle, of critical cultural representation that seeks to represent Blackness rhizomatically, with full agency and subjectivity. The late Edward Said declared,

> Gone are the binary oppositions dear to the nationalist and imperialist enterprise. Instead we begin to sense that old authority cannot simply be replaced by new authority, but that new alignments made across borders, types, nations, and essences are rapidly coming into view, and it is those new alignments that now provoke and challenge the fundamentally static notion of *identity* that has been the core of cultural thought during the era of imperialism. (1994, p. xxiv, original emphasis)

And since we are not fully out of this "era of imperialism" (see McLaren & Farahmandpur, 2005), we need to challenge this static notion of identity. Here, I hope that my introduction of the *rhizomatic process of becoming Black* is a rupture and a radical shift from this era of colonialism and imperialism where the identity Blackness is one-dimensionally represented. As we have seen with African youths, identity is not as "transparent or unproblematic" as we previously thought; it is "a 'production,' which is never complete, always in process, and always constituted within, not outside, representation" (Hall, 1990a, p. 222). *To be* for African youth is *to become*; that is, to become a rhizomatic and an ambivalent product of two, of both here *and* there, Africa *and* Canada, to become forever born in two. The role for us educators, therefore and lastly, is not only to motivate and empower students to be themselves, but also, and more importantly, to enable them to locate themselves in time and history and, at the same time, to critically interrogate the adequacy of that location. Only then can we talk about pedagogy of hope and radical love.

Notes

1 "The phrase "What's the dillio" is an "old skool" hip hop term meaning, "what's the deal," "what's up," "what's going on," or "what's happening." Essentially, the phrase is used to inquire information about the most important aspects of something" (Kuoch, 2013, p. 12).

2 Most of the time, Hassan had on elegant yet baggy clothes, thus bordering on Hip-Hop and dominant/"regular" clothes. As I have indicated, Hassan was one of the most popular and elegant students at the school.

3 As Freire (1993) puts it, Action and Reflection = word = work = praxis. Praxis, then, is the intersection of discourse and practice. For Freire, "There is no true word that is not at the same time a praxis. Thus, to speak a true word is to transform the world" (p. 68).

4 Although my primary targets are those in positions of power, I do, in fact, address everyone. I am including Black peoples here, and this may address the phenomenon of "acting White," at least in part; that is, if Black peoples can negotiate the fact that, given the multiplicity of social and class locations that Blackness may occupy, what belongs to Whites may also belong to Blacks, and vice versa. If they can expect, imagine, and therefore feel that, as C. L. R. James used to say, Beethoven belongs as much to Blacks and West Indians as he does to Germans (see Said, 2001), they must see that academic success is as much a Black phenomenon as it is a White phenomenon.

APPENDIX I

Notes on Transcription of Interviews

All names are pseudonyms. All quotations are translated from French, unless otherwise indicated.

Italics:	Denotes a foreign term: either an Arabic term; a French term that is not easily translated (enclosed in parentheses); or English terms/expressions spoken by the speaker during an interview in French.
Bold:	Indicates my own emphasis.
Ellipsis:	Omitted text, inaudible or repetitious
[Bracketed Text]:	My own added texts or comments.
Un/une professeur(e):	In the translation, the generic 'un' and 'une' posed a problem because in English 'a' is used for male and female, where as 'un' in French is masculine and 'une' is feminine. Unless indicated, I translated it literally, that is, as pronounced: *un* = male and *une* = female: a 'male teacher' and 'female teacher.'

APPENDIX II

Profiles of Students Interviewed for This Book

Aaliyah: Sixteen-year-old, grade 10 female student at Sunnyside. She was born in Canada to parents from Kenya. She was an exceptionally articulate and socially active student, and participated in many extracurricular activities, especially tutoring and offering help to ESL students. She ran an afterschool program at her church for young Kenyan students. She was planning to study English and philosophy at the University of Ottawa.

Amani: Seventeen-year-old, grade 12 female student at MV, from Somalia. She is Aziza's sister, and had two brothers who were also at Marie-Victorin. Aziza and Amani come from a well-to-do, almost bourgeois family in Somalia. She has ten brothers and sisters and was living with her single mother. In 1996 she had a sister who was attending Université Laval and a brother who was attending York University. Amani was one of the most active students at the school and was awarded *la médaille de l'élève le plus actif* (the medal of the most active student). She participated in sports (volleyball, basketball, soccer) and social activities (Black History Month, fashion show, and student council) and was the school singer.

Asma and **Ossi**: Sisters, sixteen and seventeen-years-old, respectively. They were in grades 11 and 12 at MV, come from Djibouti and were living with their single mother. Along with Samira, they dominated the school fashion show and were exceptionally active in cultural and social activities, including *réunion générale* (general assembly) and Black History Month. They also had a special affinity for anything Black, especially "Black" dress and fashion. Along with Aziza, Amani, and Samira, they formed an inseparable group, and did very well academically.

Aziza: Eighteen-year-old Ontario Academic Credit or OAC (also known as Grade 13, which was abolished in 2003) female student at MV, from Somalia. Exceptionally active, Aziza was a co-founder of the African Students' Association, a member of the school fashion show and volleyball and female basketball teams, and a co-organizer of the students' strike.

Ginette: Sixteen-year-old, grade 10 female student in Maxwell High. She moved to the school two years prior to this research in 2011. Originally from Bénin, she lived with her older brother (a twenty-one-year-old with a three-year-old daughter) and three of her siblings in a two-bedroom apartment. She was their "mother" and took care of everything in the house, from cooking to helping with school homework. She was exceptionally articulate and hoped to study at York University, where her best friend was studying criminology.

Hassan: Eighteen-year-old OAC male student at MV, born in Ethiopia but lived in Somalia and Djibouti. He was living with his single mother and was planning to attend York University, where he would study political science and international studies. Then he was planning to attend law school at the University of Ottawa. He made history by being the first Black president of the student council, was recognized by the school for three consecutive years as the most active student, and was the most popular student at the school. His academic performance was remarkable, and his political and social activism was noteworthy.

Ibri: Nineteen-year-old OAC male student at MV, from Gabon. He lived by himself and worked part-time; was awarded *la médaille d'or*—the gold prize—for being the best student in the school in mathematics and science; was planning to attend York University; and was a co-founder of *comité d'aide* (help committee).

Jean-Yves: Sixteen-year-old grade 10 male student at Maxwell High from the Democratic Republic of Congo. His parents had immigrated to Canada eight years before the time of this research. He switched from a French-language high school to Maxwell High. He was socially active and well liked by the vice principal Brian. He wanted to study biology at a bilingual university.

Jenny: Sixteen-year-old grade 10 female student at Sunnyside. She was born in Canada to parents from South Sudanese. She was proud to work for the independence of the recently formed nation South Sudan (2011). She is well known in the school for her aspiration to become a professional model. She received the Governor General of Canada Award for her social activism.

Juma: Twenty-year-old OAC male student at MV. Juma, from Senegal, was very shy, and had been in Canada for three years at the time of this research. He was living with another student, Musa, and was doing well academically. He was planning to attend York University, but he had to deal with a few troubling incidents with the school administration.

Mukhi: Eighteen-year-old OAC male student at MV, from Djibouti. He lived with his single mother. He had attended the school since grade 9, and was one of the students who felt the pressure of *le contrat* because of their age. He was a co-organizer of the students' strike and was planning to attend York University.

Musa: Nineteen-year-old OAC male student at MV, from Djibouti. He lived with three other students from the same school. It was at their home that I conducted the focus-group interview with the boys. Musa expressed his desire to attend Laurentian University and was very energetic when it came to African students' activities, especially Black History Month. He was so involved in other African students' lives that he became an authority, an "African elder," if you like, for both the students and school administration.

Najat: Fifteen-year-old, grade 9 female student at MV, from Djiboutian. She came to Canada when she was seven years old and was very much affected by her father's death when she was three years old. She was living with her single mother and her only sister, who used to attend Marie-Victorin and then transferred to an English-language school. She was humorous, which made her a popular student, and very active in cultural, musical, and social activities (especially Black History Month). She was the school's female Rapper and Hip-Hopper.

Omer: Nineteen-year-old, OAC male student at MV, from Ethiopia. He came to Canada by himself when he was fifteen years old and was living in a shelter (almost homeless) at the time of this study. Yet, he was the head organizer of the students' strike, and like Musa, Omer also acted as an "African elder," liaising between African/Black students and the administration, including teachers. He loved reggae and was considered the rasta of the school.

Phil: Seventeen-year-old, grade 11 male student at Sunnyside. He was born in Canada to Nigerian parents. He considers himself "Nigerian, Canadian, Nigerian-Canadian, Canadian-Nigerian." He famously told me, "I am Hip-Hop," by which he meant, "It is what I listen to, my head is totally Hip-Hop. I grew up with it, it is all I know." He did slam poetry and was in the process of creating a Spoken Word Club. He was a popular student and was planning to major in English.

Sam: Nineteen-year-old, OAC male student at MV, from Djibouti. He had been at the school since grade 7 and was socially and politically active and articulate. He participated in many activities pertaining to Black students, especially Black History Month. His identification with Black America was the most noticeable among the African students. Indeed, he was the Rapper of the school and the "Jordan" of the basketball court.

Samira: Sixteen-year-old grade 10 female student at MV, from Djibouti. She was *la beauté* of the fashion show and exceptionally socially active. She participated in all of the school activities: fashion shows, sports activities, Black History Month, student council's Green Committee. She was planning to attend a French-language university.

Sherifa: Fifteen-year-old grade 9 female student at Maxwell High. Born in Canada to Somali parents, Sherifa was a very active student. She was at the top of her class academically and the head of three social clubs. She had an older brother at the school and hoped to study biology and then medicine.

REFERENCES

Abdi, A. (2008). Europe and African thought systems and philosophies of education: "Re-culturing" the trans-temporal discourses. *Cultural Studies, 22*(2), 309–327.

Alim, S. (2006). *Roc the mic right: The language of hip hop culture.* New York and London: Routledge.

Alim, S., Ibrahim, A., & Pennycook, A. (2009). *Global linguistic flows: Hip-hop cultures, youth identities, and the politics of language.* London and New York: Routledge.

Alim, S., & Smitherman, G. (2012). *Articulate while Black: Barack Obama, language, and race in the U.S.* New York: Oxford University Press.

Althusser, L. (1971). *Lenin and philosophy.* London: New Left Books.

Alverman, D. (2000). Researching libraries, literacies, and lives: A rhizoanalysis. In E. St. Pierre & W. Pillow (Eds.), *Working the ruins: Feminist poststructural theory and methods in education* (pp. 114–129). New York: Routledge.

Amit-Talai, V., & Wulff, H. (Eds.). (1995). *Youth culture: A cross-cultural perspective.* London and New York: Routledge.

Amit-Talai, V. (1995). Conclusion: The 'multi' cultural of youth. In V. Amit-Talai, & H. Wulff (Eds.), *Youth culture: A cross-cultural perspective* (pp. 223-233). London and New York: Routledge.

Anderson, B. (1983). *Imagined communities: Reflections on the origin and spread of nationalism.* London: Verso.

Anthias, F., & Yuval-Davis, N. (1992). *Racialized boundaries.* London and New York: Routledge.

Appel, R. & Muysken, P. (1987/1990). *Language contact and bilingualism.* London: Edward Arnold.

Aronowitz, S., & Giroux, H. (1993). *Postmodern education.* Minneapolis: University of Minnesota Press.

Asante, M. (2002). *100 greatest African Americans: A biographical encyclopedia.* Amherst, NY: Prometheus Books.

Asante, M. (2012). *The African American people: A global history.* New York: Routledge.

Atlas, J. (2014). Subjects in becoming: Photographs in the European Black diaspora. *Cultural Studies 28*(1), 168–170.

Austin, J. (1962). *How to do things with words.* Oxford, UK: Clarendon Press.

Back, L., & Solomos, J. (Eds.). (2000). *Theories of race and racism: A reader.* London and New York: Routledge.

Baker, H., Jr. (1991). Hybridity, the rap race, and pedagogy for 1990s. In C. Penley & A. Ross (Eds.), *Technoculture* (pp. 25–34). Minneapolis: University of Minnesota Press.

Baker, H., Jr. (1993). *Black studies: Rap and the academy.* Chicago, IL: University of Chicago Press.

Bakhtin, M. (2000). *The dialogic imagination: Four essays.* Austin: University of Texas Press.

Barthes, R. (1983). *Elements of semiology.* New York: Hill and Wang.

Benett, T. (1986). The politics of "the popular" and popular culture. In T. Benett, C. Mercer, & J. Woollacott (Eds.), *Popular culture and social relations* (pp. 6–21). Milton Keynes, UK: Open University Press.

Beneviste, E. (2000). Subjectivity in language. In P. du Gay, J. Evans, & P. Redman (Eds.), *Identity: A reader* (pp. 39–43). London: Sage.

Bhabha, H. (1990). The third space: Interview with Homi Bhabha. In J. Rutherford (Ed.), *Identity: Community, culture, and difference* (pp. 26–33). London: Lawrence & Wishart.

Bhabha, H. (1994). *The location of culture*. London and New York: Routledge.

Bonilla-Silva, E. (2014). *Racism without racists: Color-blind racism and the persistence of racial inequality in America*. Lanham, MD: Rowman & Littlefield.

Bourdieu, P. (1977). *Outline of a theory of practice*. London: Cambridge University Press.

Bourdieu, P. (1991). *Language and symbolic power*. London: Polity Press.

Bourdieu, P. (2000). The biographical illusion. In P. du Gay, J. Evans, & P. Redman (Eds.), *Identity: A reader* (pp. 297–303). London: Sage.

Brake, M. (2003). *Comparative youth culture: The sociology of youth cultures and youth subcultures in America, Britain, and Canada*. London: Taylor & Francis.

Butler, J. (1997). *Excitable speech: A politics of performativity*. London and New York: Routledge.

Butler, J. (1999). *Gender trouble: Feminism and the subversion of identity*. New York: Routledge.

Butler, J. (2004). *The Judith Butler reader*. Malden, MA: Blackwell.

Butler, J. (2009). *Frames of war: When is life grievable?* New York: Verso.

Butler, J. (2011). *The power of religion in public life*. New York: Columbia University Press.

Carby, H. (1982). White women listen! Black feminism and the boundaries of sisterhood. In Centre for Contemporary Cultural Studies (Eds.), *The empire strikes back* (pp. 183–211). London: Hutchinson.

Carby, H. (1992). The multicultural wars. In G. Dent (Ed.), *Black popular culture* (pp.187–199). Seattle, WA: Bay Press.

Carspecken, F., & Walford, G. (Eds.). (2001). *Critical ethnography and education*. Amsterdam and New York : JAI Press.

Center for Contemporary Cultural Studies (CCCS). (1982). *The empire strikes back.* London: Hutchinson.

Chan, W., & Mirchandani, K. (Eds.). (2002). *Crimes of colour: Racialization and the criminal justice system in Canada*. Peterborough, ON: Broadview Press.

Chang, J. (2005). *Can't stop won't stop: A history of the hip hop generation*. New York: St. Martin's Press.

Chideya, F. (2000). *The color of our future*. New York: William Morrow.

Chomsky, N. (1965). *Aspects of the theory of syntax.* Cambridge, MA: MIT Press.

Cixous, H. (1994). *The Hélène Cixoux reader.* London and New York: Routledge.

Collins, P. H. (1990). *Black feminist thought: Knowledge, consciousness, and the politics of empowerment.* London and New York: Routledge.

Conyers, J. (Ed.). (2001). *African American jazz and rap: Social and philosophical examinations of Black expressive behavior.* Jefferson, NC: McFarland.

Cummins, J. (2004). Foreword. In S. Nieto, *Affirming diversity: The sociopolitical context of multicultural education* (pp. x–xix). Boston, MA: Pearson/ Allyn and Bacon.

Danesi, F. (1994). *Cool.* Toronto, ON: University of Toronto Press.

Danesi, M. (2009). *Dictionary of media and communications.* New York: M. E. Sharpe.

de B'béri, B. (2008). Africanicity in Black cinema. *Cultural Studies, 22*(2), 187–208.
de Certeau, M. (1997). *Culture in the plural*. Minneapolis: University of Minnesota Press.
Dei, G. (1996). *Anti-racism education: Theory and practice*. Halifax, NS: Fernwood.
Dei, G. (2009). *Teaching Africa: Towards a transgressive pedagogy*. New York: Springer.
Dei, G. (2010). *Learning to succeed: The challenges and possibilities of educational achievement for all*. Youngstown, NY: Teneo Press.
Dei, G., James, I., Karumanchery, L., James-Wilson, S., & Zine, J. (2000). *Removing the margins: The challenges and possibilities of inclusive schooling*. Toronto, ON: Canadian Scholars' Press.
Dei, G., Mazzuca, J., McIsaac, E., & Zine, J. (1997). *Reconstructing "drop-out": A critical ethnography of the dynamics of black students' disengagement from school*. Toronto, ON: University of Toronto Press.
Deleuze, G., & Guattari, F. (1987). *A thousand plateaus: Capitalism and schizophrenia*. London and New York: Continuum.
Dent, G. (Ed.). (1992). *Black popular culture*. Seattle, WA: Bay Press.
Denzin, N., & Giardina, M. (2010). *Qualitative inquiry and human rights*. Walnut Creek, CA: Left Coast Press.
Denzin, N., & Lincoln, Y. (Eds.). (2003). *Collecting and interpreting qualitative materials* (2nd ed.). Thousand Oaks, CA: Sage.
Denzin, N., Lincoln, Y., & Smith, L. (2008). *Handbook of critical and indigenous methodologies*. Thousand Oaks, CA: Sage.
DePoy, E. & Gitlin, L. (2011). *Introduction to research: Understanding and applying multiple strategies*. St. Louis, MO: Elsevier/Mosby.
Derrida, J. (1996). *Monolingualism of the other, or, the prosthesis of origin*. Stanford, CA: Stanford University Press.
Derrida, J. (2000). *Of hospitality*. Stanford, CA: Stanford University Press.
Dimitriadis, G. (2001). *Performing identity/performing culture: Hip hop as text, pedagogy, and lived practice*. New York: Peter Lang.
Du Bois, W. E. B. (1903). *The souls of Black folk*. New York: Penguin.
du Gay, P., Evans, J., & Redman, P. (Eds.). (2000). *Identity: A reader*. London: Sage.
Duncan-Andrade, J. & Morrell, E. (2008). *The art of critical pedagogy: Possibilities for moving from theory to practice in urban schools*. New York: Peter Lang.
During, S. (2005). *Cultural studies: A critical introduction*. London and New York: Routledge.
Dyson, M. (2001). *Holler if you hear me: Searching for Tupac Shakur*. New York: Basic Civitas Books.
Dyson, M. (2004). *Mercy, mercy me: The art, loves, and demons of Marvin Gaye*. New York: Basic Civitas Books.
Eagleton, T. (2000). *The idea of culture*. Oxford, UK: Blackwell.
Ebron, P. (1991). Rapping between men: Performing gender. *Radical America, 13*(4), 23–27.
Egbo, B. (2009). *Teaching for diversity in Canadian schools*. Toronto, ON: Pearson Prentice Hall.
Ellison, R. (1952). *Invisible man*. New York: Random House
Emdin, C. (2012). Yes, black males are different, but different is not deficient. *Phi Delta Kappan, 93*(5), 13.

Essed, P., & Goldberg, D. T. (Eds.). (2002). *Race critical theory.* Malden, MA: Blackwell.
Fanon, F. (1967). *Black skin/ White mask.* London: Paladin.
Fanon, F. (1963). *The wretch of the earth.* New York: Grove Press.
Faye, J. (2012). *After postmodernism: A naturalistic reconstruction of the humanities.* New York: Palgrave Macmillan.
Feagin, J., Vera, H., & Imani, N. (1996). *The agony of education: Black students at White colleges and universities.* London and New York: Routledge.
Felman, S. (1992). Education and crisis, or the vicissitudes of teaching. In S. Felman & D. Laub (Eds.), *Testimony: Crisis of witnessing in literature, psychoanalysis, and history* (pp. 1–56). London and New York: Routledge.
Fine, M., Powell, L., Weis, L., & Wong, L. (2004). *Off white: Readings on race, power, and society.* New York: Routledge.
Fisher, G., & Model, S. (2012). Cape Verdean identity in a land of Black and White. *Ethnicities, 12*(3), 354–379.
Forman, F., & Neal, M. (Eds.). (2004). *That's the joint!: The hip-hop studies.* New York: Routledge.
Foucault, M. (1972). *The archaeology of knowledge.* New York: Harper & Row.
Foucault, M. (1979). *Discipline and punish: The birth of the prison.* New York: Vintage Books.
Foucault, M. (1980). *Power/knowledge: Selected interviews and other writings.* New York: Pantheon.
Frankenberg, R. (1993). *White women, race matters: The social construction of whiteness.* Minneapolis: University of Minnesota Press.
Freire, P. (1993). *Pedagogy of the oppressed.* New York: Continuum.
Gaarder, J. (1996). *Sophie's world: A novel about the history of philosophy.* New York: Farrar, Straus & Giroux.
Garcia, E. (2005). *Student cultural diversity: Understanding and meeting the challenge* (3rd ed.). Boston, MA: Houghton Mifflin.
Gelder, K. (2007). *Subcultures: Cultural histories and social practice.* London and New York: Routledge.
Gelder, K., & Thornton, S. (Eds.). (1997). *The subcultures reader.* London and New York: Routledge.
George, N. (1998). *Hip hop America.* New York: Viking.
George, N. (2004). *Post-soul nation: The explosive, contradictory, triumphant, and tragic 1980s as experienced by African Americans (previously known as Blacks and before that Negroes).* New York: Viking.
Gibran, K. (1966). *The prophet.* New York: Knopf.
Gilroy, P. (1991). *"There ain't no black in the Union Jack": The cultural politics of race and nation.* Chicago, IL: University of Chicago Press.
Gilroy, P. (1993). *The black Atlantic: Modernity and double consciousness.* London and New York: Verso.
Gilroy, P. (2000). *Against race: Imagining political culture beyond the color line.* Cambridge, MA: Harvard University Press.

Giroux, H. (2005). *Border crossings: Cultural workers and the politics of education* (2nd ed.). New York: Routledge.

Giroux, H. (2012). *Education and the crisis of public values: Challenging the assault on teachers, students and public education.* New York: Peter Lang.

Giroux, H., & Simon, R. (1989). Popular culture as a pedagogy of pleasure and meaning. In H. Giroux & R. Simon (Eds.), *Popular culture, schooling, and everyday life* (pp. 1–29). Boston, MA: Bergin & Garvey.

Goldberg, D. (Ed.). (1994). *Multiculturalism: A critical reader.* Oxford, UK: Blackwell.

Goldstein, L. (1987). Standard English: The only target for nonnative speakers of English? *TESOL Quarterly, 21*(3), 417–438.

Gonick, M. (2010). Indigenizing girl power: The whale rider, decolonization and the project of remembering. *Feminist Media Studies, 10*(3), 305–320.

Gramsci, A. (1971). *Selections from the prison notes.* New York: International Publishers.

Griswold, W. (2012). *Cultures and societies in a changing world* (4th ed.). Thousand Oaks, CA: Sage.

Grossberg, L. (2014). Cultural studies and Deleuze-Guattari, Part I. *Cultural Studies 28*(1), 1–28

Grossberg, L., Nelson, C., & Paula, T. (Eds.). (1992). *Cultural studies.* New York: Routledge.

Gumperz, J. (1982). *Discourse strategies.* Cambridge, UK: Cambridge University Press.

Hall, S. (1986). On postmodernism and articulation. *Journal of Communication Inquiry, 10*(2), 45–60.

Hall, S. (1989). *Race, culture and the media.* Unpublished manuscript, University of Massachusetts at Amherst.

Hall, S. (1990). Cultural identity and diaspora. In J. Rutherford (Ed.), *Identity, community, culture, difference* (pp. 222–237). London: Lawrence & Wishart.

Hall, S. (1991). Ethnicity: Identity and difference. *Radical America, 13*(4), 9–20.

Hall, S. (1992). What is this "Black" in Black popular culture? In G. Dent (Ed.), *Black popular culture* (pp. 21–33). Seattle, WA: Bay Press.

Hall, S. (Ed.) (1997). *Representation: Cultural representations and signifying practices.* London: The Open University.

Hall, S. (2001). Introduction: Who needs "identity"? In S. Hall & P. du Gay (Eds.), *Questions of cultural identity* (pp. 1–17). London: Sage.

Hall, S. (2002). *Race: The floating signifier* [Video]. Northampton, MA: Media Education Foundation.

Hall, S. (2006). Old and new identities, old and new ethnicities. In P. Rothenberg (Ed.), *Beyond borders: Thinking critically about global issues* (pp. 123–131). New York: Worth Publishers.

Harding, S. (1987). *Feminism and methodology.* Bloomington and Indianapolis: Indiana University Press.

Harding, S. (2009). Standpoint theories: Productively controversial. *Hypatia, 24*(4), 192–200.

Hardt, M., & Negri, A. (2000). *Empire.* Cambridge, MA: Harvard University Press.

Harushimana, I., & Awokoya, J. (2011). African-born immigrants in U.S. schools: An intercultural perspective on schooling and diversity. *Journal of Praxis in Multicultural Education, 6*(1), 403–417.

Hassaskhah, J. (2011). *Educational theory*. New York: Nova Science Publishers.
Hebdige, D. (1979/2003). *Subculture: The meaning of style*. London: Methuen.
Hebdige, D. (1997). Posing...threats, striking...poses: Youth, surveillance, and display. In K. Gelder & S. Thornton (Eds.), *The subcultures reader* (pp. 393–405). London and New York: Routledge.
Heller, M. (1992). The politics of codeswitching and language choice. *Journal of Multilingual and Multicultural Development, 13*(1–2), 123–142.
Heller, M. (1994). *Crosswords: Language, education and ethnicity in French Ontario*. Berlin and New York: Mouton de Gruyter.
Heller, M. (2011). *Paths to post-nationalism: A critical ethnography of language and identity*. New York: Oxford University Press.
Heller, M., with Campbell, M., Dalley, P., & Patrick, D. (1999). *Linguistic minorities and modernity: A sociolinguistic ethnography*. London and New York: Longman.
Henry, A. (2012). The problematic of multiculturalism in a post-racial America: Notes from an anti-multiculturalist. In H. Wright, M. Singh, & R. Race (Eds.), *Precarious international multicultural education: Hegemony, dissent and rising alternatives* (pp. 41–60). Rotterdam: Sense.
Henry, F., Tator, C., Mattis, W., & Rees, T. (2000). *The colour of democracy: Racism in Canadian society* (2nd ed.). Toronto, ON: Harcourt Brace Canada.
Herrnstein, K., & Murray, C. (1995). *Bell curve wars: The reshaping of American life by differences of intelligence*. New York: Free Press.
Hewson, A. (2009). Changing habits: Deconstructing one convent school song. *Journal of Curriculum Theorizing, 25*(1), 14–29.
Hill, L. (2007). *The book of Negroes*. Toronto, ON: HarperCollins.
Hill, M. (2008). *Beats, rhymes, and classroom life: Hip-hop pedagogy and the politics of identity*. New York: Peter Lang.
hooks, b. (1990). *Yearning race, gender, and cultural politics*. Toronto, ON: Between the Lines.
hooks, b. (1992). *Black looks*. Boston: South End Press.
hooks, b. (1994). *Teaching to transgress: Education as the practice of freedom*. New York: Routledge.
hooks, b. (2003). *Teaching community: A pedagogy of hope*. New York: Routledge.
Huq, R. (2001). The French connection: Francophone hip-hop as an institution. *Taboo, 5*(2), 69–84.
Ibrahim, A. (1999). Becoming Black: Rap and hip-hop, race, gender, identity, and the politics of ESL learning. *TESOL Quarterly, 33*(3), 349–369.
Ibrahim, A. (2000a). "Whassup Homeboy?" Black/popular culture and the politics of "curriculum studies": Devising an anti-racism perspective. In G. J. S. Dei & A. Calliste (Eds.), *Power, knowledge and anti-racism education: A critical reader* (pp. 57–72). Halifax, NS: Fernwood.
Ibrahim, A. (2000b). "Hey, ain't I Black too?" The politics of becoming Black. In R. Walcott (Ed.), *Rude: Contemporary Black Canadian cultural criticism* (pp. 109–136). Toronto, ON: Insomniac Press.

Ibrahim, A. (2004). One is not born Black: Becoming and the phenomenon(ology) of race. *Philosophical Studies in Education*, 35, 77–87.

Ibrahim, A. (2005). The question of the question is the foreigner: Towards an economy of hospitality. *Journal of Curriculum Theorizing, 21(*2), 149–162.

Ibrahim, A. (2008). The new *flâneur*: Subaltern cultural studies, African youth in Canada, and the semiology of in-betweenness. *Cultural Studies, 22*(2), 234–253.

Ibrahim, A. (2011). Will they ever speak, with authority? Race, post-coloniality and the symbolic violence of language. *Educational Philosophy and Theory, 43*(6), 619–635.

Ibrahim, A. (2012). Global Hip-Hop Nation Language: A (semiotic) review of *Languages of Global Hip-Hop*, edited by Marina Terkourafi (Continuum, 2010), 351 pages. *Journal of Sociolinguistics 16*(4), 547-552

Ibrahim, A. (2014). Research as an act of love: Ethics, émigrés and the praxis of becoming human. *Diaspora, Indigenous and Minority Education 8*(1), 7-20.

Jackson, S., & Moody-Freeman, J. (2011). *The Black imagination, science fiction, futurism, and the speculative*. New York: Peter Lang.

Jaleh, H. (2012). *Educational theory*. New York: Nova Science Publishers.

James, C., & Shadd, A. (2001). *Talking about identity: Encounters in race, ethnicity, and language*. Toronto, ON: Between the Lines.

Jameson, F. (1991). *Postmodernism, or, the cultural logic of late capitalism*. Durham, NC: Duke University Press.

Jenks, C. (1993). *Culture*. London: Routledge.

Jiwani, Y., Steenbergen, C., & Mitchell, C. (Eds.). (2006). *Girlhood: Redefining the limits*. Montreal: Black Rose.

Johnson, A. (2006). *Privilege, power, and difference*. Boston, MA: McGraw Hill.

Johnson, T. (2004). "I secretly relished that delicious feeling of excitement": A rhizoanalysis of teacher-student attraction. *Taboo, 8*(4), 83–95.

Kailin, J. (2002). *Antiracist education: From theory to practice*. Lanham, MD: Rowman & Littlefield Publishers.

Kantor, J. (2012). For President Obama, a complex calculus of race and politics. *The New York Times*, A1. Retrieved from http://www.nytimes.com/2012/10/21/us/politics/for-president-obama-a-complex-calculus-of-race-and-politics.html?pagewanted=all.

Kennedy, R. (2002). *Nigger: The strange career of a troublesome word*. New York: Vintage Books.

Kevin, G. (2009). *Cultural studies*. Pittsburgh, PA: Carnegie Mellon University Press.

Knicheloe, J. (2008). *Critical pedagogy primer*. New York: Peter Lang.

Kitwana, B. (2002). *The hip hop generation: Young Blacks and the crisis in African American culture*. New York: Basic Civitas Books.

Klein, M. (2000). Notes on some schizoid mechanisms. In P. du Gay, J. Evans, & P. Redman (Eds.), *Identity: A reader* (pp. 130–143). London: Sage.

Kress, T. (2011). *Critical praxis research: Breathing new life into research methods for teachers*. Dordrecht, Netherlands: Springer.

Kristeva, J. (1974). *La révolution du langage poétique, l'avant-garde à la fin du 19e siècle*. Paris: Lautréament et Mallarmé.

Kristeva, J. (1989). *Language—the unknown: An initiation into linguistics*. New York: Columbia University Press.

Kuoch, P. (2013). *Hip hoe to hip hoPe: Hip hop pedagogy in a secondary language arts curriculum*. Unpublished doctoral dissertation, Simon Fraser University, Vancouver.

Labov, W. (1972). *Language in the inner city: Studies in the Black English vernacular*. Philadelphia: University of Pennsylvania Press.

Lacan, J. (1977). *Écrits: A selection*. New York: Norton.

Laclau, E., & Mouffe, C. (1986). *Hegemony and socialist strategy*. London: Verso.

Ladson-Billings, G. (1998). Just what is critical race theory and what's it doing in a nice field like education? *International Journal of Qualitative Studies in Education, 11*(1), 7–24.

Ladson-Billings, G. (2009). Education for everyday people: Obstacles and opportunities facing the Obama administration. *Harvard Educational Review, 79*(2), 345–359.

Lambert, W. (1978). Some cognitive and sociocultural consequences of being bilingual. In J. Alatis (Ed.), *Georgetown University roundtable on language and linguistics* (pp. 214–229). Washington, DC.

Lea, T., & Driscoll, C. (2012). *Girls at the centre: An evaluation of engagement and retention strategies for indigenous girls*. Sydney, AUS: Gender and Cultural Studies.

Lee, E. (1994). Anti-racist education: Panacea or palliative? *Orbit, 25*(2), 22–25.

Lemelle, A. (1995). *Black male deviance*. Westport, CT: Praeger

Lemon. (2012). LEMON 6—Lemon performs *"The era of the goon"performed at the Public Theater* [Video]. Retrieved from http://www.youtube.com/watch?v=a_BsU7SfRwo&feature=relmfu.

Levinas, E. (1998). *Entre-nous: On thinking-of-the-other*. New York: Columbia University Press.

Lin, A. (2009). "Respect for da chopstick Hip-Hop" The politics, poetics, and pedagogy of Cantonese verbal art in Hong Kong. In S. Alim, A. Ibrahim & A. Pennycook (Eds.), *Global linguistic flows: Hip-hop cultures, youth identities, and the politics of language* (pp. 137–155). London and New York: Routledge.

Lopez, D., & Espiritu, Y. (1990). Panethnicity in the United States: A theoretical framework. *Ethnic and Racial Studies*, 13, 103–121.

Love, B. (2012). *Hip hop's li'l sistas speak*. New York: Peter Lang.

Low, B. (2011). *Slam school: Learning through conflict in the hip-hop and spoken word classroom*. Stanford, CA: Stanford University Press.

Lyotard, J.-F. (1984). *The postmodern condition: A report on knowledge*. Minneapolis: University of Minnesota Press

Malcom X. (1965). *The autobiography of Malcom X as told to Alex Haley*. New York: Ballantine Books.

McAdams, D. (1993). *The stories we live by: Personal myths and the making of the self*. New York: William Morrow.

Massumi, B. (1992). *A user's guide to capitalism and schizophrenia: Deviations from Deleuze and Guattari*. Cambridge, MA: MIT Press.

McIntosh, P. (1998). White privilege: Unpacking the invisible knapsack. In P. Rothenberg (Ed.), *Race, class, and gender in the United States* (pp. 165–169). New York: St. Martin's Press.

McLaren, P. (2005). Introduction: Performance in education. In B. Alexander, G. Anderson, & B. Gallegos (Eds.), *Performance theories in education: Power, pedagogy, and the politics of identity* (pp. xv–xix). Mahwah, NJ: Lawrence Erlbaum.

McLaren, P., & Farahmandpur, R. (2005). *Teaching against global capitalism and the new imperialism: A critical pedagogy*. Lanham, MD: Rowman & Littlefield.

McRobbie, A. (1994). *Postmodernism and popular culture*. London and New York: Routledge.

McRobbie, A. (2009). *The aftermath of feminism: Gender, culture and social change*. Thousand Oaks, CA: Sage.

Meeks, B. (2007). *Culture, politics, race and diaspora: The thought of Stuart Hall*. Cambridge, UK: Cambridge University Press.

Mensah, J. (2002). *Black Canadians: History, experiences, social conditions*. Halifax, NS: Fernwood.

Mercer, K. (1994). *Welcome to the jungle: New politics in Black cultural studies*. New York and London: Routledge.

Mercer, K. (2008). *Exiles, diasporas and strangers*. London: Institute of International Visual Arts.

Middleton, J. (2002). *Culture*. Chichester, UK: Capston.

Miles, R. (2003). *Racism*. London: Routledge.

Minh-ha, T. (2011). *Elsewhere, within here: Immigration, refugeeism and the boundary event*. New York: Taylor & Francis.

Morgan, J. (2004). Hip-hop feminist. In F. Forman & M. Neal (Eds.), *That's the joint!: The hip-hop studies* (pp. 277–281). New York: Routledge.

Morrison, T. (1992). *Playing in the dark: Whiteness and the literary imagination*. Cambridge, MA: Harvard University Press.

Ndegeocello, M. (1993). *If that's your boyfriend (he wasn't last night)*. Los Angeles, CA: Maverick.

Nelson, C. (Ed.). (2010). *Ebony roots, northern soil: Perspectives on Blackness in Canada*. Newcastle upon Tyne, UK: Cambridge Scholars.

Nelson, C., & Nelson, C. (Eds.). (2004). *Racism eh? A critical inter-disciplinary anthology on race in the Canadian context*. Toronto, ON: Captus University Press.

Neuman, L. & Robson, K. (2012). *Basics of social research: Qualitative and quantitative approaches*. Toronto, ON: Pearson Canada.

Noddings, N. (1992). *The challenge to care in schools: An alternative approach to education*. New York: Teachers College Press.

Norton (Peirce), B. (1993). *Language learning, social identity, and immigrant women*. Unpublished doctoral dissertation. Toronto, ON: OISE/University of Toronto.

Norton, B. (2000). *Identity and language learning: Gender, ethnicity and educational change*. New York: Longman.

Norton, B., & Toohey, K. (Eds.). (2004). *Critical pedagogies and language learning*. Cambridge, UK and New York: Cambridge University Press.

Novak, M. (1972). *The risk of the unmeltable ethnics*. New York: Macmillan.

O'Toole, P., & Were, P. (2008). Observing places: Using space and material culture in qualitative research. *Qualitative Research, 8*(5), 616–634.

Obama, B. (1995). *Dreams from my father: A story of race and inheritance*. New York: Times Books.

Ogbu, J. (2003). *Black students in an affluent suburb: A study of academic disengagement*. Mahwah, NJ: Lawrence Erlbaum.

Ogbu, J. (1983). Minority status and schooling in plural societies. *Comparative Education Review, 27*(2), 168–190.

Ogbu, J. (1990). Minority education in comparative perspective. *Journal of Negro Education, 59*(1), 45–57.

Ogbu, J., & Fordham, S. (1986). Black students' school success: Coping with the "burden of acting white." *The Urban Review, 18*(3), 176–206.

Ogg, A., with Upshal, D. (2001). *The hip hop years: A history of rap*. New York: Fromm International.

Oladipo, O. (1992). *The idea of African philosophy: A critical study of major orientations in contemporary African philosophy*. Ibadan, Nigeria: Molecular Publishers.

Olsson, G. H. (Director). (2011). *The Black Power Mixtape 1967–1975* [Documentary]. Oslo, Sweden.

Omi, M., & Winant, H. (1994). *Racial Formation in the United States*. London and New York: Routledge.

Osumare, H. (2001). Beat streets in the global hood: Connective marginalities in the hip hop globe. *Journal of American and Comparative Cultures, 24*(1–2), 171–181.

Osumare, H. (2012). *The hiplife in Ghana: West African indigenization of hip-hop*. New York: Palgrave Macmillan.

O'Toole, P., & Were, P. (2008). Observing places: Using space and material culture in qualitative research. *Qualitative Research, 8*(5), 616–634.

Pascale, C.-M. (2012). *Social inequality and the politics of representation: A global landscape*. Thousand Oaks, CA: Sage.

Peirce, B. (1993). *Language learning, social identity, and immigrant women*. Unpublished doctoral dissertation, University of Toronto.

Pennycook, A. (2004). Performativity and language studies. *Critical Inquiry in Language Studies: An International Journal, 1*(1), 1–19.

Philip, M. N. (1991). *Harriet's daughter*. Toronto, ON: Women's Press.

Pinar, W. (2004). *What is curriculum theory?* Mahwah, NJ: Lawrence Erlbaum.

Powell, C. (1991). Rap music: An education with a beat from the street. *Journal of Negro Education, 60*(3), 245–259.

Prince, A. (2000). *Being Black*. Toronto, ON: Insomniac Press.

Rajchman, J. (1995). *The identity in question*. New York: Routledge.

Rampton, B. (1995). *Crossing: Language and ethnicity among adolescents*. London and New York: Longman.

Razack, S. (2004). *Dark threats and white knights: The Somalia affair, peacekeeping and the new imperialism*. Toronto: University of Toronto Press.

Richardson, E. (2003). *African American literacies*. London and New York: Routledge.

Rose, J. (2000). Feminine sexuality. In P. du Gay, J. Evans, & P. Redman (Eds.), *Identity: A reader* (pp. 51–68). London: Sage.

Rose, T. (1991). "Fear of a Black planet": Rap music and Black cultural politics in the 1990s. *Journal of Negro Education, 60*(3), 276–290.
Rose, T. (1994). *Black noise: Rap music and Black culture in contemporary culture*. Hanover, NH: New England University Press.
Rothenberg, P. (Ed.). (1998). *Race, class, and gender in the United States*. New York: St. Martin's Press.
Ryan, M., & Musiol, H. (2008). *Cultural studies: An anthology*. Malden, MA: Blackwell.
Sagert, K. (2010). *Flappers: A guide to an American subculture*. Santa Barbara, CA: Greenwood Press.
Said, E. (1978). *Orientalism*. New York: Vintage Books.
Said, E. (1994). *Culture and imperialism*. New York: Alfred A. Knopf.
St. Pierre, E. (1997). Circling the text: Nomadic writing practices. *Qualitative Inquiry, 3*(4), 403–417.
San Juan, E., Jr. (2002). *Racism and cultural studies: Critiques of multiculturalist ideology and the politics of difference*. Durham, NC: Duke University Press.
Sartre, J.-P. (1980). *Being and nothingness: A phenomenological essay on ontology*. New York: Pocket Books.
Savage, J. (2007). *Teenage: The creation of youth culture*. New York: Viking.
Seegars, L. (2007). *Being the token: One person cannot represent an entire race*. Retrieved from http://www.thecrimson.com/article/2007/2/23/being-the-token-being-the-token/.
Silverman, K. (2000). Suture: The cinematic model. In P. du Gay, J. Evans, & P. Redman (Eds.), *Identity: A reader* (pp. 76–86). London: Sage.
Simmons, R. (2001). *Life and def: Sex, drugs, money, God*. New York: Crown.
Simon, R. I. (1992). *Teaching against the grain*. New York: Bergin & Garvey.
Simon, R. I., & Dippo, D. (1986). On critical ethnography work. *Anthropology and Education Quarterly, 17*, 195–202.
Smitherman, G. (2000). *Black talk: Words and phrases from the hood to the amen corner*. Boston, MA: Houghton Mifflin.
Soja, E. (1996). *Thirdspace: Journeys to Los Angeles and other real-and-imagined places*. Cambridge, MA: Blackwell.
Solomon, P. (1992). *Black resistance in high school: Forging a separatist culture*. Albany: State University of New York Press.
Solomon, P., & Sekayi, D. (2007). *Urban teacher education and teaching: Innovative practices for diversity and social justice*. New York: Routledge.
Spivak, G. (1990). *Post-colonial critic: Interviews, strategies, dialogue*. New York: Routledge.
Stanley, T. (2011). *Contesting White supremacy: School segregation, anti-racism, and the making of Chinese Canadians*. Vancouver: UBC Press.
Statistics Canada. (2009). *Community profile*. Retrieved from http://www12.statcan.ca/census-recensement/2006/dp-pd/prof/92-591/index.cfm?Lang=E.
Statistics Canada. (2011). *Immigrant languages in Canada*. Retrieved from http://www12.statcan.gc.ca/census-recensement/2011/as-sa/98-314-x/98-314-x2011003_2-eng.cfm.

Statistics Canada. (2014). *Labour force characteristics by immigrant status of population aged 25 to 54 by country of birth*. Retrieved from http://www76.statcan.gc.ca/stcsr/query.html?qt=immigrant%20population&charset=utf-8&qm=1

Tatum, B. (1997). *"Why are all the Black kids sitting together in the cafeteria?" and other conversations about race*. New York: Basic Books.

Taylor, C. (1994). The politics of recognition. In D. Goldberg (Ed.), *Multiculturalism: A critical reader* (pp. 75–106). Oxford, UK: Blackwell.

Terkourafi, M. (Ed.). (2010). *Languages of global hip hop*. New York: Continuum.

Trifonas, P. (2004). Postmodernism, poststructuralism, and difference. *Journal of Curriculum Theorizing, 20*(1), 151–163.

Troman, G., Jeffrey, B. & Walford, G. (2004). *Identity, agency and social institutions in educational ethnography*. Amesterdam: Elsevier JAI.

Usher, R., & Edwards, R. (1994). *Postmodernism and education*. New York: Routledge.

van Manen, M. (1997). *Researching lived experience: Human science for an action sensitive pedagogy*. London, ON: Althouse Press.

wa Thiong'o, N. (1986). *Decolonising the mind: The politics of language in African literature*. Nairobi: Heinemann.

Walcott, R. (1995). *Performing the postmodern: Black Atlantic rap and identity in North America*. Unpublished doctoral dissertation, University of Toronto.

Walcott, R. (Ed.). (2000). *Rude: Contemporary Black Canadian cultural criticism*. Toronto, ON: Insomniac Press.

Walker, J. (1997). *A history of Blacks in Canada*. Montreal and Kingston: McGill-Queen's University Press.

Weaver, J., Dimitriadis, G., & Daspit, T. (Eds.). (2001). *Taboo: The Journal of Culture and Education* [special issue], *5*(2).

Weis, L., & Fine, M. (Eds.). (2005). *Beyond silenced voices: Class, race, and gender in United States schools*. Albany: State University of New York Press.

West, C. (2001). *Race matters*. Boston, MA: Beacon Press.

Williams, R. (1988). *Keywords: A vocabulary of culture and society*. London: Fontana Press.

Williams, S. (1992). Nostalgia for the present: Cultural resistance in Detroit, 1977–1987. In G. Dent (Ed.), *Black popular culture* (pp. 160–172). Seattle, WA: Bay Press.

Willis, P. (1977). *Learning to labor*. Farnborough, UK: Saxon House.

Wilson, C., Gutierrez, F., & Chao, L. (2013). *Racism, sexism, and the media: Multicultural issues into the new communications age* (4th ed.). Thousand Oaks, CA: Sage.

Winant, H. (2004). *The new politics of race: Globalism, difference, justice*. Minneapolis: University of Minnesota Press.

Wittig, M. (2003). One is not born a woman. In L. Alcoff & M. Eduardo (Eds.), *Identities: Race, class, gender, and nationality* (pp. 159–164). Oxford, UK: Blackwell.

Woodward, K. (Ed.). (1997). *Identity and difference*. London: The Open University.

Wright, H. (2004). *A prescience of African cultural studies: The future of literature in Africa is not what it was*. New York: Peter Lang.

Wright, M. (2004). *Becoming Black: Creating identity in the African diaspora*. Durham, NC: Duke University Press.

Wulff, H. (1995). Inter-racial friendship: Consuming youth styles, ethnicity and teenage femininity in South London. In V. Amit-Talai & H. Wulff (Eds.), *Youth culture: A cross-cultural perspective* (pp. 1–18). London and New York: Routledge.

Yon, D. (2000). *Elusive culture: Schooling, race, and identity in global times*. New York: State University of New York Press.

Žižek, S. (2000). *The ticklish subject: The absent centre of political ontology*. London and New York: Verso.

INDEX

Africa, 4, 5, 6, 8, 29, 35, 41, 42, 88, 95, 111, 123, 148, 149, 150, 176, 179, 193, 206, 213
    Blackness in Africa, 6, 8
    Colonial, 42
    Continent, 29
    Cultural Identity, 42, 141, 147, 189
    Gender, 170, 175
    Historical, 110
    Identity, 8, 147
    Language, 128, 129, 131, 141
    Origin, 41, 73, 92, 97, 115, 139, 155, 187, 206
    Political, 119, 126
    Refugee, 55
    Representation, 28, 41, 126, 131, 147, 149, 152, 207, 208
    Schooling in, 69, 88, 89, 118, 152
    Sexuality, 175, 176
    South, 5, 26, 188
African(s), 5, 28, 15, 23, 25, 26, 28, 41, 42, 44, 54, 58, 59, 63, 65, 68, 76, 82, 88, 90, 91, 92, 95, 97, 98, 111, 112, 113, 118, 126, 128, 147, 149, 152, 156, 160, 167, 170, 179, 185, 187, 189, 192, 196, 198, 203, 206, 208, 219
African American, 14, 29, 45, 123, 158, 159, 178, 179
African American Culture, 14, 15, 43, 141, 181, 188
African Canadian, 27, 29, 50, 64, 182, 187
    Continental, 3–8, 13, 14, 17, 23, 25, 29, 34–36, 69, 70, 85, 88, 123, 197
    Diasporic, 4, 8, 29, 35, 36, 42, 123, 180
    Identities, 50, 150, 178–180, 189
    Languages, 47, 58, 128, 130, 136
    Students, 69, 70, 76–83, 85–91, 93–100, 102, 104, 105, 107–109, 111, 113, 114, 117, 119, 120–123, 126–131, 133, 134, 136, 138, 140, 141, 143, 147, 149–152, 154, 155, 157, 158, 159, 162–164, 166, 167, 174–179, 181–183, 186, 191, 196, 200, 205–207, 209–212, 217, 218, 219
    African youth, 6, 13–15, 19, 24, 27, 46, 47, 49, 50, 52, 54, 55, 59, 70, 72, 96, 154, 159, 163, 177, 182, 183, 187, 188, 189, 192, 196, 198, 199, 202, 213
African American Vernacular English, 47, 58, 156
Africanist, 97, 104, 106, 123, 200, 205
Agony of Education, 114, 123
Alim, S. 4, 15, 19, 43, 44, 58, 144, 210
Althusser, L., 6, 8, 48, 49, 58, 70, 141
Amati-Talai, V., 171
Archaeology, 18
Assemblage, 3, 4, 13, 15, 29, 51, 52, 193

Back & Solomos, 31, 33, 56
Bakhtin, 27, 39, 48, 49, 54
Barthes, 7, 33, 36, 37, 38, 49, 168
Becoming Black, 2–6, 13, 15, 17–19, 22, 27, 34, 52, 53, 59, 70, 72, 80, 90, 95–98, 122, 123, 125, 152, 154, 158, 165, 166, 186, 193, 196, 197, 213
Being Black, 4, 6, 59
Being made, 13, 52, 59, 157
Bhabha, 15, 27, 38, 50, 52–55, 70
Bilingualism, 134, 136, 137, 138
Black, 1–9, 13–15, 17, 22, 23, 26, 27, 28, 32, 33, 35, 36, 40–42, 44–47, 50, 52, 54, 55, 57, 58–61, 69–75, 78–80, 84, 90–98, 100–104, 106, 108, 109, 111, 122–125, 136, 141, 143, 144, 153, 155, 156–159, 161–169, 175, 177–181, 185, 187–190, 193, 195–197, 199–203, 205, 208–211, 213, 217–219

Blackness, 1, 3, 8, 12, 13, 15, 18, 28, 29, 31–35, 45, 49, 56, 59, 72, 80, 84, 87, 112, 122, 136, 142, 143, 146, 152, 153, 157, 158, 162, 163, 165, 168, 192, 196, 197, 201, 210–213
Body, 2, 4–6, 8, 9, 11, 33, 79, 80, 85, 145, 193
Black English, 3, 13, 22, 46, 47, 58, 72, 106, 141, 142, 150, 152, 154–158, 167, 183
Black Talk, 43, 47, 58, 144, 146, 158
Body without Organs, 29
Bourdieu, P., 2, 4, 6, 24, 27, 33, 38, 46, 47, 57, 82, 87, 138
Butler, J., 1, 2, 7, 8, 34, 35, 57

Canada, 3, 4, 6, 9, 11, 18, 23–26, 40, 41, 50, 54, 55, 58, 59, 68, 70, 71, 75, 99, 102, 109, 110, 111, 115, 117, 119, 120, 122, 128, 130, 131, 134, 136, 138, 139, 141, 152, 158, 163–166, 169, 170, 175, 178, 180, 181, 187, 191, 195, 197, 203, 204, 213, 217–219
Chang, 43, 44
Culture, 2, 11, 15, 16, 18, 27, 28, 31, 35–41, 43, 45, 47, 49, 52–55, 57, 58, 66, 67, 90, 92, 94, 96, 98, 107, 109, 110, 113, 120, 126, 128, 142, 148, 150, 152–154, 159, 167, 168, 178–181, 183, 187, 189, 191, 196, 202, 203, 211
   African American, 14, 15, 42, 178, 181
   Black, 4, 5, 14, 15, 27, 36, 40, 41, 42, 50, 72, 96, 126, 131, 140, 141, 142, 143, 152, 156, 162, 189, 211, 212
   Hip-Hop, 43, 44, 45, 125, 144, 145, 176, 181
   Popular, 4, 12, 27, 38, 39, 40, 42, 57, 72, 84, 111, 126, 131, 133, 140–143, 149, 152, 189, 197, 211
   Separatist, 27, 28, 126, 150–152
   School, 96, 98, 99

Subculture, 38–40, 171
Youth, 36, 39, 40
Cummins, J., 134
Curriculum, 69, 75, 84, 98, 100, 109, 110, 111, 113, 122, 129, 130, 131, 155, 205, 211
   hidden, 110

Dance, 41, 43, 124, 143, 188
   B-boying/B-girling, 43
De Beauvoir, S., 7, 34
Dei, G., 14, 42, 56, 57, 64, 71, 74, 84, 89, 92, 107, 118, 129, 147, 198, 205, 206, 209, 211
Deleuze, G. & Guattari, F., 4, 7, 15, 17, 19, 51
Derrida, J., 2, 8, 17, 151, 192
Desire, 3, 4, 7, 9, 12, 15, 17, 19, 20, 24, 29, 33, 36, 39, 41, 44, 45, 47, 49, 50, 52, 74, 82, 84, 100, 106, 114, 118, 128, 132–134, 143, 146, 152, 154, 157, 158, 160–166, 170–173, 182, 187, 189, 193, 197, 199, 202, 212, 218
Deterritorialization, 3, 21
Diaspora, 4, 36, 40, 41, 42, 95
DJ, 43, 44, 144, 145, 157, 182, 188
Domination, 39, 202
Du Bois, W.E.B., 12
Duncan-Andrade, J. & Morrell, E., 19
Dyson, M., 43, 44

Ebron, P., 45, 159
Economy, 31, 32, 33, 34, 46, 151, 192
   Of exchange, 31, 33, 46, 200
   Of hospitality, 150, 151, 194, 196
   Of power, 32, 192
Ellison, R., 208, 209
Emdin, C., 84
Essed, P., 6, 9, 14, 33, 56, 72
Ethnicity, 27, 35, 39, 44, 51, 57, 67, 72, 90, 189
Ethnography, 1, 16, 18, 20, 22, 140, 176, 177

Fanon, F., 14, 32, 47, 94, 192
Forman, F., & Neal, M., 43, 45, 161, 212
Foucault, M., 4, 17, 19, 21, 34, 37, 38, 92, 107, 113, 170, 199, 207
Franco-Ontarian, 24, 87, 91, 133, 135, 137
Freire, P., 123, 207, 210, 213
French, 1–3, 17, 18, 21, 23–26, 42, 44, 57, 58, 61, 68–71, 73, 74, 76, 77, 78, 80, 82, 85–95, 97–111, 113, 114, 117, 118, 120, 122, 123, 126–141, 143, 145, 146, 148, 149, 151–153, 155, 158–170, 173, 174, 176–183, 186–189, 191, 194, 198–208, 216, 218, 219

George, N., 43, 44
Gilroy, P., 33, 36, 40, 41, 42, 44, 166
Giroux, H., 12, 55, 64, 93, 211
Global Hip-Hop Nation, 44
Goldberg, T., 6, 9, 14, 29, 33, 56
Golden, R., 124
Graffiti, 43
Gramsci, A., 4, 38, 39, 57
Grossberg, L., 37

Hall, S., 4, 6, 7, 29, 31, 33, 35, 37–39, 42, 44, 47, 48, 51, 52, 57, 111, 152, 161, 177, 189, 213
Hanging out, 15, 18, 19–22, 26, 140, 142
Hegemony, 38, 39, 57, 160
Heller, M., 2, 16, 46, 58, 87, 90, 107, 113, 133, 135, 176
Henry, A., 5, 32, 33, 68, 151,
Hip-Hop, 4, 11, 14, 15, 27, 28, 42–47, 52, 96, 125, 126, 140–146, 150, 152, 155, 156, 158, 159–162, 164, 166–168, 176, 181, 183, 186, 188, 189, 190, 197, 201, 202, 209, 211–213, 219
Hooks, B., 5, 35, 40, 112, 148, 151, 159, 207, 211, 212

Ibrahim, A., 4, 6, 7, 15, 20, 41, 43, 44, 46, 47, 56, 58, 92, 107, 194, 211, 212

Identification, 3, 11–15, 32, 39, 47–50, 54, 72, 84, 100, 141, 143, 146, 154, 158, 162–165, 167, 168, 181, 197, 205, 206, 219
Identity, 1–6, 8, 12, 13, 15, 17, 22, 27–32, 35, 36, 38, 40, 42, 47–53, 55, 56, 64, 84, 95, 96, 109, 110, 113, 140, 141, 143, 146, 147, 150, 152, 153, 155, 158, 162–167, 170, 176–179, 180, 183, 186–189, 193, 197, 201, 204, 208–213
   Old/New, 29, 48, 51
Immigration, 77, 83

James, C., 12, 43, 57, 69, 71, 89

Kincheloe, J., 19,
Kristeva, J., 7, 11, 27, 31, 46, 49

Language, 1–10, 12, 14, 15, 17, 18, 21–31, 33, 34–44, 46–50, 52–58, 66, 67, 69, 71, 76, 77, 81–84, 86, 87, 90–97, 106–109, 113, 114, 117, 119, 120–124, 126–141, 143–148, 150–155, 158–161, 167, 168, 170, 175–183, 186, 190, 192, 194, 197, 199, 200, 202–205, 207, 211, 212, 218, 219
   B/ESL, 3, 7, 8, 12, 13, 22, 24, 26, 27, 71, 120, 124, 140, 150, 151, 155
Le contrat, 81, 84–86, 96, 100, 120, 205, 218
LINC, 71
Line of flight, 3, 18, 51, 68, 193
Lopez, D., & Espiritu, Y., 35, 36, 57
Love, B., 42, 45, 64, 65, 67, 144, 151, 190, 212
Low, B., 43

Marie-Victorin, 1, 18, 21–23, 26, 60, 64, 68, 69, 72, 77–79, 83–85, 88, 90, 92, 97, 99, 101, 103, 110, 113, 123, 126, 150, 152, 154, 193, 194, 196, 197, 217
Massumi, B., 19

Maxwell High, 22–26, 64–66, 68, 71, 72, 75, 76, 78, 83, 84, 87, 95, 98, 100, 102, 120–126, 158, 162, 190, 193, 194, 196, 197, 217–219
McLaren, P., 93, 104, 139, 213
Methodology/Method, 12, 15–22, 140
Minority, 68, 113, 158, 159, 205, 209
Mother tongue, 7, 26, 30, 91, 126, 129, 134, 151, 153
Multiculturalism, 102–104

Negotiation, 2, 15, 55, 187–189
Noddings, N., 66–68, 75, 120
Norton, B., 16, 46, 208

Ogbu, J., 19, 56, 69, 89, 98, 151, 158, 179, 190
Olsson, G. H., 122, 125
Omi, M. & Winant, H., 35, 56
Ontario, 3, 17, 18, 23–25, 60, 65, 87, 113, 117, 120, 138, 217
Osumare, H., 42, 44
Other, 2, 6, 14, 31–33, 48, 49, 109–111, 147, 148, 198, 207, 208

Pedagogy, 13, 19, 27, 28, 67, 84, 86, 98, 109, 112, 120, 121, 192, 198, 202, 204, 208–213
Pennycook, A., 15, 43, 46
Performance, 3, 18, 22, 45, 46, 48, 89, 92, 140, 142, 143, 145, 154, 167, 177, 186, 190, 198, 218
Performativity, 7, 34, 166, 177
Politics, 2, 3, 5, 6, 15, 16, 36, 41, 44, 45–48, 50, 52, 60, 64, 100, 143, 150, 152, 154, 158, 163, 166, 168, 189, 211
Powell, C., 43
Présence africaine, 6, 27, 33

Quebec, 60, 130, 131, 136

Race, 2, 3, 7, 8, 12, 13, 16, 27, 3–36, 40, 44, 54, 56, 57, 61, 70, 72, 87, 90, 91, 93, 103, 106, 136, 142, 143, 152, 154, 157, 162, 164, 167, 176, 187, 190, 192, 197, 198, 204, 205, 209, 210
Racialization, 8, 14, 33–35, 57, 59, 96
Rampton, B., 21, 24, 46, 47, 87, 143, 181
Rap, 4, 14, 15, 27, 43–47, 126, 141–146, 153, 157-162, 164, 168, 185, 186, 190, 211, 212, 192
Rhizome/Rhizomatic, 1–5, 15, 17, 18–22, 27–29, 31, 50–55, 59, 72, 98, 117, 122, 123, 125, 152, 154, 165, 166, 172, 176, 181, 182, 186–189, 192, 193, 196–198, 209–213
　Smooth, 29, 52, 68, 72, 98, 123, 125, 126, 157, 186, 193, 194, 196, 197
　Striated, 29, 52, 68, 72, 98,123, 157, 186, 193, 194, 196, 197
Rose, J., 7, 32, 33, 43–45, 212

Said, E., 94, 123, 147, 212, 213
Sexuality, 174
Simon, R., 16, 211, 212
Smitherman, G., 4, 43, 47, 58, 144, 157, 211
Social imaginary, 13, 14, 59
Somalia/Djibouti, 26, 68, 70, 76, 79, 82, 83, 88, 91, 92, 97, 99, 101, 105, 106, 109, 110, 114, 119, 120, 126–132, 134, 136, 139, 145, 148, 151, 158, 163–165, 169, 176, 180, 188, 194, 195, 199, 203, 217–219
Stanley, T., 14, 18, 59, 110, 168
Streaming, 69, 87, 96, 100
Symbolic capital, 24, 31, 34, 87, 150, 187

Teaching, 25, 60, 64, 94, 100, 101, 120–123, 140, 158, 194, 206, 211
The strike, 93–96, 104
Third space, 15, 27, 28, 31, 50, 52–55, 154, 172, 176, 181, 182, 186–189
Translation, 2, 15, 25, 27, 31, 49, 50, 53–55, 70, 99, 139, 154, 183, 188, 189, 215

Unité dans la diversité, 23, 199

wa Thiong'o, N., 126
Walcott, R., 41, 43
Whiteness, 6, 18, 28, 31, 32, 57, 96
Woodward, K., 6, 7, 33, 48, 56, 58, 208
Wright, H., 5, 7, 42, 129, 198

Yon, D., 31, 48, 89

Žižek, S., 197, 198

ROCHELLE BROCK &
RICHARD GREGGORY JOHNSON III,
Executive Editors

Black Studies and Critical Thinking is an interdisciplinary series which examines the intellectual traditions of and cultural contributions made by people of African descent throughout the world. Whether it is in literature, art, music, science, or academics, these contributions are vast and far-reaching. As we work to stretch the boundaries of knowledge and understanding of issues critical to the Black experience, this series offers a unique opportunity to study the social, economic, and political forces that have shaped the historic experience of Black America, and that continue to determine our future. Black Studies and Critical Thinking is positioned at the forefront of research on the Black experience, and is the source for dynamic, innovative, and creative exploration of the most vital issues facing African Americans. The series invites contributions from all disciplines but is specially suited for cultural studies, anthropology, history, sociology, literature, art, and music.

Subjects of interest include (but are not limited to):

- EDUCATION
- SOCIOLOGY
- HISTORY
- MEDIA/COMMUNICATION
- RELIGION/THEOLOGY
- WOMEN'S STUDIES
- POLICY STUDIES
- ADVERTISING
- AFRICAN AMERICAN STUDIES
- POLITICAL SCIENCE
- LGBT STUDIES

For additional information about this series or for the submission of manuscripts, please contact Dr. Brock (Indiana University Northwest) at brock2@iun.edu or Dr. Johnson (University of San Francisco) at rgjohnsoniii@usfca.edu.

To order other books in this series, please contact our Customer Service Department:

(800) 770-LANG (within the U.S.)
(212) 647-7706 (outside the U.S.)
(212) 647-7707 FAX

Or browse online by series at www.peterlang.com.

www.ingramcontent.com/pod-product-compliance
Ingram Content Group UK Ltd.
Pitfield, Milton Keynes, MK11 3LW, UK
UKHW022238230426
12048UKWH00018BA/1338